EUROPE AND THE DOLLAR

EUROPE AND THE DOLLAR

CHARLES P. KINDLEBERGER

THE M.I.T. PRESS
MASSACHUSETTS INSTITUTE OF TECHNOLOGY
CAMBRIDGE, MASSACHUSETTS, AND LONDON, ENGLAND

FOR EMILE DESPRES

PREFACE

Papers that appear outside of routine scholarly channels, and therefore escape the library-indexing process, are for the most part lost. This provides the excuse, if not the justification, for collecting these papers and memoranda, covering a considerable span of years, on the central themes of international finance among the developed countries: the dollar, European currencies, world liquidity, balance-of-payments adjustment. Four of the papers were written for publication in French (Chapters Three, Twelve, Thirteen, and Fourteen); three are published in symposia (Chapters Four, Seven, and Sixteen); one was a statement before a congressional committee (Chapter Ten); one appeared in a *Festschrift* (Chapter Four); and one was written for a collection of essays which aborted before publication (Chapter Nine). Current interest in the subject provides the occasion for rescuing these and one or two other items from oblivion, despite the fact that they have not all withstood the ravages of time in all or perhaps even most respects.

Everything in the collection was written for publication except one memorandum (Chapter Six), rather formal and concise, which consists in a statement on the United States balance of payments with policy recommendations, limited to five pages, written for a group of economists. The longest essay in the volume, Chapter Fourteen, was designed for a history of Europe which is to appear in French at the hands of an Italian publisher. Written mainly in 1953, and completed in 1954, it has not yet seen the light of day — a publication lag distinguished even by United States academic standards.

Some limited amount of repetition has been eliminated and marked with brackets [. . .]. More remains. It was felt that few readers (even few reviewers?) would tackle the essays *seriatim* and become irritated by recurring and repeated themes and even phraseology.

Moreover, once started, there would be no end to modification. In addition, no attempt has been made to standardize the style of the separate papers. Contradictions abound. Some are explained by the change of circumstances over the quarter century covered by the papers. Others can be attributed to initial error or failure of understanding.

The period started out with dollar shortage and ended with dollar surfeit. It is doubtless true in the light of the latter that I overexplained the former. But there are some consistent threads running through the collection: the importance of supply; the need for international cooperation under any and all systems; the superiority of unwritten to formal constitutions in institutional machinery in a world of change with no consensus; the unimportance of the quantity of international liquidity.

It will be observed that Emile Despres is not only a coauthor of one essay (Chapter Fifteen), but is given thanks in another (Chapter Eight). Had I then understood academic courtesy more deeply, he should also have been thanked in Chapter Seventeen, as he was in my thesis in 1937. His thought and analytical abilities have left a strong imprint, as he and I have been colleagues at the Federal Reserve Bank of New York, the Board of Governors of the Federal Reserve System, the Office of Strategic Services, and the Department of State. This collection is dedicated to him — economists' economist, teachers' teacher, and friends' friend.

CHARLES P. KINDLEBERGER

Massachusetts Institute of Technology
June 1965

CONTENTS

CONTENTS

EUROPE AND THE DOLLAR

CHAPTER ONE

BALANCE-OF-PAYMENTS DEFICITS AND THE INTERNATIONAL MARKET FOR LIQUIDITY*

Ambiguity and confusion abound over the international payments position. President Johnson's balance-of-payments message, for example, devotes the first half to stating how strong the dollar is, and the second to proposals for correcting its weaknesses. Economists have been using the term "crisis" to describe the situation for at least six years, during which world trade has expanded virtually continuously. The balance of payments of the United States is puzzlingly in continuous massive deficit, but the foreign-exchange market for the dollar, with sporadic speculative exceptions, evinces no particular sign of weakness. The French, and to a lesser extent the European Economic Community as a whole, express irritation over both the duration and extent of the deficit, and the strength of American corporations, banks and other financial institutions. German opinion is unclear whether capital is scarce or abundant in that country, and whether, accordingly, the long-run normal capital flow should be outward to finance long-term foreign investment, or inward to finance the still large backlog of housing demand.

This paper contends that much of the confusion arises from a mistaken definition of balance-of-payments disequilibrium. It holds that there is no objective problem of the strength or weakness of the dollar, but a possibility of a subjective problem arising and growing by reason of faulty economic analysis, stemming from this definition. Moreover, the change in definition of a deficit proposed

* From Essays in International Finance, No. 46, (International Finance Section, Princeton University, Princeton, N.J., May 1965).

by the Bernstein Review Committee for Balance of Payments Statistics,[1] and referred to in the President's balance-of-payments message of February 10, 1965, effects no distinct improvement.

The difficulty arises from confusion between capital movements for the purpose of transferring real assets and those which have the purpose of and serve to accommodate national liquidity preferences.

I ignore President deGaulle's animadversions on the subject of gold. The analysis does, however, expose the error in the thinking on international payments of Jacques Rueff, whose thought formed the (distorted) basis of deGaulle's statement.

Definitions

The Department of Commerce or Walther Lederer definition of balance-of-payments deficit, as is well known, is the loss of gold plus the increase in certain liabilities to foreigners: specifically — all short-term liabilities and all United States government bonds and notes, including the non-marketable issues payable in dollars and foreign currencies (the so-called Roosa bonds). In some definitions, prepayments of intergovernmental indebtedness are added. On this basis, the President's balance-of-payments message stated that the deficit amounted to $3.6 billion in 1962, $3.3 billion in 1963, and $3.0 billion in 1964.

The basis for this definition has been explained at length.[2] It rests not on the solvency of the United States in international transactions but on its liquidity. Net worth can increase from year to year with a deficit, as the current account of the balance of payments, less transfers, is positive, but falls short of the long-term capital outflow and the increase in United States short-term claims on foreigners. It is assumed that the country might be called upon to pay off all its short-term liabilities to foreigners, without being able to draw on any of its short-term claims.

The difficulties with this definition have been widely noted.[3] It is asymmetrical. When banks in two countries buy foreign deposits, each in the other, to acquire an inventory of foreign exchange (perhaps each entering into a contract with the other to sell the foreign-currency assets forward), both countries are in deficit, despite the fact that there has been no capital movement. It draws far too sharp a distinction between United States assets and liabilities. Some claims of the United States on Europe and Japan are highly liquid

2

or transferable to another holder without substantial loss, whereas some minimum amount of working balances in dollars held by the countries of the "dollar bloc," will be held through thick and thin. Where a claim and a liability are closely associated, in particular, it is offensive to common sense to assume that one is a highly flighty and skittish balance likely to be withdrawn, while the other is a turgid frozen asset, which cannot be drawn upon to meet the withdrawal. When an American corporation puts a deposit, for example, in the New York branch of a Canadian bank, which in turn invests the proceeds in the New York call-money market, the United States balance of payments is in deficit on the Lederer definition, despite the fact that there has been no impact on the foreign-exchange market — the funds never having left downtown Manhattan — and that only under the most unlikely circumstances would the Canadian bank go short of dollars by the amount of the deposit, i.e., use the deposit to buy foreign exchange. The pinnacle of absurdity is reached in the case of Japan, where New York banks making short-term loans to that country require borrowers to maintain minimum balances. The deposit puts the United States balance of payments into deficit, while the asset that gave rise to the claim against this country is ignored.

The revision of the Department of Commerce definition, set out in the Bernstein Committee report, continues to ignore assets. The distinction is drawn merely between official short-term claims on the United States and unofficial claims. The deficit is now defined as losses of gold and increases in short-term official claims. It is assumed that private holders of dollars can be disregarded, because they have voluntarily chosen to lend to the United States at short term. By contrast, official dollar holders are considered to be lending to the United States under duress, or at least are much more nervous and more desirous of converting their dollars into foreign currencies or gold than private holders. The Bernstein Committee is understood to have made no change in the treatment of United States claims on foreign countries. These are still regarded as unavailable to meet withdrawals of foreign dollars from the United States, except, of course, for official United States holdings of foreign exchange which are the equivalent of gold.

This definition has the benefit of reducing the stated deficits of the years 1962, 1963, and 1964. Instead of $3.6 billion, $3.3 billion, and $3.0 billion, respectively, they are $3.3 billion, $2.3 billion, and $1.3 billion, as the President's balance-of-payments message stated. But this virtue is unaccompanied by others. Over a long period, since 1959, the two definitions produce roughly the same order of magnitude of deficit. Theoretically, the distinction between private and official holdings is not a sharp one. From time to time privately held dollars are dumped on the market and must be bought by foreign central banks. Or the Bank of Italy will seek to mop up excess domestic liquidity by selling dollars to the commercial banks under repurchase agreements which remove the exchange risk. While it is true that a good many European central banks have been inching up in their proportions of gold to total reserves, as nervousness over the international monetary mechanism has been maintained at a high level, the holdings of other countries are both substantial and steady. It might be well to make a distinction between the dollars held by the monetary authorities in Canada, Japan, Mexico, Venezuela, etc., on the one hand — which may be said to be in a "dollar bloc" — and those of France, the Netherlands, Spain and Switzerland — which deal only in or are moving rapidly toward gold — with Germany, Italy and Belgium somewhere between. In any event, the distinction between private and official holders is overdrawn. The numbers may be comforting in the short run, but the theory is erroneous.

These remarks about the definition used by the Bernstein balance-of-payments committee have been written without benefit of having seen the report. Publication is hung up for reasons which, rumor has it, stem from the strenuous objections of the Department of Commerce, and the threatened resignation of Department of Commerce officials, if the report is allowed to appear. On the basis of my analysis, the Department of Commerce definition should be discarded, and those who are committed to it must yield intellectual positions or remove themselves. But the Bernstein definition between official and private dollar liabilities of the United States is not the appropriate replacement.

Long-Term Borrowing for Liquidity

Where these definitions go wrong is in assuming that international lending by the United States, at short-term and long, should be transferred in real goods and services. This is perhaps true of

4

lending under present conditions to the less developed countries, which are interested in real assets, and not in balancing their portfolios among real and monetary assets, nor, within the monetary category, in balancing assets by maturity. But much, perhaps most, of the lending by the United States to Europe, and perhaps a third to a half of United States lending to Canada and Japan, serve an altogether different purpose: they are intended in an over-all economic sense to provide liquidity. The United States is not engaged in exchanging real goods for long-term securities, but short-term monetary liabilities for long-term monetary claims. The country, of course, is not the decision-making unit, and no conscious national portfolio-balancing decision is made. But the effect of private and public decisions is the same. Foreign countries as a whole must be added to domestic institutions as financial intermediaries.

Postulate a country like Germany with a high rate of saving and a high rate of investment. Suppose that the *ex ante* rates of saving and investment will produce an equilibrium rate of national income, which would mean, provided that capital markets were isolated, that the balance of payments was in equilibrium. In the well-known formula developed by Sidney S. Alexander, the foreign balance of a country is necessarily equal to its national product minus its domestic "absorption" of goods and services. From this equation, or rather identity, it follows that the foreign balance must be zero if and when the sum of domestically absorbed goods and services is exactly equal to the total national product.

If the savers happen to have high liquidity preference, and the investors insist on long-term obligations — the capital markets still being isolated — one will find a very high long-term rate of interest and a low short-term rate. Time deposits will yield a low return because they are abundant; bonds will have low prices because the demand for them is far to the left.

Assume then convertibility, and connect up this capital market roughly, if not perfectly, with that in a country where liquidity preference is much lower. Investors who prefer their liabilities funded at long term will borrow abroad. Savers who lose outlets for their savings domestically have no alternative but to lend abroad. The households which save are unlikely themselves to maintain time deposits in New York banks, but the effect is the same. If the savings are maintained with banks, the banks may hold foreign

5

deposits. Or, if the banks are uninterested themselves in holding foreign assets, the liquid assets held against their quick liabilities to savers must be supplied by the government or central bank, which in turn must hold the foreign assets. The financial authorities may choose to fund these assets into long-term claims on abroad. In either event there will result a long-term private inflow into the country and a long- or short-term capital outflow by the authorities. But the country has a surplus in its balance of payments in no meaningful sense.

The counterpart in the long-term lender is equally not a deficit. A country with low liquidity preference finds it profitable to exchange types of assets with a country with high liquidity preference when *ex ante* savings equals *ex ante* domestic investment in each country.

The result of connecting up European and American money and capital markets in this way can be illustrated schematically. Figure 1 shows solid lines which suggest the structures of interest rates with markets separated. The United States, with low liquidity preference, has short-term rates almost as high as long-term; Europe, with a strong demand for liquidity on the part of savers and a desire of borrowers to fund obligations, has a much steeper profile of rates. When the two markets are joined, assuming perfect mobility of capital, the two structures become identical — the dotted lines. The European structure changes more than the American, in the schematic diagram, because the United States market is larger. Arrows suggest the direction of capital movement — the upward arrows representing lending, which tightens the local market, and the downward borrowing, which lowers rates. The diagram, it should be emphasized, is highly stylized: in the real world, money and capital markets are not perfect and the arrows signify directions of movement, not discrete distances.

Observe that the distinction between official and private holdings of foreign claims in the country with high liquidity preference is a detail of no objective consequence, and one which should not make any considerable difference in the interpretation of the balance-of-payments position. The distinction between private and official institutions in the country with low liquidity preference may be equally or more significant. If this country lends long and borrows short, it makes a difference for monetary policy whether the short

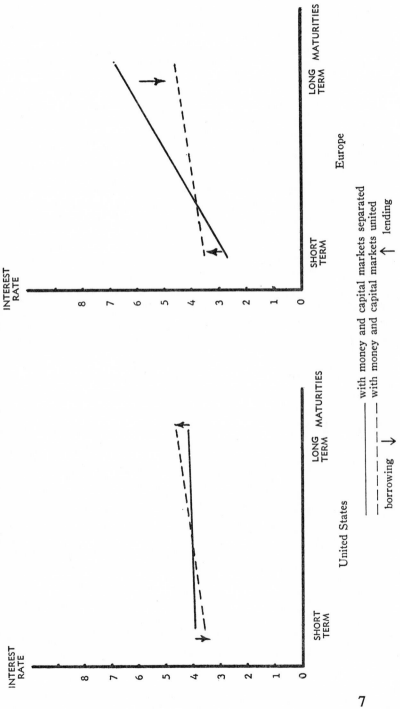

Figure 1: Market Structure of Interest Rates in United States and Europe

lending is to the central bank or to the commercial banks. Member-bank reserves are reduced, of course, when the proceeds of long-term loans in the capital market finally come to rest as deposits with the central bank. But on balance-of-payments grounds, the distinction is of no interest.

Examples of Long-Term Loans for Liquidity

Professor Triffin's criticism of the gold-exchange standard is that reserves can be added only by new gold production, which is inadequate in some sense which need not be made precise, and through deficits of the reserve-currency countries. Deficits pile up as reserves expand, and ultimately undermine the value of the reserve currency. The system is thus self-destructive.

The point that reserves under the gold-exchange standard can be created only by newly mined (or dishoarded) gold and deficits is formally correct on the definition of deficits propounded both by the Department of Commerce (Walther Lederer) and by the Bernstein balance-of-payments committee. The attempt has been made, however, to show that these definitions were not very helpful — and in fact have been harmful. Some examples of reserve creation through long-term loans may serve to illustrate how these definitions have led to and sustained confusion in this area.

First, take the case of currency swaps between central banks. This device has been used by the United States Treasury, under the leadership of former Under Secretary of the Treasury for Monetary Affairs, Robert V. Roosa, as one of the perimeter defenses. As has been mentioned, the exchange of short-term capital assets between two countries can put both in "deficit," as the increase in liabilities is counted but the offsetting increase in claims is not. The slight redefinition of the balance-of-payments deficit to include monetary authorities' holdings of foreign exchange with gold means that outright, irreversible swaps now create reserves without deficits, but when only gold and short-term liabilities were counted, reserves were created by "deficits" which were not deficits in a significant sense.

Where swaps are undertaken when a currency is under pressure, and one country sells its foreign exchange in the market, while the other holds its foreign exchange, there is of course a real deficit. The liability remains, but the asset is sold. The United States

Treasury devised currency swaps mostly as a way to acquire foreign exchange needed to meet a run. But these swaps can take place any time, among two- or multiple-currency centers, to create instant reserves without deficits, except as some irrelevant definition may decree.

Second, consider stabilization loans. The distinction between a stabilization loan and an ordinary loan is, or should be, that under ordinary circumstances a country borrows from abroad to acquire real assets, whereas a stabilization loan is contracted to raise permanently the level of foreign-exchange reserves. The hope of retaining the proceeds of the loan is not always realized, as the Anglo-American Financial Agreement of 1946 demonstrates. But countries do, from time to time, borrow long and lend short, for stabilization purposes, without the borrowers having a surplus or the lenders a deficit, except under the Department of Commerce and Bernstein definitions.

Third, take the question of the reserves of the British Commonwealth, the sterling balances held in London. In the early 1950s there was controversy over whether it was fitting for rich Britain to borrow from the poor colonies and ex-colonies through the mechanism of the sterling-area and colonial sterling balances in London. It was alleged in a series of claims, and denied, that Britain exploited these colonies by borrowing from them.[4] Balance-of-payments issues were not in the forefront of discussion at the time, and the question did not arise whether Britain had a deficit, and the colonies surpluses, when sterling balances increased. Concern was with the stocks, not the flows.

It was not of course appropriate to regard simply the gross sterling balances of the colonies in London. There were many offsets to these sums, in bank loans, commercial indebtedness, and especially bond issues in London. The claim that countries that had 100 per cent reserves for their domestic money supply, as did many of the colonies, had to achieve an export surplus to add to their local money was wrong. Money could be expanded through long-term borrowing. Sometimes colonial borrowing in London resulted in a transitional increase in the money supply as the government sold the proceeds of the loan to the Currency Board against local means of payment; when local expenditure spilled over into import surplus the money supply was drawn down again, and the increase in claims

9

on London spent to pay for the additional imports. This is the transfer mechanism at work. But money could be acquired through long-term borrowing to finance export projects, the output of which offset rising imports. The balance of payments did not turn adverse; the increase in money supply became part of the long-run structure; and the colony borrowed long and lent short to match British borrowing short and lending long. On Department of Commerce terms there was a colonial surplus and a British deficit. On any sensible basis, the balance of payments remained in equilibrium. The colonies acquired liquidity, and paid for it with the difference between the return on short-term assets and the coupon on long-term bonds. Since in London the spread between long and short rates was narrow, the liquidity was acquired cheaply.

Fourth, let us return to the case of two countries, Germany and the United States, with high and low liquidity preference, respectively. Just as the colonies did not lend to Britain by holding sterling, so Germany does not finance the United States. It is claimed, for example, that Europe finances American direct investments in Europe, and it could be held that European holders of dollar balances financed the $940 million increase in long-term U.S. bank claims on foreigners in 1964. But it can equally well be put the other way: American direct investment financed European holdings of dollars, or long-term bank loans by the United States made possible the liquidity of European money markets.

Direct investment raises another point on which the Department of Commerce statistics are grossly misleading. When Europeans think of direct investment, they inevitably have in mind the large United States corporations with enormous amounts of capital which built efficient factories and make life difficult for their competitors. They fail to realize that the Department of Commerce estimates include inter-company balances in direct investment, and that some of the rise in direct investment in recent years represents nothing more than dollar balances left on deposit in the Euro-dollar market by the European subsidiaries of American corporations to earn ¼ per cent more return than would be possible through time deposits in New York. The counterpart to Euro-dollar deposits in London by U.S. firms takes two forms. In one case, the London bank holds short-term assets in New York. The balance of payments shows a deficit on the Commerce (but not the Bernstein) definition. The

Euro-dollar balance (direct investment) is ignored, but the London claim on New York is counted. In effect, however, the London bank could be regarded as part of the New York market (like the Canadian bank already discussed). There is no effect on the exchange market, current or potential, since the liability and the claim are linked.

In the other case, the dollar funds are lent by the New York bank to a European borrower. Here it is necessary to pierce the corporate and banking veils and see what is really happening. Corporation X in the United States has dollars in London, which a London bank (possibly of American ownership) lends to a European borrower, for three, six, or maybe as much as nine months. The European borrower may be expecting a devaluation of the dollar — going short — and if his borrowing is matched by his central bank acquiring dollars, the private short position is matched by a public long one. But suppose foreign-exchange rate changes are far from his mind. His motivation is only that he can borrow more cheaply from the Euro-dollar market, and for longer periods, than he can from his local European bank. In this circumstance it is true that the European central bank finances "direct investment," in the form of dollar balances held abroad, but direct investment equally finances European liquidity.

In fact, however, we do not know how much of the slowly rising direct investment in Europe takes the form of dollar balances and how much is the acquisition of real assets. Many of the real assets, such as those to be represented by the new General Motors plant in Antwerp, involve no capital movement at all. General Motors will finance the entire project through Belgian banks, thus subtracting liquidity from the Belgian money market. It does this largely because of misguided United States concern about the United States balance of payments. But if General Motors tightens up European money markets this may put pressure on local borrowers to turn to the Euro-dollar market, which in turn will raise the demand for United States loans. The United States success in frustrating General Motors using United States funds for European investment — assuming that the company would have borrowed in the cheapest market rather than be concerned about exchange risks — may merely drive some other borrower there.

For another example, consider Dallas. Happily for our peace

of mind, we have no data showing the balance of payments between the Dallas, or 11th, Federal Reserve District and the rest of the United States. But my intuition tells me that if we had such data they would show that Dallas was in surplus and the remaining eleven districts in deficit, on the Department of Commerce definition; that, while Dallas floated many security issues in New York in order to acquire real assets, it also borrowed for liquidity purposes. As its real assets mounted, portfolio balancing required an increase in money assets, and this demand was met by "foreign loans." If the figures were before us, there is every likelihood that the eleven districts would seek to cut Federal spending in the Dallas district, to limit or tie transfers, and to adopt voluntary restrictions on capital movements to the area.

Canada is a foreign country but it is also regarded as the 13th Federal Reserve district. Canada has been borrowing heavily in the United States and its claims on the United States banking system have been rising as well. It is significant that the interest-equalization tax and the Gore amendment were not applied to Canadian transactions, as our monetary authorities instinctively understood that the Department of Commerce approach (and the Bernstein) made no sense in this area. What I have been suggesting above is that Europe is or was in process of becoming the 14th Federal Reserve district.

Finally there is Williamson's interpretation[5] of the 19th century balance-of-payments experience of the United States. His findings are opposed to the classic view of capital transfer, in which capital movements are transferred between countries first in gold and then in goods, the goods-flow real transfer reversing the monetary transfer. As he sees it, cyclical expansion in the United States (of the Kuznets variety) attracts goods and money (gold), which are both paid for in securities. In separate but linked markets, the excess demands for goods and money are matched by an excess supply of securities. Classic transfer theory (and the Commerce definition of balance-of-payments equilibrium) assumes that there are only two markets to be cleared in equilibrium, those for goods and those for securities. But modern monetary theory underlines the need for balanced portfolios in both the lending and the borrowing country. In one case real assets, in the other case securities, are balanced with money. In equilibrium, the United States borrowed through the sale of securities partly to acquire real assets, partly to increase its liquidity.

If only two markets have excess demand or supply, these need not be those for goods and securities. It is possible — the point of this paper — that they are the markets for securities on the one hand, and money on the other.

The International Market for Liquidity

Again take two money-and-capital markets with different liquidity preferences and join them together. The market with high liquidity preference will borrow long and lend short. The market with low liquidity preference will lend long and borrow short. Under the prevailing definitions, past and current, both countries are in disequilibrium, the one with a surplus, the other with a deficit. Does this make sense? The temptation is to answer no. But the temptation must be postponed until we consider the consequence of the two countries swapping loans to bring their interest-rate schedules into line.

In the country with low liquidity preference, which we can call America, short rates fall and long rates rise. In the other country, Germany, short rates rise, long rates fall. If the two countries have strong reasons for preventing these changes, there is something to be said for trying to keep the two markets separate, and to adopt a monetary policy, including a policy regarding long-term interest rates, which suits local conditions. On this score, the United States justifies low long-term rates, for fear of deflation, and Germany high long-term rates for fear of inflation. There are a number of reasons why one might resist allowing the long-term rate to be affected by foreign conditions. The demand for investment might be judged elastic with respect to interest-rate decreases, as is claimed in Germany (the real Germany). Or one may fear deflation, worry that investment is interest-elastic in the United States, or merely be unwilling to risk the chance that investment might decline if the long-term interest rate were to rise. Or one may insist on a particular mix of fiscal and monetary policy not for stability, but for growth, as does Franco Modigliani. If international money-and-capital markets are joined, and a single interest-rate structure obtains internationally, internal stability can be achieved only by fiscal policy, or by persuading international monetary authorities to adopt that set of interest rates which fits the national needs.

Another possibility is that monetary policy has only a very small role to play in domestic economic stability, and to give it up to international influences is not to lose much internally, and to gain in the international sphere. To achieve this gain, of course, it is necessary to change the definition of balance-of-payments disequilibrium.

Take America and Germany with joined money-and-capital markets. The position is akin to international trade between two countries with identical endowments, but different tastes. Equality of prices gives each a chance to benefit: Germany to satisfy its demand for liquidity (plus high investment in illiquid form), and the United States its demand for a return on financial investments. When cloth is traded for wheat and the price of each commodity is the same in both trading countries, the trade can be regarded as unbalanced only if the imports of one commodity are taken as a payment but exports of the other commodity are not regarded as a receipt.

Separating the Markets

When savings equals domestic investment in two countries, but liquidity preferences differ, so that with joined money-and-capital markets one borrows long and lends short (and vice versa for the other), there is a temptation under the Department of Commerce (and Bernstein) definitions to try to separate the money and capital markets again. This is what the United States and Europe are now trying to do, after having spent the years from World War II to 1958 in attempting to restore convertibility.

There are essentially three ways to separate the money and capital markets of the developed world: tax policy, foreign-exchange control, and exchange-rate policy. We may use as illustrations of these devices respectively the interest-equalization tax, voluntary restrictions on foreign lending, and exchange depreciation.

The interest-equalization tax has hardly been very successful. The direct issue of foreign dollar bonds for foreign account (outside of Canada and Japan, which were excepted) has declined, but foreign long-term lending by banks has increased, as well as foreign dollar bonds issued in London. Money is fungible, and to close one outlet is to increase the flow through another. New long-term lending in debt form by the United States actually increased in 1964, despite the interest-equalization tax, as increases in security loans for Canada and new bank long-term lending (of almost $1 billion) more than offset the decline in new foreign dollar bonds sold by European borrowers in New York. When and if the Gore amendment closes off this last outlet (long-term bank loans), there will still be the possibility of developing the Euro-dollar market for bonds as well as for short loans. This is said to have some $5 to $8 billion churning about in it. It is possible that continental and United States capital markets could maintain no direct contact with each other, but have their interest-rate schedules equalized via the European market for dollars and dollar bonds. Still another interesting possibility is European borrowing by way of Canada: the Canadian insurance company borrows from New York and the Canadian bank lends to Europe.

Many observers believe that unit-of-account bonds will replace dollar bonds as an international device for providing long-term funds. Since their start in 1964, $70 million of these bonds have been issued. But foreign dollar bonds are a much more important financing vehicle. Since the interest-equalization tax was announced, it has financed $400 million to September 1964.[6]

An interesting point is that Europeans not only borrow in dollar bonds; they also lend through them.[7] Long-term capital markets are so thin in Europe (outside of Switzerland and the Netherlands) that European investors are prepared to take a lower rate of interest to have bonds which are traded in a wider market, and therefore present less risk of fluctuation. Whether the foreign dollar-bond market in London can grow to the size of the 1962-63 foreign bond market in New York is an open question, though the chances are slim. Much depends upon whether the Euro-dollar market is fed from United States corporate funds. Here is where the United States government is applying foreign-exchange control, in the guise of voluntary restrictions on capital outflows, and exhortations to bring overseas funds home.

What will be the result if United States foreign-exchange control is successful? To believe that one can contain the market in one respect without producing side results is to adopt a partial-equilibrium form of analysis, and to be naive. When United States corporations return Euro-dollar funds to the United States, there are, again, two possibilities. On the one hand, the counterpart can be a reduction in United States liabilities to foreigners; the Chase Manhattan in New York has the deposits instead of the Chase Bank, London. The internal international deposit is cancelled. Nothing has happened. The Department of Commerce rejoices over the reduction of its deficit, but this is trivial. Suppose, however, that the Chase Manhattan branch in London calls a Euro-dollar loan to a European borrower. Rates of interest in Europe rise. It may be that investment is interest-elastic and investment declines. United States exchange control puts pressure on European investment, stability, and growth. This is the opposite of the European expansion which the surplus calls for, and it is action calculated to improve the European balance of payments in real terms, and hurt the United States balance.

Foreign-exchange control has an ugly sound in the United States today, but it is hard to avoid the term. The fact that it is voluntary means that it will either fail completely or it will have to be applied with legal sanctions. The voluntary sanctions applied by the Department of State on oil shipments to Italy during the Ethiopian campaign failed: the five major companies refrained from shipping oil, but thousands of small firms sprang into being practically overnight and delivered to Mussolini all the petroleum products he needed.[8] The prospect of restrictions is said to have produced a massive outflow of capital from the United States during the final quarter of 1964, and a still larger one in the first half of the first quarter of 1965, prior to the message of February 10. If the major corporations dealing in foreign trade are asked to improve their balance-of-payments contribution by 5 per cent a year, there is no guarantee, although perhaps little likelihood, that the Euro-dollar market cannot be fed by a flow of funds from small corporations, individuals, etc.

Varying exchange rates may separate international money markets. They failed to do so in the Canadian case: the flexible exchange rate of Canada from 1950 to 1961 managed to produce a stabilizing movement of short-term capital, but the system broke down because the exchange rate was ignored by long-term investors. They held the view that the Canadian dollar could not get very far

16

from the United States dollar over the lifetime of a 15- to 20-year investment, so that a one per cent differential in interest rates could not be discouraged by exchange risk. The opinion exists that foreigners are borrowing in the United States and in the Euro-dollar market, as already mentioned, because they believe the dollar is weak and want to go short of it. But foreigners are also investing in United States bonds, so that the long-term capital market may choose to ignore the exchange rate. If the dollar is weak today, as I do not believe, there is an excellent chance that it will be as strong as the French franc, the Swiss franc, the guilder and the lira five years from now — if not the strong German mark and the weak pound sterling — so that it makes no sense to make a long-term bet either way. The exchange-rate pattern is not likely to be changed much, and over the long run the exchange-rate differential becomes less important than the interest-rate spread.

Moreover, changing exchange rates threaten the possibility of destabilizing short-term speculation. They need not; and the Canadian case is reassuring at short-term if not at long. But is the risk worth taking for the possible gain in freedom to use another weapon internally — monetary policy — when the evidence to confirm its importance is cloudy? World trade and payments have done brilliantly in the last fifteen years. United States internal policy has been successful since the tax cut. It would be not only United States trade and payments that would be jeopardized by the risk of changing the slowly solidifying structure of fixed rates, but the trade and payments of many countries of the world. Rather than embark on the dubious proposition of altering the exchange-rate structure, I would recommend keeping it and changing our attitude toward international capital movements.

One recommendation for United States action continuously comes forward from bankers in the United States and from all segments of economic and financial opinion in Europe: it is that the United States should raise interest rates. The weakness of this policy, and of monetary policy generally when liquidity preferences in the markets differ sharply, is readily seen in the present analysis. It can happen that when tastes and endowments are identical in two markets, incorrect pricing in one of them will lead to trade which is not called for on economic grounds. It is possible that such is the case between New York and European money and capital

17

markets, but the likelihood is not high. And if tastes do differ, changing prices in one market to align them with those abroad is a disequilibrium measure which will not succeed.

Monetary policy is more readily applied at the short than at the long end of the market. Raising rates in New York will therefore narrow the spread between long- and short-term rates, a spread which is already too narrow in relation to liquidity preferences abroad. What is needed is not Operation Twist, to raise short rates without disturbing long, for the sake of stimulating long-term investment and employment, but Operation Reverse Twist, lowering the short rate and raising the long, or at least raising the long more than the short.

To permit New York and European money and capital markets to coalesce does mean the international determination of monetary policy. Some of the remoter sections of the capital market, as for example mortgage rates, may continue only tangentially linked, as the mortgage markets in the United States differ regionally. The surrender of some measure of economic sovereignty is not, however, cause for despair. Already exchange rates, commercial policy, and mechanisms for support in time of speculative crisis are internationally determined. In a small world, neighbors have to shape domestic policies in the light of what is going on next door. But if and when such underlying phenomena as liquidity preferences differ, it is not enough merely to change prices to match those abroad.

Europe's Gripes

I have tried to make clear that much of European impatience with the United States balance-of-payments deficit, its cause and its duration, is misguided. It is not, as many Europeans think, that we are wantonly buying up European plant and equipment and paying for them with funny money, the dollar. For the most part, we are providing Europe with liquidity it cannot or will not provide for itself.[9] It is true that there is some United States direct investment in plant and equipment, including some bought with dollars, like the minority stock of Ford in Dagenham in 1960. But British reserves are not mounting, and the Ford purchase enabled sellers of Ford stock to undertake investment in new corporations.

Most of the unhappiness is based on rising nationalism, a phenomenon which has little to do with economics, like the Swiss closing the frontier to Italian workers, the Greeks cutting off the outflow of workers, and the United States threatening to tax tourists going to Europe. It is highly significant, however, that in the two leading cases in France — General Electric's purchase of Machines Bull, and the Libby-McNeil-Libby investment in canning in the Rhone valley — the French authorities first stopped the investment and then backed down and, after face-saving gestures, allowed it in. [. . .] These American firms, whether financed from New York or locally in Europe, have technological and productivity contributions to make in Europe, which when pointed out overwhelm nationalistic and prestigious sentiments. The opposition to direct investment has little to do with concern over balance-of-payments equilibrium. It can make a contribution to breaking bottlenecks which foster monopoly profits. But it is a convenient lightning rod to attract irritation.

Balance-of-Payments Equilibrium When Liquidity Preferences Differ

An appropriate definition of balance-of-payments equilibrium when considerable differences exist in the liquidity preferences of the countries concerned can be developed by a sequence of slight modifications of the various arrangements of accounts that are implied in each of the definitions discussed. If errors and omissions be ignored, foreign investment, necessarily equivalent to the current-account balance, that is, to exports of goods and services less imports of goods and services, can be divided into long-term capital flows, short-term capital flows, and gold flows:

1.　　　　Exports of goods and services
　　less Imports of goods and services
　　————————————————
　equals Net outflow of long-term capital
　　plus Net outflow of short-term capital
　　plus Net inflow of gold.

If we transpose the movements of long-term capital above the line and find that both the three items above the line and the two

19

remaining items below the line add up to zero, we arrive at the equilibrium condition formulated by Ragnar Nurkse for "basic balance":

2.   Exports of goods and services
    less Imports of goods and services
    less Net outflow of long-term capital

equals Zero

equals Net inflow (outflow) of short-term capital
    plus Net outflow (inflow) of gold.

The Department of Commerce is not content with this and, in order to emphasize implications for changes in the international "liquidity" of the United States, divides short-term capital into two parts, depending on whether the movement takes the form of changes in assets or in liabilities. It regards movements of short-term capital through changes in foreign assets as the equivalent of movements of long-term capital — transactions that call for a real transfer through a current-account surplus or deficit. Accordingly, the arrangements of accounts in the statistics of the Commerce Department place flows of short-term capital that take the form of increases or decreases in the holdings of liquid foreign assets above the line. The equilibrium condition then looks as follows:

3.   Exports of goods and services
    less Imports of goods and services
    less Net outflow of long-term capital
    less Net outflow of short-term capital through
              increase in foreign assets

equals Zero

equals Net inflow (outflow) of short-term capital through
              increase (decrease) in foreign liabilities
    plus Net outflow (inflow) of gold.

It is implicitly assumed that changes in liquid short-term assets abroad represents movements of real capital which ought to be transferred through the current account, whereas changes in foreign liabilities are merely balancing items, like gold. There is general agreement that capital should flow from countries where its marginal physical product is relatively low to countries where its real return is higher. The definition of "balance" that is used by the Department of Commerce evidently implies a rough approximation, associating all changes in the holdings of foreign short-term assets with real capital movements, and changes in liquid liabilities to foreigners with balancing or financing transactions. One may modify this, however, by drawing another distinction, namely, between short-term capital flows called for by differences in the relative scarcity of capital in different countries and short-term capital flows of a balancing type. A more general, though less operational, view of the equilibrium condition then will take the following form:

3a. Exports of goods and services
  less Imports of goods and services
  less Net outflow of long-term capital
  less Net outflow of short-term capital
    induced by differences in capital scarcity

  equals Zero

  equals Net inflow (outflow) of short-term capital of
    a balancing type
  plus Net outflow (inflow) of gold.

This arrangement would be used, for example, if because of the greater marginal product of capital abroad than at home, the United States finances both its exports and its imports, and holds claims on foreign importers among its assets while financing domestic importers.

The Bernstein Committee's disagreement with the Department of Commerce turns on the fact that the latter treats liabilities to private foreigners and to foreign official holders of dollars alike in regarding changes in both these liabilities as short-term capital movements of the balancing type. The Bernstein Committee wants to treat liquid liabilities to private foreigners differently from liquid liabilities to official foreign creditors, and thus implicitly proposes the following arrangement as indicative of equilibrium:

4. Exports of goods and services
  less Imports of goods and services

21

  less Net outflow of long-term capital

  less Net outflow of short-term capital
      induced by differences in capital scarcity

  plus Net inflow of short-term capital through
      increase in liabilities to private foreign creditors

 equals Zero

 equals Net inflow (outflow) of short-term capital through
      increase (decrease) of liabilities to official
      foreign creditors

  plus Net outflow (inflow) of gold.

This is unsatisfactory for several reasons. To begin with, movements of short-term capital induced by differences in relative capital scarcity are not even roughly equivalent to movements in short-term capital through changes in holdings of short-term foreign assets, and movements of short-term capital of the balancing type are far from being the same as movements of short-term capital through changes in liquid liabilities; even if these items were equivalent, the division of changes in liabilities between those to private creditors and those to official creditors is almost meaningless. Most important, however, we find it necessary to divide flows of long-term capital as well as flows of short-term capital. Long-term capital flows may either be induced by differences in the relative scarcity of capital or they may serve to accommodate national liquidity preference. The most appropriate definition of balance-of-payments equilibrium is then depicted by the following arrangement of items:

5.   Exports of goods and services

  less Imports of goods and services

  less Net outflow of long-term capital
      induced by differences in capital scarcity

  less Net outflow of short-term capital
      induced by differences in capital scarcity

 equals Zero

 equals Net outflow (inflow) of long-term capital
      induced by differences in national liquidity
      preference

22

less Net inflow (outflow) of short-term capital
    induced by differences in national liquidity
    preference
less Net outflow (inflow) of gold.

The theory is simple. The problem arises in trying to divide short-term capital and long-term capital into their components. I see no easy rule of thumb. The Department of Commerce distinction between assets and liabilities in short-term capital is misleading. The Bernstein Committee's distinction between private and official movements through liabilities fails to help. What is called for is rather art than science, the banker's act of distinguishing between assets and liabilities by the mean of the probability distribution of the date on which they are likely to require payment. The functions are non-linear. It is absurd, up to a certain point, for a bank to be said to be in deficit when it makes a loan and writes a deposit on its books (the Commerce definition); but beyond a certain point, the idea ceases to be misleading and is a touchstone of great operational significance. It is a paradox that the premature adoption of the Department of Commerce definition shifts the point at which it would otherwise apply.

The distinction in the long-term capital field is even more difficult to draw than in the short-term. What long-term capital movements should serve to transfer real assets, and what are merely to trade internationally in liquidity? One possibility might seem to be by geographical region. United States long-term capital exports to the less developed countries should be transferred; some considerable part, at least, of those to Europe (and Japan?) are transactions in the liquidity market. But this is obviously wanting, if it be recalled that the British colonies under the sterling-exchange standard were interested in borrowing long and lending short.

Another clue may be found in the question whether the capital moves in the same direction or contrary to the movement of short-term capital. When long- and short-term capital move together, it is useful to have them transferred through the current account, since both seem to reflect the lower marginal product of capital at home than abroad. When they move oppositely, however, there is reason to suspect international trade in liquidity. But this is unsatisfactory. It ignores the kink. Below a certain point — which

23

shifts with time, the unfolding of events, and opinion — lending long and borrowing short, or vice versa, is merely trading in liquidity. Beyond it, the long lender is overdoing it and the short lender has the right to become increasingly nervous.

There is, then, in my judgment, no rule of thumb by which balance-of-payments equilibrium can be turned over either to the clerical staff or to the econometricians. It remains an art. Rules of thumb breed confusion and uncertainty. They shift the inflection point. They occasion trouble.

In my judgment, further, in case anyone cares, the dollar is strong today, not weak, in an objective sense, and it is important that subjective appraisals discard the terrifying definitions we have allowed to creep into the discussion, and recognize this fact. Objective circumstances of strength can be turned into chaos by subjective judgments. The need is far more for central-banker and money-market education than it is for voluntary restrictions, higher rates of interest, or new interferences through tax or exchange policy.

The Outlook

The Brookings Institution is being proved right in its forecast of the current account. Slowly, but surely, the current account of the United States has improved from $150 million in 1959 to over $6 billion in 1964. On any sophisticated view that looks ahead, it is the French franc, the Swiss franc, and the Dutch guilder that threaten weakness ahead, not the dollar.

In a sense, the years since 1961 or 1962 have been abnormal. Until that time, rapid growth took place in Europe without an increase in wages, as extra supplies of labor were mopped up. When labor became more difficult to obtain, and Mediterranean workers failed to provide the correct mix of skills, wages rose, and growth slowed down. Wages rose more than prices, and profits were squeezed. But the response to the profit squeeze was not reduced investment, as in a Keynesian system, but the Schumpeterian one of increasing investment to cut costs and maintain profit margins. The reduction in corporate profits led to pressure on weak capital markets, which spilled over to the United States because of convertibility established in 1958. Partly there was a need for real assets; but with the real assets came a need for greater liquidity, as corporations wanted to balance their portfolios of real assets with money, and to fund their obligations on a longer basis than could be provided by the liquidity preference of savers.

High investment, however, is unlikely to survive long with low profits. In the long run, the Keynesian relation is likely to prevail. Growth is likely to slow down still further, as investment declines. American balance-of-payments measures, by restricting investment and cutting down long-term lending, will accelerate the decline. If the decline becomes cumulative, Europe is likely to develop a real balance-of-payments surplus vis-à-vis the United States in place of the current phoney one, a surplus achieved at the cost of a fall in output and imports.

NOTES

[1] See Edward M. Bernstein, *The Balance of Payments Statistics of the United States: A Review and Appraisal* (special report prepared for the Bureau of the Budget; published in Washington, April 29, 1965).

[2] See, for example, Walther Lederer, *The Balance on Foreign Trans- actions: Problems of Definition and Measurement,* Special Papers in Inter- national Economics, no. 5. (International Finance Section, Princeton University, September 1963); and by the same author, "The Balance of United States Payments: A Statement of the Problem," in S. E. Harris, ed., *The Dollar in Crisis* (New York: Harcourt Brace and World, 1961), pp. 114-136.

Throughout the discussion below, the appropriate treatment of "errors and omissions" is ignored, as if all payments were known, rather than estimated by imperfect techniques.

[3] See, for example, Hal B. Lary, *Problems of the United States as World Trader and Banker* (Princeton, N.J.: Princeton University Press, 1963); Robert Triffin, "The Presentation of U.S. Balance of Payments Statistics," in American Statistical Association, 1961 *Proceedings* of the Business and Economics Statistics Section (Washington, 1962), pp. 51-57; and Walter Gardner, "An Exchange-Market Analysis of the U.S. Balance of Payments," International Monetary Fund *Staff Papers* (May 1961), pp. 195-211.

[4] See, for example, Ida Greaves, *"The Colonial Sterling Balances,"* Essays in International Finance, No. 20 (International Finance Section, Princeton University, 1954), and the discussion in the *Economic Journal* for 1953-55 among Greaves, Hazelwood, Niculescu, King.

[5] Jeffrey G. Williamson, *American Growth and the Balance of Payments, 1820-1913* (Chapel Hill: University of North Carolina Press, 1964).

[6] See "Perspectives on the New York Market: 'Capital Market Aspects,' " Remarks by Nathaniel Samuel, National Industrial Conference Board, October 14, 1964.

[7] See Chapter Five, pp. 72ff.

[8] See Herbert Feis, *Seen from E. A.: Three International Episodes* (New York: Knopf, 1947), Episode No. 3, pp. 193-276.

⁹ I discuss elsewhere the possibility that high long-term interest rates in, say, Germany are the result of monopolistic practices in capital markets and particularly the control of the bankers over lending and security issues. [. . .] See Chapter Four, pp. 54ff.

CHAPTER TWO

EUROPEAN INTEGRATION AND
THE INTERNATIONAL CORPORATION*

My thesis is that economic integration cannot be achieved by customs unions alone but requires factor movements, and that factor movements on an adequate scale to achieve or closely approach integration require institutions beyond those normal to factor markets.

In particular, to make substantial progress toward economic integration probably necessitates the development of corporations that are equally at home in the various political entities party to the integration attempt. Ideally in the European integration contemplated by the Rome Treaty, it would be a European corporation, reconstituted under European charter or resulting from mergers that transcended national lines to create a truly European, not a national, decision-making entity. Or the effective institution might be an international corporation with a home base outside the Common Market, and therefore indifferent in its dealings with one or another country of the Six. At the moment, when provision for European incorporation in the European Economic Community has been tabled, it looks as though the international corporation, typically that with headquarters in the United States, is the leading prospect for the effective instrument of European integration. If the Common Market repulses the American giant corporation and fails to establish European incorporation, the European movement may fall short of real integration.

But it is necessary to proceed more systematically. Permit me

* This is a slightly revised version of the Ascher Isaacs Memorial Lecture in International Economics, delivered at the University of Pittsburgh on April 1, 1965. Published in the *Columbia Journal of World Business*, Vol. I, No. 1 (Winter, 1965-66).

to discuss the two substantives in the title of this lecture separately before I develop the connection. Economic integration I define as factor-price equalization, that is, the equalization of wages, interest, and profits. This definition is more far-reaching than those which emphasize merely the elimination of restrictions on the movement of goods. It makes integration a standard, like absolute zero in temperature, which can be approached or moved away from, but is seldom if ever reached.

Of course, freedom of goods movement is an important ingredient of integration, as the factor-price-equalization theorem suggests. If two countries produce goods in the same way, equalization of goods-prices will result in equalization of the prices of factor inputs — land, labor, and capital — provided certain rather restrictive assumptions are met about the unimportance of transport costs, the identification of certain goods with certain factors, the production of every good in all the countries, perfect competition, constant returns to scale, etc. So restrictive are the assumptions, however, that few economists believe that goods-movements alone can produce economic integration as here defined. It probably requires as well the movements of factors which the classic economists thought did not occur in international, as contrasted with domestic, trade.

The Rome Treaty establishing the European Economic Community provided for freedom of factor movements. Yet large-scale movements of capital have not taken place within the Common Market. To the extent that the capital markets of Europe are joined, it was, before the announcement that the President would seek passage of an Interest Equalization Tax in July 1963, principally by means of New York.[1] European borrowers would sell bonds in New York, and European lenders would buy bonds. Some of the bonds were identical, i.e., bought by Europeans from Europeans in New York. [. . .]

Another institution for moving capital from one national money or capital market in the EEC to another is the large American bank with branches in the separate countries. This device is not available for integration in the United States, since branch banking is forbidden in most states. Nor has it gone far elsewhere. But it is interesting to observe that there are no European-wide commercial banks except the Chase Manhattan, the First National City,

28

the Bank of America, and the Morgan Guaranty. French, German, Italian, Dutch, and Belgian commercial banks cooperate, and sometimes form consortia regularly for successive loans; but the identity of interest is limited. A new decision is made each time for each operation; there is no mechanism for borrowing in one market and lending in another automatically, such as occurs in the single bank which receives deposits here and makes loans there.

Integration through factor movements also takes place by means of movements of labor, and these, too, operate in Europe largely by outside mechanisms. It is true that Italy has provided the largest number of foreign workers for Germany, France, and Belgium (leaving out Switzerland, which has half a million Italians but is not a member of the Common Market). But the numbers of border workers who cross from Belgium into France, or the Netherlands and France into Germany, are trivial compared to the large inflow from Eastern Germany to the West, from North Africa to France, and from Portugal, Spain, Greece, and Turkey into Germany, France, and Belgium.

Moreover, the outsiders with no roots are more mobile than Bretons are in France or East Bavarians in Germany and far more mobile than nationals between the separate countries. It has been noted that wage equalization is taking place between Southern and Northern Italy by means of Switzerland and Germany. Southern Italians go to Switzerland and Germany at the same time that Italian employers are recruiting Italian workers in those countries to bring them to North Italy. Similarly, 12,000 Moroccans leaving Northern France for the Ruhr when their contracts in the French coal mines are up raise wages in France and lower them in Germany, a step in the direction of wage equalization.

But the tendency toward equalization of factor prices does not always occur through organized markets — for goods or for labor and capital. In the United States an important contribution to integration has been the national corporation. This borrows in New York and invests where it can assemble materials and labor in least-cost combinations, relative to market outlets. [. . .] The economic historian, Alfred Chandler, dates the rise of the national corporation in the United States at the 1890's, and observes, interestingly, that with the change of scale and horizon, there was also a change in behavior, as the national corporation took marketing back from wholesalers and discharged the function itself. A national corporation that shuts down production in a high-cost and expands in a low-cost location provides a mechanism of integration connected with but significantly differentiated from the markets for goods and factors.

The rise of the international corporation is more difficult to date. Some American companies "went international" shortly after becoming national, at the turn of the century. By 1929 there was a sizable list. But it was not until the development of the aircraft, and especially the jet aircraft, that the international corporation came into its own. As Stephen Hymer has pointed out,[2] international operations are expensive. They require face-to-face contact, expensive communication by telegram and telephone. They involve misunderstandings and loss. They can be undertaken, therefore, only when they offer a particularly high return. Hymer's point is that direct investment is not simple capital movement. That could take place more cheaply through capital markets. Direct investment implies coordination of company operations to take advantage of superprofits. The basis of the higher-than-normal profits may be a monopoly in technology, or access to extra large amounts of capital, or capacity to coordinate operations in several parts of the world in ways which cannot be managed through the free play of market forces.

A few further remarks about the international corporation before coming to grips with the connections between it and European integration. There is a theorem set out by Irving Brecher and S. S. Reisman that since people in the same position trying to maximize profits will necessarily behave in identical fashion, it makes no difference whether a given company in Canada is Canadian or American: the economic result will be the same. I doubt this. Two decision-making units trying to maximize profits within the same horizon, spatially and through time, will behave in the same fashion — assuming equal intelligence and managerial capacity — but if one is a national corporation and the other an international one, their horizons will differ, and so may their behavior. The international corporation will be keeping an eye on profit opportunities, governmental intervention, political pressures, and so on all over the world. To meet a local demand, the local company will expand in the local area. The international corporation might well supply the demand from abroad. Moreover, if demand contracts in the market, the local corporation is likely to cut production and dig in. The international corporation may close down altogether. [. . .]

The differences between the national and the international corporations explain why joint ventures are such failures as an answer to the problem of direct investment — one partner wants income and the other wants capital gains, or one partner wants profits from refining and distribution and the other wants profits from selling the basic material. They also explain why the international corporation's answer to the demand for local participation — why don't you buy shares in the parent corporation — usually falls on deaf ears. (Note the exception of the Libby-McNeil-Libby case in France, however.) Local capital is limited to a local horizon. It sees a local profitable enterprise owned abroad, and it wants a piece of it, including the wealth that comes from capitalizing the superprofits from the particular operation. On Hymer's principle of the need to overcome costs of foreign operations, direct investment must earn not only a higher return than the company could earn at home, but also a higher return — owing to the monopoly — than a local company can make in the host country. Since they operate with different horizons, the international corporation and the local investor or government have a hard time agreeing on what constitutes optimal behavior.

Now to join up European integration and the international corporation. As noted at the start of this lecture, my hypothesis is that if European integration is really to be achieved, there must develop European corporations, maximizing profits over some appropriate time profile, within the geographical limits of the Common Market. I do not see such corporations coming into being [. . .]. To the extent that international corporations operate in the Common Market, the bulk of them will be American, with most of their interests outside. But I doubt that there will be enough American corporations operating in the Common Market to achieve much of the indicated integration by this mechanism.

There are some European corporations, to be sure. The 1964 merger of Agfa and Gevaert in the photographic-film field, a German corporation and a Belgian, was viewed by some as the beginning. But the two firms maintain separate identities for their

31

products, separate boards of directors, separate bodies for decision-making. It is said that they will start by merging their distribution facilities, and move on after that to research. The test of a merger, however, is whether there is finally one decision-making unit, and whether the decision can be taken to close out an activity in one location (read country) when it is found less efficient than in another location where operations can be expanded. Cooperation between two locations that are both maintained stops short of integration in the sense I mean it. The forms of integration may be adopted without the substance.

To illustrate, let me cite the story of a Sloan Fellow at M.I.T. — a junior executive studying for a year — who wrote a master's thesis on oil imports. Like most Sloan Fellows, he liked to interview — it gives one a chance of looking over the rest of the industry with a good cover. In New York he asked the assistant to the chairman of a large oil company what its views on oil imports were, and was told that the company had none. Expressing incredulity, he was told more candidly that the company had two views which the board of directors was unable to reconcile, one of the domestic and one of the foreign-operating subsidiary. The fact that the foreign subsidiary earned a higher return on its investment than the domestic subsidiary might have been expected to push the board of directors in favor of its position. But the domestic subsidiary was not without its strengths. For one thing, it had support in the Congress of the United States, which neither the foreign subsidiary nor the main company could muster. This was not a merger into a single company, but an alliance of sovereigns.

The United Steel in Britain, which maintained inefficient production at Cumberland and hesitated to expand efficient capacity in the East Midlands between the wars, may provide another example.[3] While it is too soon to estimate how the Agfa-Gevaert merger will develop, the initial arrangement, which perpetuates both companies under the direction of a joint board, suggests that decisions will not be taken solely on the basis of profitability, regardless of where that standard leads.

There have been many international corporations of European origin. Some of the most impressive of these, where integration is complete, have been Anglo-Dutch in character, especially the Shell and Unilever companies. These breach the lines of division between the Common Market and the European Free Trade Area under British aegis. Others have had a purely national base, like Philips, Siemens, Solvay, or Dunlop. Still others — ARBED of Luxembourg in iron, or Alsthom in electrical products — are most clearly international in character.

For a while in 1963 and 1964, it looked as if the Agfa-Gevaert merger would be followed by many others. Citroën bought into the German firm NSU, which owns the patents to the Wankel gas-turbine engine, and plans were laid in 1965 to construct an engine plant in Germany and a chassis factory in France. Henschel in Kassel and Berliet in Lyon cooperate in trucks. Alfa Romeo and Renault and a number of other pairs of automobile companies have marketing agreements. Philips is talking to Siemens, and joint actions have been taken by Société Carbochimique of Belgium and Société Chimique d'Auby of France, Royal Dutch Shell and Monetcatini. But agreements, talks, and cooperation are not mergers in which the identity of the parent company is mingled with those of other nationality; nor is this true when new joint subsidiaries are created. Rheinische-Westphalische Oel is a new subsidiary, owned jointly by Shell and I. G. Leverkusen, and Shell and Badische Anilin, another I. G. Farben descendant, cooperate in plastics. But these efforts are not only limited, as compared with complete mergers; they are confined for the most part to pairs of national companies. When Shell and Badische Anilin tried to form a subsidiary in France to make polyethylene, the Minister of Finance reminded them icily that authorization was required for foreign firms to operate in France.[4]

The fact is that the European tradition calls not for merger but for business agreement, or cartels. The Rome Treaty forbids cartels, but the European Economic Commission, in the course of applying the provisions of the Treaty, has chosen to distinguish between good agreements and bad ones. In the early period of the Common Market a number of agreements between national firms were made in the interests of rationalization. One company would make this product, and the other that. The need to maintain a complete line behind a tariff wall gave way to specialization and exchange within the Common Market, with large economies of scale, according to observers like Herbert Giersch, arising from rationalization cartels. But when Nordhoff of Volkswagen publicly proposed that the

33

various national companies of Europe specialize by model size[5] as a means of meeting American competition, he was indignantly refused. Professor Valletta, of Fiat, who had earlier suggested an agreement of the European producers for pricing, purchasing (especially steel), and selling as a means of heading off American competition, but was turned down because his scheme was obviously in contravention of the Rome Treaty, rejected the Nordhoff proposal. Fiat has a full line of cars, and Volkswagen has specialized. The Volkswagen proposal for specialization patently favors Volkswagen and hurts producers with a more balanced set of models.

The automobile industry furnishes an excellent example of the problem. The United States, with a single market of 194 million consumers, has three or possibly four producers. Europe, with more than 200 million consumers, has had 40 altogether and possibly 15 to 20 substantial producers, but is surely going to find itself reduced to a smaller number. A semimerger is currently taking place in France between Citroën and Peugeot, which are forming a special company, a fifty-fifty subsidiary to produce parts common to both, including certain transmissions and truck engines.[6] Volkswagen originally bought up DKW but has since sold it to Mercedes-Benz. It is significant that these are national mergers. Italian, French, and even German interests are fearful of American "monsters," but the answer to them seems thus far to have been merger at the national level rather than the development of the European corporation. Apart from the Citroën interest in Wankel with NSU and Henschel-Berliet in trucks, there have been no international mergers.

Contrast the position of the American Big Three. General Motors has the fast-rising Opel in Germany and Vauxhall in Britain, and has announced a $100 million expansion of its Belgian assembly plant in Antwerp. Ford is well established in Germany and England with local models, with a new plant in Belgium. Chrysler has acquired interests in Simca in France, Rootes in England, and a Spanish subsidiary, and is said to be looking for a suitable company to buy in Germany. These firms are already in position to adjust production internationally.

Europe generally is made unhappy by the size of American corporations. It is pointed out that General Motors alone grosses as much as the thirteen largest German companies, and that this is 10 per cent larger than the gross national product of the Netherlands; or that General Motors' profit has been larger than Renault's turnover. This was in 1963, before its record $1¾ billion profit in 1964. Among the world's 60 biggest corporations, 49 are American and only 11 European,[7] and of the 100 top firms in turnover in 1962 Germany placed only 13, with its largest, Volkswagen, thirty-fifth on the list.[8] Of the giant companies of the world, the Americans listed average five times larger in size than the leading British or German corporations in their field, and ten times larger than the French companies.[9]

But these figures, as economists know, are not only difficult to interpret, depending upon whether one chooses assets, net worth, turnover, profits, or cash flow; they are also of doubtful relevance. The amount of funds which an American company will invest in Europe is limited, and it is this limited portion of assets, profits, sales, cash flow, or whatever which should be compared with European companies. Even so, the comparison is frightening for Europe.

France objects to the American companies on more than mere size. These companies, it is held, can frustrate the French Plan. The Plan is implemented to a considerable degree through the control which the Commissariat du Plan exercises over the flow of government funds and public savings. With an underdeveloped capital market, savings move from household to French business largely through government institutions. This is especially true when profits are squeezed by rising costs so that investment depends more on outside and less on internal funds. Foreign corporations with access to outside sources of capital can escape governmental control.

The other concern of the French is that the technological fallout of international corporations will occur outside of France. When General Electric buys Machines Bull and Olivetti, the research will be done in Schenectady rather than in Paris or Ivrea.

Neither of these objections is very compelling. As to the first, the Plan has thus far been a success because it pushed for expansion. To worry that investment may occur which is not wanted is to anticipate a shift in the thrust of planning to restraint, higher prices, less growth. There have been symptoms of this attitude in France from time to time, but happily they have been fleeting. If American companies want to invest their own money or money borrowed outside France, they are sensible or foolish. If they are sensible, France benefits, as well as the company; if foolish, it is their money which is lost, not French, unless their expansion led to intense competition and losses for other manufacturers.

The more fundamental reason, it seems to me, is that the French are unwilling yet to be truly international, nor even, as I shall suggest in more detail shortly, truly European in their economic life. This attitude is not solely French, by any means. Industrial associations in Germany last winter were studying whether European industry should be delivered to United States capital power. The great German banker, Herman Abs, is said to be restive under the threat of United States direct selling of securities by American brokers to Europeans, instead of through German banks, and German banks dislike the international corporation because it weakens their monopoly on capital by providing the firm with access to credit abroad. The Dutch are regarded as international and maintain strong ties to Britain and the United States, but this sometimes appears less as a positive attitude of faith in internationalism than a counterpoise to the domination of Germany and France in the Common Market. There are times, exemplified by their attitude toward Mediterranean labor to which they have not extended a warm welcome, when they seem slightly nationalistic too. But the French are outstanding in independence of trans-Channel or trans-Atlantic suggestion or leadership, and we can use them to illustrate the vestigial importance of national life in the Common Market.

The French opposition to the international (read American) corporation is partly its freedom from capital control, and partly the fact of technological fallout abroad. But fundamentally the trouble with these corporations is that they are not French. The French want a French and not an international technology, just as they want a French and not an international deterrent. This is true in atomic energy, in supersonic aircraft, in computer technology and everything else. It is widely believed by American officials in Europe that the French opposition to American "monsters" is a smoke screen under which the Conseil du Patronat Français hopes to soften up the Community's antimerger and anticartel actions. But this is too subtle. The point is that the French are not

36

ready for the European corporation, much less for the international corporation.

This can be demonstrated partly by the absence of international mergers in Europe involving French and partner companies. It is also mirrored in the actions of others. Take the attitude of American corporations. When the Common Market was initially organized, it was believed that American firms operating in the separate markets would rationalize their operations. IBM, for example, was said to have maintained plants in separate countries assembling separate machines, the components of which were produced in several other countries. This layout was believed to minimize the danger of nationalization, since no country taking over a plant would acquire an integrated operation. When the Common Market took effect, this rather expensive arrangement could be abandoned for a more efficient organization of production. Or in the case of companies making a single line, scale economies might make it sensible to substitute one plant for five after the internal protective tariffs were eliminated.

The notions of investment creation and investment diversion were evolved to parallel (verbally, though not analytically) trade creation and trade diversion in the economic analysis of customs unions. Investment creation was the response by the outside producer to the stimulus of trade diversion. Unable to lick them, he joined them, establishing a plant inside the Common Market to fill the market from which discrimination cut him off. This was the widespread American response to the Rome Treaty and is completely analogous to a tariff factory — that is, a manufacturing operation called into being by a tariff on finished products. Much of the effect of the Common Market in attracting United States investment was not investment creation in the sense that investments in Europe which were not profitable with internal tariffs separating the four countries and the Belgian-Luxembourg customs union became profitable when these were removed. It came from the attention which the Common Market drew to investment opportunities in Europe which had previously passed unnoticed, having lain beyond the horizon of the American businessman still preoccupied after the war with the American market.

Investment diversion, as contrasted with investment creation, was to stem from the anticipated reorganization of the European investment of outside companies that were already established in Europe to take advantage of newly arisen opportunities for economies of scale and specialization. The creation and the diversion effects could be intermingled. The Common Market could lead to both expansion and reorganization. But investment diversion, so far as is observable from the outside, is negligible. American companies seem to have decided that the anticipated opportunity to rationalize was illusory. It was put to me once in 1964: "To sell in France, build a factory in France." General Motors Frigidaire incurred the displeasure of the French government when it closed down its small plant at Gennevilliers in 1962. This was required by the force of Italian competition in automatic refrigerators. If the cause had been company rationalization, the indignation would doubtless have been greater. It is true that there is considerable interplant exchange between Ford of Limburg in Belgium and Ford of Cologne — enough, it is said, to have increased the ratio of Belgian foreign trade to national income in recent years (without affecting the balance of trade). The General Motors investment in Antwerp may be more than a mere duplication of Opel and Vauxhall facilities in Germany and Britain, respectively. But investment diversion by American plants does not seem to have been significant.

It is not only the international companies of American origin which encounter problems in France. The rebuff to Shell-Badische Anilin has been mentioned. At the time of the General Electric purchase into Machines Bull of France, it is said that a private banker had tried to interest Siemens and Philips, separately, in the venture. These two companies, like General Electric, have need of a ready-made entry into the computer field in which they have fallen behind. Capital problems may have contributed to the decision not to pursue the matter, but it is said that each company lacked the assurance that it would be treated in the long run as a national in France.

Trade discrimination is possible under GATT because the world has made provision within the most-favored-nation clause for customs unions and free-trade areas, to bridge the gap between free trade (in the national market) and tariffs. In the corporate field, no such discrimination has been possible. The standard here is national treatment, in which foreign corporations are treated like national corporations.

For example, national treatment of each other's corporations is provided by the Franco-American Convention of Commerce, Friendship, and Navigation, the latest of which was signed in November, 1959, even though the French have disregarded it in announcing restrictions on foreign investment in April 1965. Foreign corporations can be discriminated against as a class by legislation or by administrative action. But while it is possible *administratively* to favor corporations from some foreign countries over those of others, there has been in the past no recognized right *in law* to discriminate in favor of the corporations of one nation over those of another. This right is now claimed by Article 52 of the Treaty of Rome, which grants national treatment to the companies of partner countries but not to those of outsiders, a claim which has still to be tested in diplomacy and in international law. If it is successfully defended, and if the conditions for establishing corporations are made uniform in the Community, as has been sought but tabled in 1961, there would be created in effect a European corporation.

Note that the concept of a European corporation presupposes the development of a corps of European executives who are mobile from Catania to Friesland. The European bureaucrat has been developed, ready for quick relocation to Brussels, Paris, Geneva, and, with less grace, Luxembourg and Strasbourg, but the European executive is less inclined to pull up stakes — and far less inclined than the business school graduate in the middle rank of executives in the United States, who is prepared to transplant his family and chattels from San Diego or Miami to Seattle or even Calais. Despite the readiness of American executives to follow orders from the vice-president in charge of foreign operations, unless the international corporation is assured of national treatment over a wide area, it can have no greater mobility than the single domestic company. If risks attach to the mobility, rather than extra profits, the international corporation will operate a series of separate foreign investments rather than a single efficient and factor-price-equalizing one.

Would the United States object to discrimination in the Common Market in favor of Common Market corporations? The subject is evidently complex and involves legal considerations of a sort that a mere economist hesitates to contemplate. There are those who think retrospectively that this Country made a mistake in encouraging the Common Market with its trade discrimination against United States exports. They, and doubtless others, would insist that while the goal is national treatment for foreign-owned corporations, there must be at minimum nondiscriminatory treatment of foreign-owned corporations. This would make the European corporation wait until there was a European sovereignty. The question is academic in view of French hesitation to take a European rather than a French view of economic, social, and political life in the Common Market. But it may not remain so.

NOTES

[1] See Chapter Five of this volume.

[2] S. Hymer, "The International Operations of National Firms: A Study of Direct Investment," unpublished doctoral dissertation, Massachusetts Institute of Technology, Department of Economics, 1960.

[3] See Philip Andrews' *Capital Development in Steel,* Oxford, Blackwell, 1951.

[4] *The New York Times,* Paris edition, July 24, 1964.

[5] *Le Monde,* July 26–27, 1964.

[6] *France Actuelle,* November 15, 1964.

[7] *The New York Times,* July 28, 1964.

[8] German Embassy, *The Bulletin,* September 22, 1964.

[9] *France Actuelle, op. cit.*

`

CHAPTER THREE

PROSPECTS FOR
THE FRENCH ECONOMY*

As in so many aspects of French life, the French economy offers the world a series of paradoxes. It has a Plan to expand economic activity, and a stabilization program to hold it down. Agriculture is shrinking, but producing embarrassing surpluses. The budget is balanced for the first time in years, but taxes have not been raised and the taxpayer grumbles about the quest for prestige in the Concorde, atomic energy at Pierrelatte, and an independent nuclear striking force. The French government objects to enormous American firms and is concerned with overexpansion of the European automobile market, but, if *The New York Times* account is correct, sought to attract to Strasbourg the $100 million General Motors plant which is going to Antwerp. French economic policy is European, so long as European means French, and international without much collaboration with the rest of the world in monetary, foreign aid, or trade affairs.

It is arguable that there is no apparent conflict between the IVth and Vth Plans and stabilization. The Plan expands supply, the stabilization program restrains demand, and together they achieve equilibrium, which is growth with price stability. But ambiguity has long been apparent in the Plan itself. Total emphasis has been on expansion, but the Commissariat has been concerned over possible overproduction in automobiles, steel, wheat, soap powders, and shipbuilding. In 1964 textiles have been added to the list, and steel which has sold well in the European Economic Community taken off. The dilemma is seen in the application of credit restrictions to the purchase of automobiles when Renault and Peugeot are work-

* Published in *Les Echos,* February 23, 1965.

ing short time. This is the dilemma which the United States and Britain have long faced, the choice between inflation and growth, but one which Continental Europe, especially France, Germany, and Italy, had been free from until about 1963.

In my judgment, the important change which has come over the Continent has been the loss of the highly elastic labor supply which has held down wages, relatively at least, and enabled profits to be maintained. The present profit squeeze cuts investment. Where technological progress is high, exports can be maintained. (France has also benefited in its balance of payments from high exports of food, arising from rapid increases in productivity in the agricultural sector which has been losing labor.) But the best of all possible worlds in the late fifties and early sixties of rapid expansion, a favorable balance of payments and relative price stability owing to either expansion of the labor supply (Germany and Italy) or more efficient use of labor (France) has come to an end. The "stop-go" choice which Britain faced confronted Italy in 1964, and confronts France and Germany in 1965 and 1966.

France has a long-run asset over the rest of Europe — its high birthrate beginning in 1946 which will shortly add much larger classes to the labor force. But it is not without handicaps. One is the difficulty of competing with Germany and even Belgium for foreign labor. French wages may be competitive, but French housing is not. France has perhaps an advantage in recruiting Spanish and Portuguese workers, inasmuch as it is both Latin and nearer. But Belgium has more adequate housing for foreign workers, and Germany is rapidly constructing it. European integration has not gone far in stimulating movements of French, Dutch, Belgian, or German workers from one country to another, despite the increasing border movement across the Rhine; but the Italian and other Mediterranean workers in the North are mobile where the local population is not, and in economics it takes only a small movement at the margin to change the price of a large inframarginal mass. French wages are no longer subject to French stabilization policy but are a function of intra-European migration.

One way to hold down prices is technical progress, and here France's postwar record is particularly brilliant: the Mystère, Caravelle, DS19, high-voltage transmission, desulfurization at Lacq, etc. These achievements have brought French science and industry great prestige. Viewed from afar, however, it seems that the French government is currently in danger of confusing shadow and substance, seeking scientific and technical advances not for themselves but for the prestige they bring, and wanting an independent technology, rather than building on the achievements of others in the normal fashion. On occasion, as in the Machines Bull–G.E. deal, it will have no choice. But where it deliberately embarks on large prestigious scientific investments, it runs the risk of losing in both science and prestige.

Americans today are particularly conscious of one paradox of French policy: the government's view that the dollar is too weak to hold but American firms too strong to be permitted to compete, whereas French firms are weak, but the franc strong. In my view three of these statements are misleading. The dollar is not weak: the definition of deficit which excludes billions of dollar loans under five years from United States assets is a silly one. American firms are strong, but the portion of their strength which they can afford to use in competition with European firms is a small fraction of their total. French industry is perhaps small by United States standards, but size and strength are by no means identical, and its technical performance makes French industry strong. The only true statement is that the franc is strong.

My opinions on politics and military matters are not relevant, but I find it regrettable that the French government which collaborated with the other members of the O.E.C.D. so long in international monetary matters has lately adopted an independent posture in this field. The categorical imperative of Kant calls for acting only in a way which can be generalized to others. France can adopt an independent policy in international monetary matters so long as the rest of the world collaborates closely to stabilize the position. The boat is safe with one man rocking it, so long as the others trim ship. But while such a policy is conspicuous, I doubt that it is the efficient way in the long run to acquire prestige.

CHAPTER FOUR

GERMANY'S PERSISTENT
BALANCE-OF-PAYMENTS
DISEQUILIBRIUM*

Once bitten, twice shy. Having explained the persistent bal-ance-of-payments surplus of the United States, I have for years been expecting the German surplus to go away, as my colleague, Paul Samuelson, continuously reminds me. Perhaps an attempt to "ex-plain" this surplus would exorcise it, too, in medieval fashion. This paper, however, is more a catalogue of explanations than a positive statement. It may have value as a review of balance-of-payments-adjustment analysis, if that subject can be said to need further attention after the Brookings report and its exegesis. We start with a list of explanations, by no means mutually exclusive.

1. Inflation abroad
2. Beggar-thy-neighbor policies by Germany
3. The structure of German trade
4. The German propensity to export
5. The docility of German labor
6. Competition in German markets
7. The German propensities to save, or not to absorb

* Published in *Trade, Growth and the Balance of Payments,* Essays in Honor of Professor Gottfried Haberler, R. E. Caves, H. G. Johnson, P. B. Kenen, eds., Chicago, Ill., Rand McNally & Co., 1965 (written in July 1964). This paper was written in the course of research undertaken with the support — gratefully acknowledged — of the Center of International Affairs, Harvard University. Thanks are due to a considerable number of economists with whom I have discussed the topic. The list is too long to set out in full, but I cannot forbear from mention of Professors Herbert Giersch and Hans Möller, of the Universities of Saarbrucken and Munich, respectively.

8. Deficiencies of the German capital market
9. German innovation and technical progress

1. *Inflation Abroad*

Gottfried Haberler thought that the persistent balance-of-payments surplus of the United States after the war was in important respects a result of inflation "pure and simple."[1] More would agree that the German surplus of 1963 and 1964 follows from inflations in Italy, France, and the Netherlands. DM 2.4 billion out of the DM 3.0 billion increase in the merchandise surplus in 1963 over 1962, for example, were with the E.E.C. countries, and much of the 1963 private capital inflow was Italian. If the surplus of the 1950's is taken as corrected by the appreciation of 1961 — see the loss of Bundesbank reserves in 1961 and 1962 — the case can be made that 1963 and 1964 present us with a new and different surplus, entirely the consequence of foreign inflation.

But the problem is to explain the 1950's; and why adjustment took so long then, and why inflation should have occurred in Italy, France, and the Netherlands, rather than in Germany with its strained use of resources. The new surplus may be a pure accident, though Nature and social science abhor such explanation. It is likely that there is an asymmetry in the system somewhere, which makes Germany come out with surpluses each time, rather than now a surplus, now a deficit.[2] The asymmetry may lie in the skills of the authorities, in their sensitivity to price changes, in the way the economic system responds to surpluses and deficits — in the German case, slowly to the former and rapidly to the latter. Inflation is part of the explanation, to be sure, but it is not an explanation in itself, and it fails to cover the 1950's.

2. *Beggar-Thy-Neighbor Policies by Germany*

The German balance-of-payments surpluses are characterized by Thomas Balogh as "beggar-thy-neighbor," but as he has not yet developed his thought on the subject, it is not clear why.[3] The economy was not depressed during the 1950's. Apart from the 1951 to 1953 period, there was a continuous inflationary gap. Efforts were made to get rid of the surplus, in unilateral tariff reductions in 1956, which had no effect on the net surplus, and in the 5 per cent revaluation of 1961, where the effect is more debatable.

45

The export drive begun during the Korean-boom deficit of 1950 was virtually abandoned in 1955. Wells states that "no substantial part of the German export effort can be explained in terms of specific government fiscal aid."[4]

We shall have occasion to discuss monetary, fiscal, exchange, and trade policies later, but it seems clear that the Germans worked hard to rid themselves of the surplus, consistent with policies addressed to other objectives. Without these efforts, the surplus might have been larger.

Something more sophisticated by way of explanation, then, is required than merely foreign stupidity or German guile.

3. *The Structure of German Exports*

Economists from less developed countries argue that it is the export structure that counts. It counts, they say, against them in primary products. As a manufacturer of capital equipment and consumers' durables, Germany was lucky. In a world of reconstruction from war and self-conscious development, the demand for capital equipment moves rapidly to the right. In Europe, where automobiles are the symbol of the rising level of living, high growth abroad produces higher growth in automobile exports. Germany's short-run comparative advantage lay in the same lines as its long-run, in contrast, say, with Belgium, where a short-run comparative advantage in capital-intensive, semifinished, industrial materials — steel, glass, soda ash, nitrogenous fertilizers — was continuously being eroded in the long run by higher foreign demands for, and higher gains of, productivity in other lines of activity.[5] But a couple of points are worth making.

In the first place, international-trade theorists of the Heckscher-Ohlin persuasion, as most of us are, would have been wrong in thinking that Germany with its large capital losses and gains of population after the war should have changed to more labor-intensive lines of export activity.[6] It is easy to underestimate the hysteresis effect which virtually requires cities to be built on the same sites after destruction, block by block, and economies to specialize in the same directions. Capital as a whole may be suddenly scarce and labor abundant, but the marginal product of new investment is highest in the familiar lines, where it combines with surviving equipment and trained labor and management. Second, as has widely been remarked, Germany not only did not lose economically by having the agricultural portions of East Germany lopped off at Potsdam; it improved its terms of trade with the world by buying its food more cheaply, and increased its degree of specialization in the heavy industry of the Ruhr and the mechanical and chemical industries of Frankfurt and Stuttgart. Third, however, and this perhaps is the main point, Germany responded to its market opportunities by increasing its specialization still further. In the 1950's, 74 per cent of the exports were manufactures; in the 1960's, 89 per cent. Whereas total exports of manufactures expanded sevenfold over the decade, machinery and transport equipment rose tenfold.

Finally, it must be stated here in the next several sections and in homilies to the less developed countries, that structure is not necessarily related to equilibrium. The absorption approach is addressed in Section 7, but note should be taken of it now and in the interim.

4. *The German Propensity to Export*

If Germany was favored by its export structure, the individual entrepreneur pushed hard in selling abroad. The high status of exporting goes back to the "Export or Die" period at the end of the nineteenth century, and has often been remarked.[7] But specific reasons are advanced for the German interest in exports today. For almost twenty years, from 1931 to 1950, the German businessman was perforce turned inward. Moreover, starting from scratch in 1950, he found it difficult to enter new foreign markets, with the necessity to incur costs to build dealer organizations, to gear production to foreign requirements, etc. (Incidentally, he may have been aided by the demise over the twenty years of the old merchanting houses which used to stand between the producer and his customer, and which now make direct selling mandatory.) Export markets, so hard to enter or re-enter, once entered were the last to be abandoned.

Whatever the explanation, there seems to be little doubt about the facts. German businessmen reacted to the slight recession of 1961–1962 with a strong drive to sell exports. One aspect of this drive was dumping, more politely referred to as price differentiation or price concessions for foreign customers.

An important and interesting puzzle is presented by the disparate behavior of export unit values and the general price level in the United States, on the one hand, and in European countries and Japan, on the other. Prices have been rising more outside the United States than in that country since 1958, but the development of export unit values has not been parallel. A striking diagram is set out in *Lloyd's Bank Review* for April 1964, showing export prices of manufactures above consumer prices and unit wage costs in manufacturing in the United States, but below them in the United Kingdom, Germany, Italy, France, and Japan. The *Review* states: "The recent upsurge in costs and prices on the Continent has found little reflection in export prices."[8]

Impressions are cheap; facts, elusive. The disparate behavior of external and internal prices may be due to differences in productivity, or in competition, between the export sector and the domestic market. If the export sector is subject to decreasing costs and domestic output, including services, to increasing, the general picture for all but the United States could be explained. United States experience in turn may be explained by the nature of competition in steel, discussed in Section 6 below. But price differentiation between the export and the home market does occur. An outstanding example is furnished by the automobile industry. In April 1962, Volkswagen raised its domestic prices by $60 to $97, but kept its export prices unchanged. It was followed by the rest of the industry in May, despite the strong adverse reaction of (then) Economics Minister Erhard.[9] The *Monthly Report of the Deutsche Bundesbank* for January 1964 states explicitly:

> In some measure the increase of foreign demand continued to be due to the fact that, under pressure of insufficiently employed capacities, some industries tried to expand their foreign sales even at the cost of price concessions.[10]

The German export drive of 1950 to 1955 has been mentioned. Present means of stimulating exports — guaranteed medium-term credits, remission of turnover taxes on exports and the application of a cascaded tax to imports — may be no greater than those of European countries in general, but the export interests have forced Chancellor Erhard to state categorically that he will not again revalue the mark. Exchange policy in Germany can be regarded as a contest between the savings banks, which favor flexible exchange rates as a means of stabilizing the internal price level, on the one hand, and export interests, which want the rate kept stable, on the other.[11] As of the summer of 1964, the export interests were winning.

5. *The Docility of German Labor*

An early explanation for the German economic miracle was love of work.[12] Today it is denied by a German sociologist that his countrymen are particularly industrious,[13] and one can even hear echoes in Germany of dislike of Italians because they work too hard at piece-rate jobs. But it remains true that German labor is unaggressive in pushing for higher pay. An early postwar labor leader, Hans Boechler, is regarded in the German press as "unforgettable" because he sold German labor on moderation in wage demands. German industrialists and public opinion find Rosenberg, the top leader — and even Otto Brenner of the metal workers who cultivates an image of militancy — fundamentally ready to hold back where exports are threatened or domestic price increases. It was feared that the 1962 settlement of the metal workers, which was regarded as eminently reasonable — a two-year contract with 6 per cent increases annually instead of 10 and 12 per cent of the earlier years — would be followed in 1964 by an enormous push, especially in view of high profits and a statement by the Economics Minister that the productivity increase in 1964 had reached a new record. Instead, the metal workers surprised even German public opinion by their moderation,[14] a fifteen-month contract of great complexity, which came to a 7.3 per cent increase a year, and agreement to postpone for another year the reduction in the working week.

It is difficult for an economist to enter into the discussion as to whether labor is unusually submissive; takes a long-run rather than a short-run view of its economic advantage, and is really maximizing with low time-preference; is deeply disturbed that present rapidly improving conditions will not last, so that nothing must be done to upset the applecart; or whether the lag of wages behind profits is merely longer than in most countries. Informed opinion in Germany, however, is persuaded that labor organizations, like businessmen, are sensitive to competitive conditions on export markets and rising prices on the home front, in a way which is true of few other countries. This is income policy from below.[15]

One view is that it is not self-restraint which limits the grasp of labor unions, but competition. This may have applied to the 1950's, with their initially large number of unemployed, of movements off the farm and of refugees from the East before the Wall, and before the need to import foreign labor, expensive because of its special needs. With long contracts, imperfect competition may hold down wages, and more competition would bid them up, as wage drift that exists in Germany implies. In a competitive market in which labor maximized its short-run advantage, wages would have gone far higher.

The importance of labor docility is of course in holding down costs and maintaining the growth of exports. Beyond this, however, it has relevance for an implicit model in which income distribution plays a critical role in balance-of-payments adjustment. Robert Mundell once said[16] that a rising share of wages in national income is followed by a worsening of the balance of payments. We shall see later that this model does not apply to Germany. But what is impressive is that the share of wages in income rose so modestly — from 59.1 per cent in 1950 to only 60.9 per cent in 1960 — and since then to 64.8 per cent in 1963[17] after the exhaustion of labor reserves.

6. *Competition in German Markets*

Egon Sohmen believes that the big difference between the economic performances of Germany and other countries lies in the competitiveness of their markets. In one paper he emphasizes the importance of competition for German growth;[18] another focuses more narrowly on flexible exchange rates.[19] Between the lines in both papers, however, and explicitly in his new book,[20] he states that competition leads to lower goods prices, which, with high elasticities, lead to export surpluses.

In steel he has a case that competition is stronger in Europe than in the United States. A decline in capacity utilization from 75 to 45 per cent in the United States fails to disturb the internal price structure, whereas the 1962 decline from 95 to 85 per cent utilization in Europe produced a substantial price decline.[21] But the implications of this for the balance of payments are unclear.

Steel prices in the United States have doubtless helped to raise the export unit values above general prices, as already discussed. In Europe, however, the market is highly competitive within the E.C.S.C. area, but prices within the Community are detached from those without. In 1963 German orders for iron and steel showed a very small gain with the E.C.S.C. and a large drop outside.

Price differentiation between the home and foreign markets suggests that the home market is imperfectly rather than highly competitive. So does the widespread discussion in Germany of retail price maintenance. In his earliest paper, Sohmen worried lest gathering cartelization in industry and banking might weaken the basis for German growth.[22] Rationalization cartels which distribute production between firms by differentiated items and which are believed to have been formed across national lines in the Common Market may lead to lower costs and prices through internal economies of scale. These would increase competition in one sense and reduce it in another. France, Italy, and Austria all experienced export surpluses during substantial stretches of the postwar period without well-developed policies of improving competition — on the contrary. The relations between market organization and export surpluses are thus difficult to establish.

"Competitiveness" is used in a wider sense by Angus Maddison to refer merely to the maintenance of competitive prices in foreign trade. In his *Economic Growth in the West*,[23] Maddison states that the German authorities followed a vigorous line of action in each of three major aspects of growth policy: management of demand, maintenance of competitiveness, and fostering output potential by policies favoring high investment and foreign trade (p. 102). Maintenance of demand means promotion of expenditure for high utilization of capacity, and while Maddison suggests that the German government may have fallen somewhat short of optimum policies in this respect during the early part of the 1950's, he gives it high marks thereafter (*passim*, esp. pp. 151–152). But it is not so clear what he means by competitiveness. On occasion this seems to imply holding demand down, rather than up, applying restrictive monetary policies each time inflation threatened (p. 138). For the rest, however, it refers to only vaguely described policies directed specifically to prices and incomes in a world of high-demand elasticities (p. 187). Germany is said to have better domestic defenses against inflation than other countries (p. 180) and a more successful policy generally (p. 185), although the measures to raise imports and reduce the surplus are acknowledged to have been unsuccessful (p. 180). Maddison recognizes that the problem of controlling inflation in Germany was more easily resolved than elsewhere for a number of reasons — the psychological shock of monetary reform, the weak position of the unions, and the rapid rise of productivity (p. 138). But so intent is he on making the point of the importance of policies to control of demand that he makes little allowance for the objective conditions of supply.

What seems to have been the case in Germany is that supply has been highly elastic without regard to market organization or monetary and fiscal policy. It is not only the authorities who are anxious to avoid inflation but the entire population. Germany's Phillips curve, that is, is virtually horizontal, with prices rising very little as unemployment moves to zero. Wide differences in Phillips curves between countries, if they exist, are more important for balance-of-payments changes among competing countries, where the elasticities are high, than differences in policy arising from differences in intelligence or political courage.

7. *The German Propensities to Save, or Not to Absorb*

As is well known, and as we have recently been reminded by Johnson's trenchant review of the Brookings report,[24] it is not enough to expand exports to enjoy an export surplus. A country must refrain from importing in an equal amount; it must not spend and respend all the income earned from exports until it spills over into imports; that is, it must save. Export surplus equals net savings, or domestic savings minus domestic investment. So much is identity, but it is also possible to look at the savings as producing the export surplus, rather than the export surplus the savings. And, to repeat, no net savings, no export surplus.

In the early period after 1951, the large net savings came from a government surplus established by the Finance Minister, Dr. Schaeffer, who levied taxes for Germany's contribution to the European defense effort well in advance of the ultimate expenditure, building up a secret government reserve. This hoard, which grew to nearly DM 6 billion in 1953, became known as the "Julius Turm" after the tower in Spandau in which some of the gold received as part of the French indemnity of 1871 was covertly stored as a war chest.[25] It was easy, at this stage, to regard the export surplus as an inadvertent consequence of fiscal policy, and to anticipate that it would disappear when the government books were balanced again.

But when government savings declined, undivided corporate profits stepped into the breach. Later, with a profit squeeze, savings of private households took over. Savings climb each year, but the distribution of savings by sector varies widely, as the following Table 1[26] shows.

Table 1. The Formation of Savings in Germany (F.R.), Selected Years (in per cent of current domestic savings)

Year	Households	Enterprises (undistributed profits)	Government (surplus on current account)
1950	21	47	31
1953	25	26	49
1958	33	36	32
1960	27	34	41
1963 prel.	37	21	43

The savings of households increase almost consistently, as does the ratio of private savings to disposable income, which has risen from 3 per cent in the early 1950's to 5½ per cent in 1956, 8 per cent in 1957, 8½ per cent in 1962 and 9½ per cent in 1963. In 1963 disposable income rose by 6.7 per cent and savings by 20 per cent for an impressive income elasticity of 3. While the Deutsche Bundesbank believes that some of the savings may be due to transitional factors, such as hesitation in buying consumer durables, it finds the phenomenon remarkable.[27]

Recall that household savings are rising as a per cent of a disposable income with a redistribution of income in favor of labor, not property owners. Many reasons are adduced for the high marginal propensity to save of the German, but most of these apply to the middle-class household rather than the wage earner: the Pigou effect, or trying to restore the asset position after the losses imposed by inflation, deflation, war, and expulsion or flight from the East; wealth illusion, arising from the absence of a national debt;[28] the postwar quest for a sense of identity, which sociologists believe deeply affects German thought and action. Or possibly the German

53

worker merely is convinced that the gain in his level of living is too good to last, and operating on a Friedman consumption function, he spends only his permanent income. If so, he differs remarkably from the French and Italian working classes, who want more income, and are prepared to spend even more than these income gains.

The erratic behavior of government surplus and undistributed corporate profits, however, casts considerable doubt on the absorption approach to balance-of-payments equilibrium, at least in the short run. The balance-of-payments surplus equals net savings *ex post,* but there need be no automatic mechanism to bring them into equilibrium *ex ante.* In fact, if government, business, and households all fear inflation and react to rising prices by spending less, not more, the income mechanism which is supposed to adjust *ex ante* savings and *ex ante* investment in a closed economy will not function. A case might be made that the current-account deficit of 1962 was the result of the decline in undistributed corporate profits from DM 19.3 billion in 1960 and DM 16.5 billion in 1961 to DM 13.8 billion in 1962. But these profits go still lower in 1963, especially during the first half, and rebound only after the new export surge of the second half of 1963. *Ex post* nonabsorption equals *ex post* export surplus through some such mechanism as windfall profits and losses and unintended investment and disinvestment in inventories which bring savings and investment into line in a closed economy. In the short run, the absorption theory is no use. In the long, the high propensity to export and the high propensity to save are identical. Goods are produced which cannot be sold at home and therefore must be sold abroad. Or high exports threaten inflation which produces the response of increased savings.

Note in passing, the inapplicability of the Mundell model to Germany. With income redistribution nothing happens because wage earners save like capitalists.

8. *Deficiencies of the German Capital Market*

Important opinion, ranging from the United States Treasury to members of the staff of the E.E.C. and individual German economists, argues that the problem lies not in the German current-account surplus, which is a consequence of high productivity and high propensities to save, but in the inadequate capacity of the

German capital market to fund this surplus in appropriate form. Private capital movements, in fact, have been inward, except in 1958 and 1959, requiring official capital exports to hold down increases in official reserves. In one view, the trouble lies in the high liquidity preference of the German saver who holds rates on long-term securities at a high level where they are attractive to foreign investors. Savers want only demand or savings deposits; banks are therefore obliged to stay liquid and keep large deposits with the Bundesbank; the Bundesbank must in turn stay liquid with gold and foreign exchange. The liquid form of the savings means that they are in considerable part held in liquid claims on the world. Or in the other version, the difficulty stems from the oligopolistic behavior of the banking system:[29] the banks like to have industrial corporations dependent on them, and issue securities only at high commissions. In addition, the Land governments protect their access to the market by a 2½ per cent tax on private issues.[30] Firms are financed through open-book credits from banks and undistributed profits. In 1963, for example, DM 60 billion of gross investment by enterprises outside of housing were financed with the issue of DM 2 billion of fixed-interest securities and DM 1.3 billion of shares. The major items (in billions of DM) were: depreciation (31); undistributed profits (16); medium- and long-term bank credit (9); short-term bank credit (3.3); capital transfers, largely from government (3.8); direct government credit (3.9). Against the bank loans there was an increase of deposits with banks (6.9).[31] And the rates on bank loans ranged upward from 5 to 9 and 10 per cent, nominal.[32]

Government direct advances to industry (and housing) are necessary for lack of a capital market, and tax advantages in depreciation. Lacking a government debt, it is impossible to use government surpluses to retire securities which investors can replace with private issues. But the high long-term rate — on this showing, a product of oligopoly among the dominant banks — encourages capital inflows and discourages capital outflows in long-term securities, which make the Bundesbank hold in liquid reserves that part of the surplus which the government does not fund.

A wide range for debate exists between those who say that Germany still has a shortage of capital and should be borrowing from abroad, and those who regard the export surplus as "natural," in the state of savings and investment needs, and conclude that the fault lies in the capital items. Should capital adjust to the current account, or vice versa? The debate is an ancient one. If one looks beyond balance-of-payments theory and compares Germany with the United States, one can argue that German investment needs, especially in housing but also in infrastructure and in further modernization of production and especially distribution, may exceed its savings capacity. This view also supports government savings in excess both of its own investment and of the countercyclical behavior of social security funds. But if Germany is compared with the rest of the world — Europe, but especially the less developed countries — Germany should be a capital exporter, and the task is to find better instrumentalities for distributing gross savings inside the country and net savings abroad.

It takes two to tango, to be sure, and one should not forget Sohmen's warning that further capital exports by Germany might be matched by an addition to the current-account surplus, not its funding.[33]

It is hard to resolve the debate. Interest rates on long-term securities have been coming down very slowly, as compared with the short-term market in Germany. In May, 1962, when the lowest yield was reached, 6 per cent bonds of public authorities which sold for 92.7 in 1957 went as high as 102.8 but have since gone back to 100. Some experts insist that moving the long-term rate toward 5 per cent would unleash heavy borrowing which would be inflationary — though it is hard to see any impact of the 1962 decline in the data for new issues. The interest rate may be high in Germany because of a high marginal efficiency of capital, or because of low liquidity preference and/or oligopoly in banking, but the identification problem remains.

9. *German Innovation and Technical Progress*

Innovation is again subject to differences of opinion. According to Maddison, technical progress cannot be given any substantial independent role in explaining differences in economic growth in Europe (and presumably also in balance-of-payments behavior),[34] though at another point he observes that the productivity achievements of Germany, France, and Italy were due to special factors.[35] The Economic Commission for Europe, on the other hand, states that the contribution of technical progress and innovation to the high productivity of capital and labor, which distinguishes German performance, must have been considerable.[36] As the remark implies, direct evidence is missing. Most data on productivity derive from dividing indexes of output by indexes of input; the relation of the resultant time series to new products and new processes, apart from the gains from using factors more efficiently at higher capacity utilization, is obscure. The E.C.E. study cites a series of specific reasons which might account for increased technical efficiency — technical assistance, joint ventures and licensing, encouragement of research, and, of course, the high rate of gross capital formation. The impact of high-capacity utilization can be argued: a backlog of orders can produce real gains in efficiency if the entrepreneur is able to organize production in ways which minimize changing machinery settings, and hence reduce knock-down time. On the other hand, in some instances, a heavy order book disrupts production, as all customers are in a hurry and the entrepreneur is forced by exigent demands to turn from one to another to equalize customer impatience at the margin, properly weighted for the importance of the buyer, thus raising costs.

The importance of the subject turns on the belief that the export-led model of growth has positive feedback built into it. Nothing exceeds like excess. Growth gives increasing returns to scale and lower costs, which leads to exports, which leads through savings and investment to more growth, lower prices, more exports, more growth.[37] As Balassa points out, however, this model requires something to hold down wages;[38] either unlimited supplies of labor, or perfect labor mobility, or that euphemism for wage stability — incomes policy. An economic journalist has extended the analysis to two sectors, one of which is efficient and exports, experiencing declining costs; the other is inefficient, with rising costs and low income elasticity of demand. To cut back demand, he suggests, raises prices by cutting output in the decreasing-cost industry, with highly elastic demand, without much cutting demand or output or reducing prices in the inefficient sector. Monopoly in factor and goods markets may even drive up prices in the archaic sector with demand cut. In his non-Euclidian, non-Keynesian, non-Phillipsian world, increased demand lowers prices (or at least rates of price increase), and decreased demand raises them.[39] There may be some-

57

thing to this picture. As Wells puts it, investment was higher in Germany; it was concentrated in the export industries; growth of demand led to rationalization of production and ultimately to lower costs; the secret of German success in exports lay in its rate of growth, and the secret of the rate of growth lay in exports.[40]

This brings us back, eleven years later, to Hicks' *Inaugural Lecture,* with export-biased growth (*cum* dumping), with the addition of Johnson's amendment for demand elasticities greater than one, such as apply, particularly, in the competitive situation of trade among industrial countries. This was, it will be remembered, a Keynesian under-employment model, in which supplies were infinite, and there was no problem of financing the surplus at home or abroad. With limited resources and full employment, it should behave differently; but, given the complexity of general equilibrium, it is difficult to say exactly how. The curious thing about the German economy is that it behaves as if it were a Keynesian economy, when all the world can see that it is at full employment with 660,000 unfilled jobs and 110,000 unemployed (June 30, 1964). It even eliminates the problem of financing the surplus at home — though unhappily the international problem remains. What remains baffling is why labor is so restrained in putting up its price when the demand curve moves to the right, and, second, why it saves so much of its income.

Of the nine listed explanations with which we started, we exclude but one — beggar-thy-neighbor policies by Germany. The rest fit into a unified picture in which relative inflation abroad, if not absolute, is accounted for in part by high elasticities of supply in Germany, in the short-run as in the long. The export structure is right, but German innovation and push make it more so. Labor turns out product without pushing up costs, and releases a large share of that product for export by refraining from consumption. Government saves, along with industry and labor.

Two points stand out in conclusion, both of which run counter to the strongly asserted conclusions of Maddison on growth: one, it is supply, rather than demand. To coin a phrase, demand is necessary, but not sufficient. Two, without disparaging the skill of the German authorities, it seems to have been not policy but the *force des choses* which produced the German results. Here is the critical asymmetry: policy directed to expand exports, hold down prices, curb domestic spending, etc., works like a charm; policy to increase imports or improve the functioning of the capital market is unsuccessful. Like flowers and diamonds in the indifference curves of young ladies, policy is nice, but elastic supply is an economy's best friend.

NOTES

[1] See "Dollar Shortage" in *Foreign Economic Policy for the United States* (S. E. Harris, ed.), Cambridge, Mass., Harvard University Press, 1948, p. 434.

[2] See Chapter Thirteen, p. 182.

[3] Thomas Balogh, *Unequal Partners*, Vol. II, Oxford, Blackwell, 1963, p. 25, note 3.

[4] S. J. Wells, *British Export Performance: A Comparative Study*, Cambridge, University Press, 1964, p. 81.

[5] See A. Lamfalussy, *Investment and Growth in Mature Economies: The Case of Belgium*, London, Macmillan, 1961.

[6] See, among others, K. W. Roskamp, "Factor Proportions and Foreign Trade: the Case of West Germany," *Weltwirtschaftliches Archiv*, Band 91, Heft 2, 1963, pp. 319–326.

[7] See W. N. Parker, "Entrepreneurial Opportunities and Response in the German Economy," *Explorations in Entrepreneurial History*, Vol. 7, No. 1, October 1954, p. 16; Henry C. Wallich, *Mainsprings of German Revival*, New Haven, Yale University Press, 1955, pp. 244ff. For a contrary statement about French incapacity for exporting, see my *Foreign Trade and the National Economy*, New Haven, Yale University Press, 1962, p. 230. The success of the French in exporting after 1958, despite a "built-in aversion for exports," throws doubt on the validity of such generalization.

[8] P. 54. The effect is most marked for the 1950's, and a similar diagram based on 1961, rather than 1953 as in the *Review*, shows United States unit values also below consumer prices and (in this comparison) industrial wholesale prices. See *Monthly Report of the Deutsche Bundesbank*, Vol. 16, No. 1, January 1964, p. 31. But the gap in the United States series is narrower than that for the other countries.

[9] *The New York Times*, May 31, 1962.

[10] *Op. cit.*, p. 31. See also the statement of Ifo-Institut für Wirtschaftsforschung in its Ifo-Schnelldienst *Berichte zur Wirtschaftslage* for April 10, 1964, under the heading "Anhaltend starkes Exportwachstum" (Continued Strong Growth of Exports), p. 1: "For the first time in a long while it was anticipated in many industrial circles that export prices would rise more than inland prices."

[11] See "Savers Prefer Devaluation," *The Economist*, Vol. CCXII, No. 6314, August 28, 1964, p. 840. For a detailed statement of the export point of view, see the article "No Fear of Export Surplus" in *Die Welt* of Hamburg, February 1, 1964, translated in the *German Tribune*, February 22, 1964.

[12] See, *e.g.*, Wallich, *op. cit.*, Chapter 12, esp. pp. 332–334, 340, 341.

[13] Ralf Dahrendorf, "The New Germanies," *Encounter*, April 1964, p. 56.

[14] *Frankfurter Allgemeine Zeitung*, July 8, 1964.

[15] But note that Chancellor Erhard held a meeting of business and labor leaders, along with the economic and financial leaders of the government, to discuss wage policy (*Frankfurter Allgemeine Zeitung*, July 10, 1964). This was after the metal workers' settlement in which government intervention, if any, was not overt.

[16] In a seminar at M.I.T.

[17] *Wirtschaft u. Statistik*, Heft 5, 1960, p. 258; 1964, Heft 1, p. 8.

[18] "Competition and Growth: the Lessons of West Germany," *American Economic Review*, Vol. XLIX, No. 5, December, 1959, pp. 986–1,003. See also the comments by K. W. Roskamp, A. I. MacBean, and W. G. Shepherd, and R. G. Opie, and Professor Sohmen's reply in *idem*, Vol. I, No. 5, December 1960, pp. 1,015–1,031.

[19] "The Dollar and the Mark," in *The Dollar in Crisis*, S. E. Harris, ed., New York, Harcourt Brace & World, Inc., 1961, pp. 185–200.

[20] *Internationale Währungsprobleme*, Frankfurt-am-Main, Fritz-Knapp Verlag, 1964.

[21] *Ibid.*

[22] "Competition and Growth," *op. cit.*, pp. 998–1,000.

[23] New York, The Twentieth Century Fund, 1964.

[24] Harry G. Johnson, "The International Competitive Position of the United States and the Balance of Payments for 1968: A Review Article," *Review of Economics and Statistics*, Vol. XLVI, No. 1, February 1964, pp. 14–32.

[25] See Frederick G. Reuss, *Fiscal Policy for Growth without Inflation: the German Experiment*, Baltimore, Johns Hopkins Press, 1963, pp. 157–158.

[26] *Wirtschaft und Statistik*, Vol. 12, Heft 12, December, 1960, p. 710; and *Monthly Report of the Deutsches Bundesbank*, Vol. 16, No. 4, April 1964, p. 5. The two series joined may not be strictly comparable.

[27] *Ibid.* and *idem*, Vol. 16, No. 2, February 1964, pp. 6–8.

[28] This could presumably be corrected by a capital subsidy. Note that losses through inflation and war typically are thought to make people save less, rather than more.

[29] See Joint Economic Committee, Economic Practices and Policies, Paper No. 3, *A Description and Analysis of Certain European Capital Markets*, Washington, D. C., U.S. Government Printing Office, 1964, esp. p. 130: "It would appear, therefore, that there is very little competition in issuing of bonds." And: "These arrangements for issuing bonds may contribute materially to the high cost of raising capital in Germany."

[30] Kurt Richebächer, "Germany's Unsought Surplus," *The Banker*, April 1964, p. 225, argues that this should be immediately repealed.

[31] See the excellent article on "Wealth Formation and Its Financing in 1963" in *Monthly Report of the Bundesbank*, April 1964, *op. cit.*, and the table on p. 14.

[32] *Ibid.*, Table 2, p. 70.

[33] Sohmen, "The Dollar and the Mark," *op. cit.*

[34] *Economic Growth in the West*, *op. cit.*, p. 81.

[35] *Ibid.*, p. 156.

[36] United Nations, Economic Commission for Europe, *Some Factors in Economic Growth in Europe during the 1950's*, Geneva, 1964, Chapter VI, p. 6.

[37] This model was set out by A. Lamfalussy, in *The United Kingdom and the Six: An Essay on Economic Growth in Western Europe,* Homewood, Ill., Irwin, 1963. The theme is also found in Sir Roy Harrod's *The British Economy,* New York, McGraw-Hill, 1963. See also W. Beckerman, "Projecting Europe's Growth," *Economic Journal,* Vol. LXXII, No. 288, December, 1962, pp. 912–925, and Bela Balassa, "Some Observations on Mr. Beckerman's 'Export-Propelled' Growth Model," and Mr. Beckerman's "Reply," *Economic Journal,* Vol. LXXIII, No. 292, December 1963, pp. 781–787.

[38] *Ibid.*

[39] Norman Macrae, *Sunshades in October,* London, Allen and Unwin, 1963.

[40] Wells, *op. cit.,* pp. 74–82.

CHAPTER FIVE

EUROPEAN ECONOMIC INTEGRATION AND THE DEVELOPMENT OF A SINGLE FINANCIAL CENTER FOR LONG-TERM CAPITAL*

1. Introduction

This paper will deal with the definition, process, and prospects of economic integration in long-term capital markets in Europe which might lead to the development of a single center for long-term capital. The subject has some heuristic value as an example of functional integration. It further raises the interesting question whether functional integration in one field — trade, taxes, agriculture, labor market, etc. — leads inevitably to parallel steps in other functions. But the integration of capital markets is not without interest in its own right. In recent years the world's major financial markets have offered a number of paradoxes:

(1) The United States, with a weak balance of payments and obliged to borrow at short term, is lending at long term; Europe, with a strong balance of payments and lending short, is borrowing long. Europe finds the explanation in the long-term rate of interest in New York which is too low; United States officials comment that the trouble lies in the restrictions on capital movements which remain in force in Europe.

(2) Europe is prepaying long-term governmental debt to the United States government but borrowing on private account. This

* From *Weltwirtschaftliches Archiv,* Band 90, Heft 2, July 1963, pp. 189-209.

Remark: I acknowledge with thanks the critical comments on the previous draft of Bela Balassa, James C. Ingram, Paul Meek, Robert A. Mundell, Scott Pardee, and George H. Willis.

suggests that the capital markets function differently for private and government funds.

(3)   Not only do European borrowers sell securities in the New York capital market; European investors buy a sizeable portion of these securities there. In interconnected markets one would expect European capitalists either to borrow or to lend in New York, but not both. We examine this apparent anomaly for the light it throws on the question of integration.

II. Integration Defined

With some oversimplification one can establish definitions of integration of increasing rigor as:

(a)   Free trade (the major element in the Tinbergen prescription)[1];

(b)   The absence of all forms of discrimination (Balassa)[2] presumably going beyond merely free trade into wage, tax, and other aspects of economic policy which might impinge on trade;

(c)   Factor price equalization (Myrdal).[3]

With appropriate qualification, all these definitions can amount to the same thing. Under certain limiting assumptions, free trade will bring about factor price equalization. Balassa points out that his definition presupposes an active economic intercourse, since an absence of discrimination between Iceland and New Zealand would hardly lead to economic integration in the absence of a substantial amount of foreign trade — perhaps enough to fulfill the requirements of the factor-price-equalization theorem. Equality of factor prices, which is seldom if ever achieved between trading countries, has the disability as a definition of being somewhat nonoperational. It helps, however, in showing the connections among economic, social, and political integration — the Negro, Jew, and other minority groups can be said not to be fully integrated into the United States community until their factor rewards are identical with those of native-born Protestant whites of equal inherent capacity; and so for other factors. Moreover, where factors are capable of moving, as in finance, the equality of factor returns becomes an operational definition: "Indeed, the best evidence of the complete integration of a capital market is the absence of differences in security yields according to the region where the firm issuing the security operates."[4]

The relevance of the distinction between freedom to move and movement of a sufficient degree to equalize factor returns can be illustrated from Benelux experience. Meade notes that the various steps undertaken to permit freedom of movement of workers between Belgium and the Netherlands failed to result in much movement; the Dutchman continued to emigrate, when he did, to North America or Australia rather than to Belgium.[5] In these circumstances it is inappropriate to define economic integration for labor as freedom to migrate, or the absence of discriminating regulations. The labor itself discriminates, which results in the absence of equalization of wages. Only if the Dutch and Belgians felt equally at home in each others' countries, and were willing to move freely about both countries in search of higher remuneration, could the labor markets be called integrated on the present definition. It is recognized that few national economies are integrated in this sense, but it is useful to have a standard against which various degrees of integration can be objectively compared — rather like absolute zero in chemistry which serves as a basis for measurement though it is not often achieved.

But even if we accept factor price equalization as a benchmark of integration, there may be room for finer distinctions, at least as concerns capital markets. The price of capital can be equalized between countries by the excess supply in Country A being matched against the excess demand in Country B, as in the familiar partial-equilibrium diagram shown in the following figure. Notice that with this sort of capital movement, the bulk of the demand in the capital-importing country is met from local supply, and only the excess demand is met by imported capital. But demand and supply in two geographically distinct markets can be added together without regard to their geographical location.[6] The supramarginal demander in either location may have his demand filled by an inframarginal supplier in either location. Total demand is matched against total supply rather than excess demand against excess supply. This may be said to be an even purer form of integration than price equalization through factor movement.

This higher form of integration may be possible only for capital and not for goods or labor because of costs of transfer. Move-

Figure 1. *Equalization of Interest Rates Through Interconnected Markets*

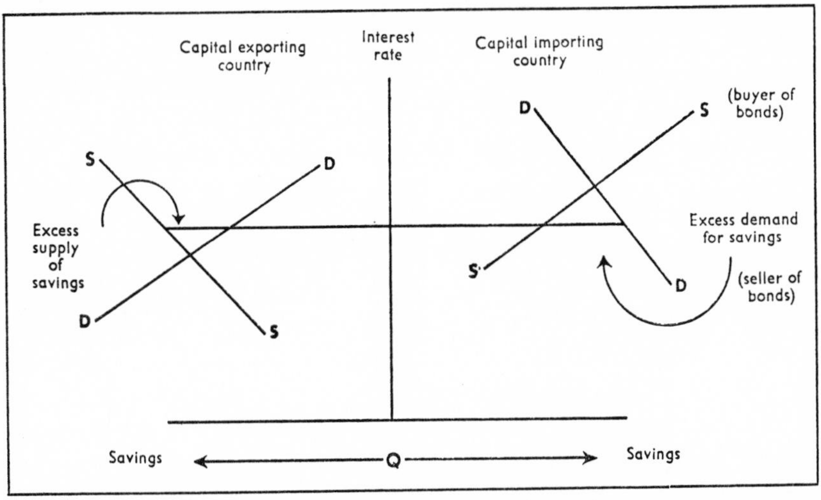

ments of capital are virtually costless; markets for goods and labor are separated regionally and nationally by positive costs of movement.[7] In the United States "only the market for marketable securities is fully integrated, with about 80 per cent of such securities dealt in on the New York stock and curb exchanges."[8]

The technical means of integration can be the physical transfer of purchases and sales to a single location, as in New York, or the spread of the major brokers and dealers to all significant financial centers, which thereby become merged. In Switzerland, for example, it makes no difference that the Swiss Bank Corporation has its head office in Basle and the Crédit Suisse in Zurich. Zurich, Basle, and Geneva are unified into a single capital market by reason of the fact that the major financial institutions are located in all of them and maintain constant and instantaneous communication among one another. An order to buy or sell placed at any single locality may be matched by another order originating in another locality without funneling all orders into, say, Zurich, as would be the case in New York. Similarly the branch banking system in Canada unifies Toronto and Montreal to such an extent that while Montreal leads as a financial center it does not dominate to the same extent as New York does in the United States.

Integration in the sense of aggregating demanders and suppliers into a single demand curve and supply curve, respectively, is not

65

only institutionally different from matching the excess demand against the excess supply. It is different economically. Capital markets integrated in this sense demonstrate economies of scale which mean that the seller of bonds gets a higher price, and the buyer of bonds is willing to pay a higher price, than if the markets had been kept apart except for excess demand and supply. The benefit to the seller is that he faces a broader market, including investors interested in diversification of risk. The benefit to the buyer is that with a broader market his liquidity is increased. When the State of California, for example, has a large bond issue to place, it sells it in New York; and California investors go to New York to buy a substantial share of it. Both buyer and seller are better off than if the bonds had been sold locally — seller because of the better rate and wider placement, buyer because of the broader market with enhanced liquidity. Rather than simply adding the supply curves in the foregoing figure, integration in this sense adds them and then shifts them downward and to the right because the more liquid bond is really a different form for savings.

These economies of scale exist not only for the buyer but for the underwriter. On a larger issue in a larger market, the underwriting commission should be lower per bond. Unfortunately, we have little aggregated information on the point. Meek points out that the underwriting spreads on foreign bonds issued in 1958 ranged from 1 point on shorter term issues to 3½ points for longer ones, with the gross compensation averaging 2¾ per cent of the proceeds to the borrowers. Meek contrasts this with the bankers' spread of more than 4.5 per cent on European long-term bonds in 1915 to 1929.[9] It has been asserted that one private United States borrower who sold bonds in Switzerland allegedly would not again go back to that source of capital because, while the coupon rate was low, the commission was high. On the other hand, borrowing in the New York market should include the expense and trouble of the Securities and Exchange Commission registration statement on the initial issue.[10]

The increasing returns to scale in a financial center mean that a substantial lead achieved by one center is difficult to overcome. New York has been the dominant financial center of the United States since about 1840, when it overtook Philadelphia.[11] It is suggestive that the First Boston Corporation, one of the largest investment bankers, has its main offices in New York City.[12]

We propose to discuss the prospects for the integration of long-term capital markets in terms of this rigorous definition of integration: where buyers and sellers are assembled in a single market, located in a single center, or tightly bound by unified institutions. But first it is useful to examine the data on recent international long-term lending in the United States and Europe.

III. Recent Experience

It is not difficult to show that world long-term capital markets are not integrated, and that within the world total the capital markets of Europe are not. It is sufficient to show interest rates, as set out in Table 1.

Table 1. Bond Yields in Selected Countries, Second Quarter of 1962 (per cent per annum)[13]

Country	Central Government Bond average yields to maturity on issues with at least 12 years' life	IBRD Bonds yields to maturity on specified issues	
		issue	yield
United States	3.89	3¼ of 1981	4.28
Canada	4.91	3½ of 1969	5.43
United Kingdom	6.18	3½ of 1974	5.50
Continental Europe			
Belgium	4.34	5 of 1969	5.30
France	5.12		
Germany	5.80[a]	5 of 1974	5.03
Italy	5.27	5 of 1976	5.31
Netherlands	4.27	3½ of 1975	4.09
Sweden	4.40		
Switzerland	3.22	3½ of 1976	3.45
Other			
Australia	4.93		
New Zealand	5.27		

[a] Covers bonds of all public authorities, including some with lives of less than 12 years.

The spread in government bond yields is wider than that in IBRD bonds: for the low-interest rate countries — the United States,

Belgium, and Switzerland especially — the IBRD bonds yield more than government issues; for the high-yield countries — especially the United Kingdom and Germany — less. Canada and Italy are exceptions to this generalization in one direction; the Netherlands in the other. (Some influence may arise from differing maturities on the IBRD bonds, though its nature is not apparent.)

The IBRD has not been trying to minimize its borrowing cost, so much as to stimulate international long-term lending by borrowing on its established credit standing in a wide number of currencies. Table 2 shows that, apart from the *DM* equivalent of $ 125

Table 2. New Issues of 5-Year or More Maturity by the International Bank for Reconstruction and Development, 1947 to 1961, by Currency Issue (millions of dollars)[14]

Year	All currencies	United States Dollars	Canadian	Swiss Francs	Sterling	Guilders	Deutsche Marks	Belgian Francs	Lire
1947	250.0	250.0	—	—	—	—	—	—	—
1948	4.0	—	—	4.0	—	—	—	—	—
1949	—	—	—	—	—	—	—	—	—
1950	106.6	100.0	—	6.6	—	—	—	—	—
1951	175.6	150.0	—	11.6	14.0	—	—	—	—
1952	135.2	110.0	13.6	11.6	—	—	—	—	—
1953	23.2	—	—	23.2	—	—	—	—	—
1954	208.8	150.0	22.7	11.6	14.0	10.5	—	—	—
1955	35.7	—	13.6	11.6	—	10.5	—	—	—
1956	75.0	75.0	—	—	—	—	—	—	—
1957	321.5	275.0	—	46.5	—	—	—	—	—
1958	475.0	475.0	—	—	—	—	—	—	—
1959	108.9	—	—	23.3	28.0	—	47.6	10.0	—
1960	353.2	200.2	—	28.0	—	—	125.0	—	—
1961	61.0	—	—	23.3	—	13.8	—	—	24.0
Total	2,333.8	1,785.2	49.9	201.3	56.0	34.8	172.6	10.0	24.0

million borrowed in Germany in 1960, the amounts acquired by long-term issues in markets other than New York have been small. Borrowing in Switzerland has been persistent, but generally subject to the informal Swiss restraint which limits single issues, for which permission must be sought on each occasion, to SF 60 million, or $ 11 million. I am informed by the International Bank that roughly 5 per cent of new issues placed in the United States were bought for foreign account; that subsequent open-market trading has resulted in the holding by foreigners of about 12 per cent of New York

IBRD issues, apart from a number of dollar issues privately placed outside the United States.[15] The Bank observes that there has been very little purchasing of European currency issues by foreigners outside the country of issue.

If the IBRD has other concerns than minimizing its cost of funds, there is no evidence to suggest that Australia and Norway do. These countries, including Norwegian local governments and private industry, have been avid for capital and borrowed in a wide number of capital markets. If we omit refunding on a substantial scale in London and New York, Australia started its borrowing in the Swiss market with the equivalent of $ 14 million (nominal amount) in each of 1953 and 1955, before placing two small issues in the New York market in 1956 and 1957, and borrowing on a more substantial scale in 1958. In that year the equivalent of $ 43 million was placed in London, and $ 50 million in New York. In 1959, $ 25 million more were borrowed in New York. In 1960 borrowings were Switzerland, $ 14 million; the United Kingdom, $ 34 million; the United States, $ 50 million. In 1961 the amounts were Canada, $ 20 million; Netherlands, $ 11 million; Switzerland, $ 14 million; the United States, $ 25 million. Bond sales took place in the traditional capital source — London — when this was available. Small sums were obtained from the rationed capital markets of Switzerland and Amsterdam, the latter when its prohibition of foreign lending was removed. A Commonwealth partner was approached for a limited sum; but the main borrowing, spaced out to maintain Australia's credit standing, was to New York.

Norwegian borrowing in the New York market was less extensive. If we limit ourselves to the last few years, various government and private Norwegian borrowers obtained $ 28.5 million in the United States in 1958, $ 10 million in 1960, and $ 18 million in 1961. But this experience illustrates a separate truth about international capital markets. Capital flows in channels, like irrigation ditches, rather than like sheets of water which have spilled over riverbanks. This held true in the nineteenth century, when Britain switched its lending from Europe to the Empire and the New World after the revolutions of 1848. It is true on the periphery of the world capital market today. Norway has borrowed the equivalent of $ 6.8 million in Sweden in 1957 and again in 1958 and in 1961, and $ 12 million in 1960. This is the only foreign lending Sweden has undertaken. This is partial integration of the Norwegian and Swedish capital markets, the latter of which is not well integrated with the rest of the world.

Table 3 summarizes the record of long-term new issues for new money in major international financial centers from 1947 to 1961. The table omits about $ 1,800 million of borrowing in New York

Table 3. Foreign Bonds Publicly Issued for New Funds in Germany, Netherlands, Sweden, Switzerland, the United Kingdom and the United States, 1947 to 1961 (excluding refunding and issues in the United States for Canadian and Israeli borrowers) (millions of dollars)[16]

Year	Total	Germany	Nether-lands	Sweden	Switzer-land	United King-dom	United States
1947	97.6	—	—	13.9	13.2	50.0	20.5
1948	40.3	—	—	5.4	11.6	23.3	—
1949	45.5	—	—	—	12.4	33.1	—
1950	85.3	—	—	—	48.9	36.4	—
1951	31.6	—	—	—	—	31.6	—
1952	66.5	—	—	—	45.5	21.0	—
1953	94.4	—	—	9.7	27.3	56.0	1.4
1954	183.7	—	16.1	9.7	87.9	70.0	—
1955	220.2	—	62.9	—	81.3	28.0	48.0
1956	91.3	—	—	6.2	64.1	14.0	7.0
1957	67.3	—	5.0	6.2	3.2	—	52.9
1958	410.0	10.0	—	—	32.7	126.0	241.3
1959	356.0	33.9	—	—	95.9	30.2	196.0
1960	325.1	14.3	—	12.0	132.3	81.5	85.0
1961	613.9	3.3	146.1	6.8	217.7	112.0	128.0
Total	2,728.7	61.5	230.1	69.9	874.0	713.1	780.1

on Canadian account, because of the special ties running between Canada and the United States capital market; and another $ 500 million of Israeli bonds which are sold on only quasi-commercial terms.[17] The table emphasizes the recent character of United States lending (and the exiguous German), the continuous activity in Switzerland, the sporadic behavior of Sweden and the Netherlands.

The amounts borrowed in Switzerland are not only impressive overall. They have been growing. But the business is on a different scale than that in New York. In 1959, for example, the New York figure of $ 196 million represents 8 loans as compared with 9 for the Swiss figure of half the sum. Switzerland offers a small capital market with a large proportion of foreign lending: it achieves diversification by lending to many borrowers for small amounts. New York is a large capital market with only a small interest in foreign lending: its diversification is largely domestic.

IV. *The Capital Market in Europe*

Eight years after the Treaty of Rome there is virtually no sign of integration of the long-term capital markets of Europe, whether in the lower form of equalized interest rates or the more advanced one of fully merged markets in a single center or through unified institutions. Individual capital markets are looking up in Germany and the Netherlands. There is a flourishing Swiss market, as we have said for individual foreign borrowers and limited amounts. But the interconnections among the various markets are thin. This is partly because of administrative obstacles in the way of new issues. Trading in outstanding securities has been relaxed and much direct investment, but not new issues.[18] In part it seems to be due to institutional obstacles and economic barriers. Investors are not particularly interested in participating in the narrow capital markets of countries other than their own. In the few cases when a number of European countries lend simultaneously to a single borrower, it is contrived rather than the result of merged market forces.

Argentina, with a weak credit standing, borrowed $ 25 million in Europe in 1961. The rate was 6½ per cent, and interest and principal were made payable at fixed rates in seven currencies. $ 7.4 million were taken by the market in Switzerland, $ 3 million in Germany, and the rest were privately placed in Belgium, France, Italy, the Netherlands, and the United Kingdom. In 1961, a Portuguese petroleum refinery placed a $ 5 million issue: $ 0.3 million in Germany, $ 0.5 million in the Netherlands, $ 1.0 million in Switzerland, $ 2.0 million in Belgium and $ 1.2 million in Luxemburg. A *DM* 60 million ($ 14.3 million) 5¾ per cent Fonds des Routes 15-year bond, guaranteed by the Kingdom of Belgium and payable in *DM* or dollars, was sold in January 1960, but only *DM* 14 million was taken in Germany and the remainder was placed in unstated amounts in Belgium-Luxemburg, the Netherlands, Switzerland, France and elsewhere. In all these loans, the fact that national *tranches* had to be arranged by the underwriters — and for what were over-all small amounts — makes clear that a smoothly working long-term European capital market has not been realized.

V. Europe and the New York Capital Market

On the other hand, as already stated, not only the smaller European countries but the institutions of the new Europe have been selling and buying bonds in New York. We discuss the selling first, and then the buying.

The European Coal and Steel Community has placed loans of $ 13.8 million in the Netherlands in 1961, following the sale of $ 11.7 million in Switzerland in 1956. Its major borrowing, however, has been in New York: $ 35 million in 1956; $ 50 million in 1958; $ 25 million in 1960, and $ 25 million in 1962.

The European Investment Bank has borrowed only $ 13.8 million (50 million guilders). This sum was obtained in the Netherlands in 1961.

The Société de Pipe-Line Sud-Européen, a private French company but European in spirit, borrowed $ 13.8 million in the Netherlands in 1961, but placed two $ 20 million issues in New York in 1962.

A similar private company with a European mission, Eurofima (Société Européenne pour le Financement de Matériel Ferroviaire) has placed one standard size issue in the Netherlands in 1961 ($ 13.8 million). In August 1962 it borrowed $ 5 million in a term loan from a New York bank; the newspaper account of the transaction[19] suggested that the firm would presently undertake to borrow larger amounts on the New York bond market.

These bonds are sold in the New York market because net rates there are below any in Europe except for the Netherlands and Switzerland, and the latter markets are rationed in amount. There is little difficulty in understanding why European organizations sell bonds in New York. The question is why they buy them.

First, it is necessary to establish the fact. Estimates differ. A. N. Overby, vice president of the First Boston Corporation, states that there are no firm estimates of the amount of foreign dollar bonds taken by foreign investors, but that in some cases the amounts have been "very large."[20] Samuel Pizer, assistant chief of the Balance of Payments Division, Department of Commerce, has estimated that in rough terms about half of the European bonds sold in New York in 1961 and probably in the first six months of 1962 have been taken by Europeans.[21] Paul Meek, manager of the Public Information Department of the Federal Reserve Bank of New York, has written[22]: "From incomplete private and Department of Commerce data it appears that foreign investors took two-thirds or more of the publicly offered and underwritten issues in 1958–1959." These estimates may be high, and I have been given to understand in official Washington circles that downward revision may bring them ultimately to one-third.

A variety of reasons can be offered to explain why Europeans buy European bonds in the New York market, but as Overby indicates, is is difficult to assess their relative weight. Some of these reasons are offered to explain why European buyers are more interested in these bonds than American investors: European investors have a better appreciation of the credit standing of the borrower, more sophistication and experience in lending, and pay lower rates of income tax on bond interest that United States holders. Overby cites these three reasons why European and other non-United States investors may have a greater interest in foreign dollar bonds than the United States investor. His three other reasons are addressed to a slightly different problem: why European investors want dollar obligations rather than European bonds. This is the more relevant question for our purposes. Overby's answers (without relative weights) are interest in obtaining a dollar obligation of his own country, lack of United States withholding tax on interest paid to nonresident holders of foreign dollar bonds, and in some cases a higher return than is obtainable on bonds available in his own market.[23]

Pizer's testimony before the Joint Economic Committee serves to amplify what Overby may have meant by the interest in a dollar obligation. His stress is on the marketability of the securities: "Of course, when an issuer can offer a bond to the public in the United States, the instrument becomes a much more highly marketable liquid instrument than if we had brought it out in a smaller capital market. There is that inducement of structure of the market here, even though perhaps the issuer expects only half of it to be taken in the United States market."[24]

Meek's statement on the point in the Mikesell study is terse[25]: "Foreign dollar bonds have offered to overseas investors excellent

73

marketability, exemption from United States withholding tax on the interest paid, and strong sinking and protective call features."

In private correspondence in October 1962, Meek has modified this statement and tentatively emphasized the rate of return. The chief European buyers of foreign dollar bonds according to his information place their orders through Belgium, the Netherlands, and Switzerland, countries which restrict or regulate the access of foreign borrowers to their capital markets and where rates are on the whole below those in New York. Marketability, on this showing, is not of great importance as compared with yield. The wealthy investors in Europe may even be unable to obtain foreign bond issues floated in Amsterdam and Zurich, since these are allocated to a privileged list of banks and insurance companies. In consequence, their demands spill over their national boundaries.[26]

The explanation that some Europeans borrow in New York because rates are higher than in their national markets, while others sell new issues because they can obtain funds cheaper, might seem to dispose of the paradox that Europeans both buy and sell bonds here and its resolution in the face of broader markets with greater marketability. But of course it does not. It merely shifts the subject to be explained to the reluctance of the European investors to buy German bonds with rates close to 6 per cent, or French bonds at 5 ¼, or British at more than 6. The dollar obligations are wanted despite their lower yield than national bond issues available in Europe because of the breadth of the market and the greater marketability or liquidity of these issues.

It also suggests that the official United States view that capital market restrictions in Europe put pressure on the United States balance of payments by diverting demand for savings to New York[27] is not very compelling. Reform of the underwriting and distributing facilities for long-term capital issues in Britain, France, Italy, and Germany will not alter the relative scarcity of capital in those markets[28]; eliminating the limits on new issues in the thin markets of Switzerland and the Netherlands would be virtually certain to raise yields rapidly in those markets without providing much more capital net from domestic savers. Zurich or Amsterdam could perhaps become a European capital center for large bond issues at reduced commissions sold to an international group of purchasers. The domestic authorities are opposed to altering the present diversification of domestic savings being placed in a number of small issues, sold by the underwriters at substantial mark-ups. The foreign borrowers, moreover, would doubtless be wary of risking a big issue on the narrow domestic market even if the official limitations were not there.

A Swiss economist suggested to the Joint Economic Committee that the United States should take a leaf out of the Swiss authorities' book and limit foreign access to the New York bond market.[29] This recommendation rests on the national view of the connection between foreign lending and the balance of payments, and overlooks the function of a financial center in providing a market for foreign lenders as well as foreign borrowers, with negligible effect on the balance.

Some interest attaches to the more intense preoccupation with liquidity in Europe than in the United States, a preoccupation which seems to inhibit the investment of excess short-term balances in long-term domestic bonds. It may be that liquidity preference, like other forms of taste, *non disputandum est* but the American official view runs to the effect that greater institutional efforts could be undertaken, by freeing markets of restrictions, providing medium-term obligations and stimulating competition among lenders, to induce European capitalists to part with their liquidity in exchange for bonds. On the other hand, it may be that the capital markets for bonds which provide too little diversification for lenders, and thereby induce them to hold cash, are narrow and unconnected by reason of investor attitudes, not official restrictions.

VI. *Prospective Europe Financial Integration*

If the financial centers of Switzerland and Amsterdam will not, and probably could not, provide the central market necessary for financial integration, what of the rest of Europe? It is the thesis of this paper that New York is the most likely center of long-term financial integration for Europe, that its head start over any potential competitor is one which cannot be overcome, and that the financial integration of the European Economic Community, with or without the adherence of the United Kingdom, will be effected through the Euro-dollar for short-term funds and the dollar bond for long. Short-term integration has made great progress since the war; long-term finance much less. To the extent that the long-term capital market becomes integrated, however, it seems probable that interest rates in Frankfurt and Paris will be equalized not by direct capital movements between France and Germany, but by those through New York.[30]

This is not the usual view. Representative Widnall of the Joint Economic Committee asked, "Would not the Common Market eventually provide greater ability to finance within the Common Market so that there would be no necessity to come to the United States?" to which D. D. Humphrey replied, "The British are very much hoping. If they join, they hope London will become the capital center...."[31]

In an important study, Paul Meek states[32]: "The advance of economic integration as an emerging reality in Western Europe is likely to be accompanied by a financial integration of European money and capital markets." And again[33]: "The growing integration of the European economy provides the central challenge to New York's present position. The breaking down of national economic barriers is inescapably going to be paralleled by an integration of national money and capital markets. . . . If the United Kingdom joins the Common Market and London should develop as the financial center of a United Europe, New York would have a very powerful competitor indeed. And the world might then have two financial centers more nearly equal in size."

Meek recognizes the possibility that the Common Market may fail to develop a single financial center, or a completely integrated capital market united by common banking institutions like those in the Swiss market. His discussion of this possibility runs mainly in terms of the effectiveness of New York in keeping commissions low and easing the rigors of registration with the Securities and Exchange Commission.[34] There is little description of the dynamic process by which a dominant market would gain ascendancy in Europe.

VII. The Emergence of a Dominant Center

It is hard to see how the London market would acquire dominance in the long-term capital market of Europe if and when Britain joins the Common Market. London rates are high; the demand for capital in Britain is large; sources of savings have dried up. The City is no longer providing capital for the Commonwealth on a significant scale, having deferred to the Colonial Office, the IBRD and New York. The channels connecting the London capital market to European centers silted up after 1848, and there is no apparent reason to expect them to open up.

It is true that London has played a major rôle in European short-term banking, partly through the Euro-dollar market where its rôle is central.[35] Several critics of the first draft of this paper have thought that I unduly emphasize the need for London to contribute savings to an international financial center, as opposed to the institutional facilities so handy to the Continent, and that if European countries hold liquid reserves in London, the practice might easily develop of centralizing purchases and sales of long-term bond issues there. This may be so. But if there are economies of scale in long-term financial markets, as I believe, a base of abundant domestic savings is needed to get started. Without this base I do not see how the first borrowers can be induced to sell issues at rates competitive with Zurich for small issues and with New York for substantial ones. With economies of scale, the problem is to achieve scale. How would London do it?

One critic, Robert Mundell, contends that London's high interest rates reflect less a relative scarcity of capital than a relatively persistent inflation. Once this inflation is cured, it follows that abundant domestic savings will lower interest rates, attract borrowers, and with broader markets, savers as well. Possible, but unlikely in my judgment, since I doubt whether the savings are really there. Income redistribution, modest profits, consumption of capital gains, middle-class dissavings and so on have undermined the bases for substantial personal savings which have not been replaced by institutional savings through insurance, pension funds, etc. But this is of course impressionistic.[36]

The emergence of another center — Frankfurt, Paris, Amsterdam, Brussels, Milan, or outside the EEC itself, Zurich, is possible but not likely. Switzerland and Amsterdam virtually eliminate themselves. Of the other four, there is no reason to expect financial energy to be attracted more to one than another. Perhaps Milan can be ruled out on the grounds of Italian capital needs, which leave little savings available for export. Brussels is small. Between Paris and Frankfurt, one would expect perhaps the demand for capital to fall relatively to the supply, first in Germany rather than France, but the German tradition in lending in bonds is slight — term loans to support exports have deeper roots in the foreign field. The French tradition in bonds, moreover, is one to forget.

How would one center pull ahead of the other? It would pull financial energy, as New York did in its rise ahead of Philadelphia. Benjamin Franklin was attracted from Boston to Philadelphia in 1726; Alexander Hamilton and Aaron Burr from the Antilles and Albany, in 1772 and 1783 respectively, to New York. The success of Paris in defeating the challenge of Lyon in the second half of the nineteenth century is vividly described by the biographer of the early years of the *Crédit Lyonnais*.[37] Established in Lyon in 1863, this great bank transferred its center of power to the Paris office, and with it the person of its energetic president, Henri Germain, during the 1870's. In 1881 the transfer was complete and Germain did not visit the Lyon office once during the year.[38]

Another possibility would be for leading European banks and investment bankers to establish a network of branches throughout the Common Market. It is not enough for certain banks to work together for particular purposes, as is said to be the case among the *Deutsche Bank,* the *Crédit Lyonnais,* the *Banca Commerciale Italiana* and the *Morgan Guaranty Trust Company.* The interests of a syndicate may be merged for particular purposes and for periods of time, but they remain divergent in ways which those of a single institution with branches in separate portions of the market would not. The private bankers — Rothschild, Lazard Frères, Schroeder — would perhaps serve the purpose if the funds at their disposal were somewhat bigger in relation to the totals. It is worth noting that of the commercial banks it is the United States institutions — Morgan Guaranty Trust Company, Chase Manhattan, the First National City, in particular — which are represented in the several countries of the Common Market rather than European institutions.

One further possibility for integrating the capital market is industrial firms using direct investment. In the United States, the marginal efficiencies of capital and of labor have been equalized throughout the country, in some considerable part, by the operations of national firms, borrowing in New York and investing where the marginal efficiency of capital was high and the cost of labor low. But this result only followed after an integrated capital market had been established. Stephen Hymer has asserted as a theoretical proposition which is persuasive that industrial firms are not likely to move capital more efficiently than long-term capital markets — which is why they characteristically attempt to borrow the maximum possible capital locally.[39] But in any event it is largely United States firms which have subsidiaries in several Common Market countries, and a few British.[40] As in banking, European firms typically form loose associations rather than merge or establish wholly-owned subsidiaries in one another's markets.

I conclude on the basis of this analysis that trade integration does not necessarily lead to financial integration; that long-term capital markets are now more integrated between the separate countries of Europe and the United States than among each other, with further integration likely to emerge in this direction rather than within the Common Market (with or without the British); that the same pattern is likely to be true of short-term capital markets, but to a lesser extent, with the Euro-dollar market taking the place of the New York bond market. It follows that economic integration in one field (trade) does not necessarily lead to integration in other aspects within the identical group of countries, and that the European Economic Community may continue to discriminate against outside countries in trade but be integrated with them in other respects. The flow of Dutch labor to Canada and Australia mentioned by Meade is one example. It is predicted that another will be increasingly found in capital markets.

A final point: Professor James Ingram believes that financial integration is desirable not only because of its effect on resource allocation but because it improves the efficiency of the balance-of-payments adjustment mechanism.[41] His studies, especially of the payments mechanism between Puerto Rico and the United States suggest that changes in ownership of long-term assets, as well as in short-term claims and liabilities, may play an important rôle in bringing about smooth and effortless balance-of-payments adjustment of the sort so frequently found within but not between countries. This may be so, though I have doubts.[42] The present exercise is one in positive, rather than normative, economics. I am not urging financial integration within the Atlantic partnership but forecasting its emergence.

NOTES

[1] Tinbergen's definition is given in more general terms as "the creation of the most desirable structure of international economy" (Jan Tinbergen, *International Economic Integration,* 2nd, Completely Rev., Ed. of *International Economic Co-operation,* Amsterdam, 1954, p. 95), but in his subsequent discussion the major instrument for achieving this structure, after the establishment of national policies for full employment, etc., is the removal of quantitative restrictions and import duties (*ibid.,* p. 119).

[2] Bela Balassa, *The Theory of Economic Integration,* Homewood, Ill., and London, 1961, p. 1. — See also his "Toward a Theory of Economic Integration", *Kyklos,* Vol. XIV, Basel, 1961, pp. 1sqq., which discusses various definitions.

[3] See Gunnar Myrdal, *An International Economy, Problems and Prospects,* New York, 1956, p. 11. Myrdal puts the stress on equality of opportunity, but adds that the remuneration paid for productive services must be equal, regardless of racial, social and cultural differences. These differences, of course, are of more importance for labor than for capital.

[4] Tibor Scitovsky, *Economic Theory and Western European Integration,* London, 1958, p. 88, note 2. This definition should perhaps be extended to comprehend as well the absence of differences in yield on similar securities issued in two physically separate markets by a single borrower. (See Table 1, below for the experience of the International Bank for Reconstruction and Development in this connection.) For a discussion which runs entirely in terms of movements, rather than of yields in capital markets, see Hans O. Lundström, *Capital Movements and Economic Integration, A Study of the Rôle of International Long-Term Capital Movements in International Economic Integration With Particular Reference to Europe,* European Aspects, Series B: Economics, No. 4, Leyden, 1961.

[5] James E. Meade, *Negotiations for Benelux,* Princeton Studies in International Finance, No. 6, Princeton, 1957, p. 78.

[6] See Scitovsky, *op. cit.,* p. 88: "An integrated capital market may discriminate among borrowers according to the nature and riskiness of their business, the size of their assets, their past financial record, and other such factors, but not according to the region where they operate."

[7] The possibility of a change in the exchange rate may also be more important for goods than for long-term capital, or at least it was in the Canadian case, where long-term capital movements ignored variations in the exchange rate between 1950 and 1961, and again in trans-Atlantic movements where European capital borrowing and lending in New York appear to ignore the short-term view of the dollar. There is some opinion in the United States that the "overvaluation" has stimulated the outflow of capital, as long-term borrowers went short of the dollar. But this explanation must account for the lenders who go long. On balance, the safer hypothesis is that investors dealing in long-term bonds ignore possible changes in the exchange rate, since the mean of a probability distribution of changes in exchange rates converted to return in per cent per annum over the life of the contract is likely to be very small as compared to differences in interest rates. It is true that two-way movements in capital, and their net, might be much larger if investors entertained inelastic expectations regarding the present exchange-rate structure. Despite the doubts of my critics, how-

80

ever, and based on the findings of Helleiner and Rhomberg in Yale doctoral dissertations examining the Canadian flexible exchange rate experience, I think the conclusion must be that while short-term capital movements respond sensitively to changes in exchange rates, long-term capital movements do not.

For a view that national demands and supplies for goods should be added into world demand and supply curves, and that the national offer curve has no operational meaning, see Frank D. Graham, *The Theory of International Values,* Princeton, 1948, p. 158: "The price of any freely traded good is unaffected by the national origin of sellers or buyers and there is, in consequence, no occasion for grouping buyers or sellers into more or less antagonistic national sectors." But this ignores transfer costs, and the possibility of exchange-rate changes.

[8] Scitovsky, *op. cit.,* p. 90.

[9] See Paul Meek, "United States Investment in Foreign Securities (Excluding Canadian and IBRD Issues)", in *United States Private and Government Investment Abroad,* R. F. Mikesell, ed., Eugene, Ore., 1962, p. 253.

[10] For an interesting account of the registration process, its costs and its usefulness, see E. Nevin, "Some Reflections in the New York New Issues Market," *Oxford Economic Papers,* Vol. XIII, 1961, pp. 84 sqq.

[11] For an analysis of how New York surpassed Philadelphia, which had been the dominant financial center from about 1750, see Bray Hammond, *Banks and Politics in America From the Revolution to the Civil War,* Princeton, New Jersey, 1957, esp. pp. 149, 351sqq. Hammond lays stress not only on New York's physical advantages — the greater commodiousness of her harbor, and the Erie Canal — but also on the energy and ingenuity of her enterprise. — See also Margaret G. Myers, *The New York Money Market,* Vol. I: *Origins and Development,* New York, 1931, Chapter I.

[12] A leading contender, if never dominant, Boston suffered a setback in the hard winter of 1816 which closed Boston Harbor to shipping. This is the year known in American annals as "Eighteen-hundred and froze-to-death."

[13] *Source:* IMF, *International Financial Statistics,* Vol. XVI, Washington, D.C., 1963, No. 2, p. 29.

[14] *Source:* IBRD, *Annual Reports to the Board of Governors,* Washington, D.C.

[15] By private letter.

[16] *Source:* Compiled from unpublished summaries made available by the International Bank for Reconstruction and Development.

[17] The table also omits private placements of foreign bonds in New York which picked up after 1958 from very small beginnings and culminated in an $100 million issue for a Mexican governmental company placed with a private insurance company in 1960. For a table of such placements including $100 millions for European borrowers, see Meek, *op. cit.,* p. 254.

[18] See: De Nederlandsche Bank, NV, *Report for the Year 1961,* Amsterdam, p. 21.

[19] *The New York Times,* August 16, 1962, p. 35, column 6.

[20] See his address, "Investment Banking and International Finance," before the Forty-Seventh National Foreign Trade Convention, New York, November 14, 1960, p. 5 of the mimeographed version. This paper was generously communicated to me by Mr. Overby.

[21] See his testimony before the Joint Economic Committee, Congress of the United States, on August 14, 1962, in: *Hearings on the State of the Economy and Policies for Full Employment* (August 7–10, 13–17, 20, 21 and 22, 1962), p. 489. — See also the testimony of Professor Philip W. Bell on the same subject, *ibid.*, pp. 490sqq., to the effect that the movement of long-term capital to Europe is exaggerated because of the proportion of the new issues bought by Europeans.

[22] See Meek, *op. cit.*, p. 251.

[23] Overby, *op. cit.*, p. 6.

[24] Pizer, *op. cit.*, p. 489.

[25] Meek, *op. cit.*, pp. 251sq. The statement is footnoted with a reference to Moody's Investor Service, *Bond Survey*, New York, October 27, 1958, p. 226.

[26] Letter from Paul Meek, October 17, 1962, paraphrased by generous permission. This explanation would apply more fully, it would seem, to Switzerland than to the Netherlands, judging by the interest yields in Table 1, and more fully to both of these than to Belgium, on the same ground and in view of Belgium's experience as a borrower on long-term bond account for new issues, rather than a lender.

[27] See Speeches of Secretary of the Treasury Dillon before the American Bankers Association at Rome, Italy, May 18, 1962 (mimeographed), p. 10; and of Deputy Under-Secretary J. Dewey Daane before the American Chamber of Commerce in the Netherlands, Scheveningen, the Netherlands, June 26, 1962 (mimeographed), p. 4. Secretary Dillon recognizes that a large proportion of the publicly floated issues in New York have been bought by Europeans but holds that the "burden is nonetheless real."

[28] Asked to comment on the Dillon speech at the Joint Economic Committee *Hearings*, F. H. Klopstock, manager, Research Department, Federal Reserve Bank of New York, combined organization of the market with its capacity without indicating their relative weights: ". . . to a considerable extent the motive for placing bonds in our capital market is that the absorptive capacity and the organization of the European capital market are inadequate to take care of these placements." (*Hearings, op. cit.*, p. 489.)

[29] See the testimony of Jurg Niehans before the Joint Economic Committee, *Hearings, op. cit.*, pp. 387sq. Niehans describes the Swiss restrictions which apply to loans over SF 10 million, characterizes them as one of the most useful instruments of Swiss credit policy, and quotes a director of the Swiss National Bank that if the United States had had such restrictions, there would be a world dollar shortage.

[30] Note the contradiction between this view and the statement of Franz Gehrels ("Monetary Systems for the Common Market", *Journal of Finance*, Vol. XIV, Chicago, Ill., 1959, p. 313, quoted by Balassa, *Theory of Economic Integration, op. cit.*, p. 259) that "an inflow of funds from Paris to Frankfurt might be easier to bring about than one from San Francisco to Kansas City." San Francisco and Kansas City are integrated financially, of course, not by direct links between them but through the integration of each with New York. And such is likely to be the case for Paris and Frankfurt.

[31] *Hearings, op. cit.*, p. 490.

[32] Paul Meek, *New York — International Financial Center* (mimeographed, draft of April, 1962), pp. 89sq.

[33] *Ibid.*, pp. 92sq.

[34] *Ibid.,* pp. 93sqq.

[35] See O. L. Altman, "Recent Developments in Foreign Markets for Dollars and Other Currencies", in *Factors Affecting the United States Balance of Payments,* Materials Prepared for the Subcommittee on International Exchange and Payments of the Joint Economic Committee, Congress of the United States, p. 6: *Longrun Prospects, Capital Movements, American Dollars Abroad,* Washington, 1962, pp. 483sqq.

[36] For a journalistic account which attributes significance to institutions for collecting savings, however, see Anthony Sampson, *Anatomy of Britain,* New York and Evanston, 1962, P. II, and esp. Chapter 25.

[37] Jean Bouvier, *Le Crédit Lyonnais de 1863 à 1882, Les années de formation d'une banque de dépôts,* Ecole pratique des hautes études, VIe Section, Centre de recherches historiques, Affaires et gens d'affaires, XXIII, Paris, 1961, T. I, Chapter IV: "Une banque bicéphale: Rôles respectifs du siège social et de la succursale de Paris."

[38] *Ibid.,* p. 275.

[39] See Stephen Hymer, *Direct Investment and the International Operations of National Firms,* unpublished doctoral dissertation, Massachusetts Institute of Technology, 1960.

[40] British restrictions on direct investment in the little budget of July, 1961, reaffirmed in the April 9, 1962, budget, militate against the development of widespread interconnections among the European Common Market countries through British firms.

[41] See James C. Ingram, "State and Regional Payments Mechanisms", *The Quarterly Journal of Economics,* Vol. LXXIII, Cambridge, Mass., 1959, pp. 619sqq. — Idem, "A Proposal for Financial Integration in the Atlantic Community", in *Factors Affecting the United States Balance of Payments, op. cit.,* P. 3: *The International Monetary System: Defects and Remedies,* pp. 175sqq., which suggests that the balance-of-payments disequilibrium of the United States and the need for international liquidity seen by Triffin can both be met by more effective interconnections between European and United States capital markets.

[42] See "Comment" by R. L. Pfister and Ingram's "Reply", *The Quarterly Journal of Economics,* Vol. LXXIV, 1960, pp. 641sqq. I sympathize with the Pfister position that the varying regional incidence of governmental expenditure and taxation plays a major rôle in interregional adjustment. It also seems likely to me that financial integration in short-term money markets can ease the adjustment mechanism (if it works right), though it reduces the possibility of reliance on monetary policy for internal purposes. In the one major international case where long-term capital markets were integrated — Canada and the United States — this fact did not help with adjustment.

CHAPTER SIX

SUMMARY OF VIEWS ON
U.S. BALANCE-OF-PAYMENTS
POSITION AND POLICY*

Analysis

1. The real problem is the basic balance and not the over-all balance, and the basic balance redefined so as to view United States government prepayments and borrowings of more than one year as compensatory rather than autonomous. (In this, as in much else, I agree with Lary's *Problems of the United States as World Trader and Banker.*) Short-term capital is responsive to interest-rate differences (I favor Kenen's position over Bell's and Lederer's).

2. It is a mistake to blame the basic deficit on any one item in the balance of payments, e.g., on the merchandise account, the long-term capital movement, direct investment, military expenditure, etc. The difficulty arises from the failure of the dependent variables to adjust to the autonomous. In my judgment, however, the deep-seated cause of difficulty is the loss of technological lead over the rest of the world, compounded of some cost-push inflation in steel.

3. While the dollar has been somewhat overvalued in recent years, partly as a result of the new availability of supplies abroad at old low prices, the degree of overvaluation, taking availabilities into account, has not been serious since 1960 and has been pro-gressively reduced (except vis-à-vis Canada) by the March 1961 revaluations and by price increases in Europe. (The Japanese econ-omy has behaved somewhat erratically and should perhaps also constitute an exception.) Cost-of-living indexes in the last twelve

* Summary Memorandum submitted as a private individual to a govern-ment consulting group, April 2, 1963.

months show increases of Spain 8 per cent, Italy 7 per cent, France and Japan 5 per cent, Germany and the Netherlands 4 per cent, Austria and Switzerland 3 per cent, compared with 1 per cent for the United States. The forces of adjustment have been working slowly, but they are working.

4. While the United States' basic deficit has responded to the automatic adjustment mechanism only slowly, the position may be helped by the fact that the persistent surpluses of Germany, the Netherlands, and Italy are broadly corrected, and the counterpart of the U.S. deficit is the less-likely-to-be persistent surpluses of Canada, Spain, Austria, South Africa, and Japan, in addition to France and Switzerland. Present French labor difficulties may assist in the correction of that surplus, and the loss of forward motion in the EEC as a whole is likely to slow down the flow of U.S. direct investment.

5. I do not believe that the United States has been seriously handicapped in its domestic policy by the balance of payments, nor that it should be except insofar as the balance limits the capability of using monetary policy. It is true that fiscal policy is subject to congressional agreement, whereas monetary policy is not; but I have doubts that investment in the United States is very interest-elastic, and I believe that the congressional and public opposition to tax cuts is on the grounds of dogma rather than balance-of-payments fears. In a world crisscrossed by broad channels through which capital flows, it may be necessary to abandon or greatly modify national independence of monetary policy (just as the Federal Reserve districts have done). This is a cost, but I judge it less than the benefit.

6. While the basic balance has been adjusting only slowly, and that of the United States more slowly than those in Europe, the machinery for coping with speculative crises has been broadened since March 1961 and tested on Canada, Cuba, and recently sterling. The only serious weakness in the short-run international payments mechanism is the tendency, evident in the first half of 1962 but recently absent, of some central banks to inch up their gold ratio to total reserves.

Balance-of-Payments Policy

7. My general line on the basic balance is to ignore it except insofar as it constrains monetary policy. The tax cut should go

forward; it may hurt the merchandise balance through imports, but it should help overall by restraining private capital exports. The adjustment mechanism is working abroad. A cumulated deficit of another $10 or $20 billion properly financed is of no great importance, compared with national income of $500 billion a year. Nor is it wise to risk a major blow to the world payments mechanism which finances $120 billion of trade annually for a $2 billion deficit.

In particular, I oppose:

a. Devaluation of the dollar. Present overvaluation is declining. In any event, the remedy for overvaluation is likely to be worse than the disease. Devaluation may not be allowed to be effective vis-à-vis Germany, France, Italy, and much less Britain, Canada, Spain, Austria, Japan. To change the rate at all will require a new world system of holding exchange reserves, at a cost in disruption of payments arrangements. We are reaching a position where the exchange rates of the major countries must be regarded as fixed even for structural changes in balances of payments. In the case of the United States, this is not a question of prestige (or should not be) but of support for the world payments mechanism. This mechanism must be maintained at some direct cost to the United States in analogous fashion to our defense support for the free world. It produces long-run benefits, and it is cheaper than any alternative.

b. A floating exchange rate.

c. Substantial cutbacks in aid or defense-expenditure abroad for balance-of-payments reasons. Payments difficulties may usefully call attention to inappropriate aid and defense sharing arrangements or levels of expenditure. In the balance of payments, U.S. expenditure on these items should be autonomous and not dependent upon our year-to-year position.

d. Tying aid and Buying American on military expenditure, not to mention contemplated tax remission for exports, etc. Here again, there may be possible gains in efficiency from new procurement agreements, and illiberal measures by the United States may serve a tactical purpose in helping to promote liberal steps abroad. The measures themselves are undesirable and their cost in loss of United States leadership is high.

e. Restrictions on capital outflows. I do not share the Treasury view that greater liberalization of capital markets in Europe will ease the strain here and achieve a healthy freedom from New York. New York is becoming a world capital center where borrowers sell bonds and investors buy them — borrowers and investors from all over the world. The dependence of the world on United States dollar deposits — directly and via the Euro-dollar market — is healthy for the world payments system, even though it involves some cost for this country. So is the two-way dependence on the capital market. This is financial integration of the Free World, or primarily of the Atlantic Partnership. It is desirable, not a pathological condition to be overcome.

International Liquidity Policy

8. The international payments system is much more stable, in my view, than it is regarded by many economists and journalists. I do not see any problems outside the United States and Britain which would be helped by a great deal more liquidity. Underdeveloped countries need resources, not liquidity. Britain would doubtless be happier with higher reserves under her control, rather than being forced to rely solely on international collaboration in exchange crises. Once the United States solves the basic deficit, additions to international reserves can be created at will by accepting surpluses in foreign exchange, rather than gold. On this score there is no useful purpose to be served by a major overhaul of the IMF, until there is a consensus on how much financial sovereignty should be committed to an international institution.

9. Pending the correction of its basic deficit, the United States can rely on its perimeter defenses, plus the responsiveness of short-term capital to changes in interest rates. It would be useful if a structural change in the liquidity position could be added to these, say, through a large, long-term government loan placed in Europe and paid for either with foreign dollars held in New York, or foreign currencies paid to the United States. A multiple-currency obligation which provided an exchange guarantee to the bondholders is worth exploring. The present fifteen-month borrowing arrangements are too limited in time to serve the purpose adequately.

10. By perimeter defenses, I mean not necessarily the specific arrangements of the Treasury but the general class of arrangements

under which central banks and treasuries acquire and hold the currency of a country under speculative bear attack as exemplified in the Basle Agreement. It may be argued that central bankers are uncomfortable with such ill-defined arrangements; this is unfortunate but inescapable. [. . .]

11. Exchange guarantees raise questions which cannot be settled in *ex ante* negotiation. What can be agreed beforehand is only the diffuse obligation not to let a central bank that has behaved correctly in the international interest be unduly hurt thereby. How this would be done will take some ingenuity in particular cases, but such ingenuity is cheap, as Lend-Lease and the Marshall Plan have demonstrated.

12. It would be well to limit possible inching by central banks to increase their gold to total reserve ratios by negotiating something like the Posthuma Plan. I have no particular interest in retaining gold in the system but see risks from any attempt to drive it out precipitously.

CHAPTER SEVEN

THE PROSPECTS FOR INTERNATIONAL LIQUIDITY AND THE FUTURE EVOLUTION OF THE INTERNATIONAL PAYMENTS SYSTEM*

I. Introduction

It is now more than three years since the Suez monetary crisis came to an end, and economists and financiers have turned their attention to the so-called problem of international monetary liquidity. Interest was drawn to the question by Sir Oliver Franks in his report as chairman of Lloyds Bank in February 1958. It was sustained by an issue of *The Economist* at the end of May in the same year, balance of payments difficulties of the United States on trade account in 1959, and owing to an outflow short-term capital in the last half of 1960 did nothing to change the subject, partly as a result of the important contribution of Robert Triffin in his various articles of 1959 and his book, *Gold and the Dollar Crisis,* of 1960. Today world monetary liquidity is 'Hit Tune Number One' in the repertoire of the international trade and monetary economist, and a host of bankers, journalists and men of affairs.

This is perhaps not curious. Economics, like female dress and much else, moves in waves of fashion, continuously discarding the old for the 'New Look'. And like female dress, the new styles seldom involve much change in basic matter. I am reluctantly prepared to recognize that there may be a world liquidity problem. But I would claim that it is rather unimportant compared with the issues with which it is currently confused.

* From *International Trade Theory in a Developing World,* Proceedings of a Conference held by the International Economic Association, Roy Harrod and Douglas Hague, eds., London, Macmillan & Co., Ltd., 1963, pp. 372-392 (Conference held in September 1961).

Analytically, one can separate out perhaps five distinct questions: obdurate or massive balance of payments difficulties of individual countries; simultaneous world deflation of all industrial countries; hot-money or short-term capital flows on a large scale; the international reserve positions of individual countries; and world liquidity. I propose in this paper to devote attention to each of these in turn, and to demonstrate that:

a. Persistent or massive balance of payments deficits and surpluses remain a matter for continuous world concern and action by a variety of means in separate countries.

b. Simultaneous world industrial deflation, which I shall call the Balogh problem, is not a current question, nor is it likely in my judgment to be; but it is important potentially, and thought, if not action, is now required to meet it should it arise; it is unwise, however, to act as if it were certain to arise, or had arisen.

c. The instability of the gold exchange standard — hot-money or the Triffin problem — is real, and requires action, but the steps needed are much less drastic than the Triffin proposal, which runs the risk of rendering more difficult the solution to persistent balance of payments deficits.

d. There may be merit in increasing the reserves of individual countries, whose persistent balance of payments deficits have been cured; the qualification makes clear, however, that no general or across-the-board measure is called for.

e. If any world liquidity problem remains — as seen, for example, by the quantity theorists who want to enlarge the volume of international reserves annually by a percentage determined by some projected growth rate of world trade — it can readily be dealt with when and if it arises; again, it is dangerous to anticipate.

It is clear, I hope, that there is work to be done. The world system for resolving international payments difficulties is not perfect. But progress has been made in recent years; and future progress is possible, in separate, discreet steps, meeting specific needs as they arise, rather than attempting to solve all with one sovereign remedy. It is especially desirable not to subject the present system to the strain on confidence of a prolonged spate of constitution writing for an entirely new system. Constitutions, in my judgment, should be written, if at all, only after the system has evolved into satisfactory form, not in advance, to anticipate and meet all forms of possible disaster.

There is work to be done because the world has moved, and in directions which, however satisfactory from many points of view, require adjustments.

(i) *Persistent or Massive Balance of Payments Difficulties.* On balance of payments account, the persistent dollar surplus on current account in excess of its long-term lendings and compensatory transfers has been corrected. Transfers have changed from a compensatory item to an autonomous one. Some claim that such a persistent surplus never existed, or existed only because of erroneous monetary policies in the United States or abroad. This may be so, but I doubt it. The record of lend-lease, post-war economic assistance, the British loan and Marshall Plan, to say nothing of the early operations of the Bretton Woods institutions, suggest that a gap existed to be filled. There have since been changes: the technological lead of the United States over foreign industrial countries has been narrowed, and in some commodities closed or reversed. Reluctance to lend abroad has been overcome. The United States has replaced earlier under-investment, under-consumption and under-importing with overspending on defence, relative to the rest of the world, and accepting an unduly large share of responsibility for economic development. Consumption has also increased. Keynes' analysis of 1946 has proved to be only fifteen years and $50 billion premature. Whether he was right or wrong depends upon one's intellectual rate of interest.

But by no means all persistent balance of payments problems have been solved. Eliminating the biggest one is a long step forward, but it does not dispose of the issue intellectually, as many economists seem to think. The German persistent surplus remains, and underlying British weakness. French, Italian and Japanese surpluses correct themselves but slowly. Under-developed countries like India, Turkey, Brazil, Argentina have deficits which correct themselves hardly at all.

(ii) *Hot Money.* Hot money, which raged from 1925 to 1939 but subsided after World War II, has taken a new lease of life. This is where Triffin has made his most penetrating analysis. Prior to World War I there was no hot money because the world was willing

91

to hold uncovered only one foreign currency apart from the national one, sterling. With stable exchange rates it was useless, too, to speculate between sterling and gold, although gold transfers took place between Britain and the sterling area on the one hand, and gold reserve countries on the other. It is also worth noting that the system was stable from 1945 to 1959 when, apart from limited sums held in Switzerland, Germany and the sterling area, the world held only dollars on an uncovered basis.

The asymmetry between dollars and other currencies has now gone, or in some cases opened up in the other direction, with speculators covering their dollar holdings and maintaining open positions in sterling, marks, or Swiss francs. Speculation also takes place between national currencies and gold. Willingness to speculate in more than one currency brings short-term capital movements back into play, whether as a destabilizing element, or, potentially, as stabilizing. Rediscovery of money on the internal front, the need felt to manipulate short-term rates of interest for domestic monetary stabilization, and renewed responsiveness of international short-term capital movements to interest rate differentials open up a conflict between internal and foreign monetary policy which, however celebrated in textbooks, has been virtually dormant in practice, for the last fifteen years, save for a few centres like Germany.

(iii) *International Reserve Positions of Individual Countries.* Liquidity problems of individual countries have been affected since 1914 by two major changes: the cutting of the links between the money supply and international reserves, on the one hand, and on the other the limitation of long-term borrowing to specific investment projects. The first is familiar in developed countries; bit by bit, however, the system has altered so that under-developed countries, including former colonies, with their high marginal propensity to import, have now established central banks to replace currency boards, and issue fiduciary currency in contrast to the former system of either using foreign currency in domestic payments, or maintaining a 1:1 relationship between local means of payments and international reserves. This is true not only of Malaya, Indonesia, Ghana, and the British colonies, but also of Cuba and Haiti which had previously operated respectively with parity with the United States' dollar and 100 per cent reserves in French francs.

One hundred per cent reserves have been attacked in an interest-ing and relatively neglected series of exchanges in the *Economic Journal* in the early 1950s as lending from poor countries to rich, and hand exploitation. But, as Ida Greaves points out, the system included not only short-term lending by colony to currency centre, but also long-term borrowing. The money supply of the colony could be expanded by long-term foreign borrowing, and selling bonds abroad for local expenditure, which had the effect of adding to reserves and expanding the domestic monetary supply, was a normal operating procedure. Insistence that long-term loans be made for fixed capital only, and limited to their foreign exchange content, apart from a few exceptional loans designed to finance general balance of payments deficits arising from particular invest-ment spending, has greatly altered the pre-1914 system when for-eign borrowing was undertaken for the same purposes as domestic borrowing — whether local investment, deficit spending, or specific projects — with temporary or even permanent changes in the inter-national reserve position and the domestic money supply.

These changes are relevant to the widely held view that the supply of the world's major currencies can only be expanded by deficits, or contracted by surpluses. The answer turns on the definition of 'deficit', to which we recur below; but if deficit and surplus be limited to the net of the balance of payments on current account, transfers and long-term loans for real investment, the claim is invalid. Countries can add to their reserves through borrowing, as well as through export surpluses, and major currencies can be lent for stabilization purposes as well as for spending.

(iv) *World Liquidity.* Finally, there are those who claim that the world liquidity problem has been altered in ways which call for action by (*a*) the threat of a new world depression in the industrial countries; and (*b*) the doubling in the world price level when the price of gold remained unchanged. On the first score one can accept the importance of the issue, but doubt the facts; on the second, one can admit the facts, but reject the analysis which attributes signifi-cance to them.

In the foregoing real changes, it is worth underlining that the position of the United States has altered from a highly asymmetrical one in which it held a persistent surplus, and operated the only currency in which the world was willing to hold long positions. The

93

passing of these asymmetries requires modification of some of the distortions in the system, which had grown up to match them: the fact, for example, that the United States was unwilling to hold other currencies, but only gold among its reserves. Or that other countries left to the United States the responsibility for managing and underwriting the payments system, and persistent deficits where they occur — the role played by Britain in the period before 1914. The system must evolve into one in which responsibility for world payments, and the burden of the world's load of defence and development expense are more widely shared. There are difficulties of sharing. The process requires a deep-seated sense of social and political cohesion. But it is a necessity. The necessity for a sense of cohesion does not produce it, of course; but it is permissible to cite it as an argument in favour of efforts to operate the system on the basis of widely diffused participation in shared responsibilities, as opposed to strict contractual obligations.

The fact that the 'world liquidity problem' is best analysed as four separate problems does not imply that these problems are unrelated.

(i) Persistent disequilibrium in the single key currency or in one of two or more key currencies on the gold exchange standard leads to an acceleration of hot-money flows. A deficit both feeds liquidity to the market and attacks the confidence in the key currency needed to make it acceptable. Heilperin goes further and thinks that the gold exchange standard, even with a single key currency, leads inexorably to persistent deficits, as the country issuing the key currency fails to take the necessary corrective steps when the deficit is financed by an increase in liabilities.[1]

(ii) Speculation in exchange can alter slightly and become speculation in primary commodities or in foreign company shares, disguising what is a problem of speculation as a trade problem or as long-term capital flow. When a country's merchants switch out of cash into imported primary products, or the reverse, this appears to be a balance of payments imbalance, or camouflages one that already exists.

(iii) The adequacy of reserves of different countries is related to the adequacy of world reserves. But the relationship is not simply additive. World reserves may be badly distributed, so that an adequate over-all amount leaves many individual countries inadequately provided for, or adequate provision for all countries requires an excessive total. In addition, a solution of the hot-money problem will, it is claimed, eliminate most of the 'world problem' but still leave national problems which really exist.

(iv) One connection stressed by Triffin and Lamfalussy[2] does not appeal to me, the attempt to relate the problem of liquidity to the economic development of under-developed countries by using long-term loans for development as the backing for short-term liabilities which serve as international reserves. But this requires detailed discussion.

II. The Persistent Balance of Payments Problem

There is a balance of payments problem, in the sense in which we use the term, when the balance on current account, plus transfers, plus long-term capital movements — appropriate account being taken of algebraic sign — departs from zero. A current-account surplus requires outward transfers or capital exports. And the reserve is required for current-account deficits. Any net payments or net receipts we can call a persistent 'deficit' or 'surplus', which is distinguished from the current-account deficit or surplus.

The definition relates to extended periods of time, and not to seasonal or cyclical fluctuations around a balanced position. This means, of course, that there are difficulties of recognition and identification.

And there will be occasions when it is desirable to omit 'compensatory' transfers or long-term capital movements from counting in the deficit or surplus. Rescue operations, for example, whether from international institutions and the key currencies to India or Turkey, or in the form of pre-payment of debts by Germany to the United States, should not be subtracted from the deficit or surplus, no matter what specific form they take. There is no unique criterion for measuring the 'deficit', under all circumstances, just as the International Monetary Fund learned that there was no reliable measure 'of compensatory' movements in the balance of payments. To recognize the problem occasionally, and to measure it, always calls for the application of art, after the scientific criteria have taken observers as far as they can go.

This definition leaves out short-term capital movements and gold, which, in equilibrium, and apart from the theoretical qualifications of the last paragraph, by definition are zero. It also ignores the practical question, whether Errors and Omissions, if its size is significant, is really long-term capital, short-term, or trade.

The normal definition includes all long-term capital. But some long-term capital in form — like speculation in shares — is short-term in intention, and some changes in short-term deposits are permanent. It might be desirable under particular conditions to count permanent additions to liquid reserves, acquired by long-term borrowing, as a long-term loan, with no long-term net movements to this extent. This supposes, of course, from the side of the long-term lender, that the currency borrowed is the currency added to reserves, such as would be true in a two-country model. Where one currency is borrowed, and another held as reserves, the reserve centres cannot net the movements. It is not a sin against the canons of finance to lend long and borrow short from the same party, when the latter understands that the short-term borrowing is for a permanent increase in reserves, and if drawn down will be quickly reconstituted. But it is dangerous to lend long and borrow short, when the short-term borrowing is undertaken from a third party who does not share that understanding.

Balance of payments problems of under-developed countries may be persistent and serious, but they have almost nothing to do with the world liquidity problem as it is generally formulated. More or less deliberately, these countries have chosen to convert liquid reserves into real investment. In so choosing, they have possibly underestimated the negative but real value of foreign exchange reserves, much as they underrate the importance of real liquid capital in inventories in their preference for fixed assets. Like insurance, foreign exchange reserves have a cost, but like insurance, they pay their way. Reserves enable a country subject to short-term fluctuations in export proceeds or long-term borrowing, around some average rate, to import at a continuous rate without interruptions, which are expensive, whether in rendering unfinished capital projects temporarily useless, even though their capital cost continues, or in encouraging destabilizing speculation in inventories of consumers' goods and raw materials against such interruptions.

Apart from the insurance value of reserves, however, the existence of persistent debtors running balance of payments deficits on current account in excess of long-term loans renders any system of international payments unworkable. The brilliant success of the European Payments Union should not delude us into thinking that the system could have solved the payments problems of 1950 had it not been (i) for the readiness of the United States to finance the persistent debit positions of Austria, Turkey, and Greece for years; (ii) for the readiness of the members to enlarge first the German quota on the debtor side, and then on the creditor side the quotas of both Belgium and Germany; and (iii) for the financing, outside the payments system, of the lumpy mass of debits accumulated by France.

It is equally true that a new multilateral payments system, contrived or evolved, will break down if persistent debtors and persistent creditors exist. The Triffin view that deficits and surpluses are needed to enlarge reserves analytically overlooks the possibilities of enlarging reserves by swapping short-term liabilities, on the one hand, and adding to reserves through long-term loans on the other. But even apart from the analytical point here, it is a weakness of the Triffin scheme that he expects to use it to finance persistent deficits of under-developed countries with rising reserves of an international payments medium held by the developed countries.

Quantities will be discussed shortly. Here the point is merely that the reconstituted International Monetary Fund would become increasingly saturated with 'phoney' assets — claims on the under-developed countries which no one expected them to requite — and the International Monetary Fund would increasingly become frozen. It can be argued that this would be unimportant, for its liabilities would be required to be accepted. But under the Triffin scheme, and every other propounded, countries which do not like to acquire the liabilities of a frozen institution which may not for ever remain acceptable, have the option of insisting on gold. Then this system, too, could break down. Aside from Senator Monroney and the World Bank which has responded to him on political grounds, practically no one takes seriously the view that the local currencies accumulated by the United States in its Point IV programme are an appropriate basis for international monetary operations.

Lamfalussy suggests that in a world of under-employment it is appropriate to finance investment through money creation, exactly as deficit spending financed by a central bank is appropriate in an under-employed economy. There are, however, these differences:

97

central banks create spending power for governments with power to convert debts into legal tender — within their own borders to be sure — and power to tax as well. In addition there is likely to be some mobility of resources within a country, so that an excess of spending in one area will spill over elsewhere or attract under-employed resources from other areas. In a multi-country world, these features are lacking. An international central bank creating new means of payment because of under-employment in the United States might find under-developed countries more disposed to spend in Germany, itself with relatively full employment and subjectively adequate reserves. This could be regarded as persistent disequilibrium in the balance of payments of the United States, or of Germany, if you like, but it suggests that Lamfalussy's analysis is better suited to a two-country model than the multilateral world. In the case cited, it would create less disturbance if Germany were to provide new loans out of savings, whether spent in Germany or the United States, or if the United States were to undertake loans or transfers abroad on a tied basis.

Persistent balance of payments deficits are serious, and I see no easy solution or sovereign remedy for them. In support of expanding markets, as free as possible, and the best possible allocation of resources, one must rule out foreign-exchange controls, trade restrictions, restrictions over foreign lending, unilateral cuts in military spending or aid. Balance of payments difficulties may none the less attract attention to an obsolete basis of dividing the world's burdens, which should be distributed according to some approximation of capacity to pay. Exchange rate changes around a given average price of gold may be desirable from time to time — one or more countries raising the price of gold and others lowering it, so as not to distort the money-gold relation. But these call for skill and nerve, more of both perhaps than was shown by Germany in the 5 per cent revaluation of February 1961 which was interpreted by the market as a first bite of the cherry. And they call for co-operation. A country's foreign exchange rate, like the composition of a country's reserve holdings, is more and more an international rather than a national question.

Moreover, discrete foreign exchange changes may not be open to all key currencies. If the dollar had been devalued as some foreign exchange markets thought likely in 1960, most of the other key currencies of the world would have followed suit, and gold would have been the only gainer — in the short run.

It is not my place to discuss flexible exchange rates, but I cannot forbear from offering the conclusion of other occasions that, however attractive or unattractive this may appear to the single country, it cannot constitute a world system of payments. Perhaps if no country interfered with its rate and all let markets clear themselves without recourse to intervention — or for that matter reserves — the system might work without interference. The instability of rates under these conditions seems to me a major depressant of trade and productive capital movements although I concede that there is room for debate. But, with reserves and market intervention, there is a need to concert moves, or monetary authorities might find themselves working at cross purposes, each of two currencies seeking to be depreciated against the other at the same time. It is of great help to a flexible exchange rate system to have a standard to work against; one key currency should be fixed in terms of gold to enable exchange rates and gold prices to be determinate at a given instant in time. If this is so, the system has to be managed at least to the extent of preventing all currencies from being depreciated or appreciated against the key currency when such a move is contrary to its authorities' view of interest. Other arguments against the adoption of a flexible exchange rate by a single country seem to me on balance, and for most countries, to have the edge. My present concern is rather with the system.

I have admitted the possibility of tied aid. It is a better-than-nothing solution and one which should be avoided if at all possible. This applies as well to redividing aid each time the balance of payments changes and much more strongly to foreign exchange control. But I can imagine circumstances in which it would seem appropriate to make use of these devices and none of them can be ruled out rigorously, no matter how much we would want to.

In short, there is no way, in my judgment, in which we can claim to dispose of balance of payments problems of separate countries, whether because they are inconsequential or because the adoption of a special brand of patent medicine would eliminate them. Different kinds of disequilibria require different sorts of treatment, and the same for qualitatively different troubles in the fields of merchandise, services, long-term lending and transfers. I see no reason to be discouraged; on the contrary. We have come a long way. And the adjustment mechanism is by no means deprived of all effectiveness. The balance of payments deficit of the United States in 1959 has been corrected, although the speculative market was late in recognizing it. Persistent German, Italian, French and Japanese surpluses have diminished, although more by expedients than by action which goes to the root of the problem. Yet we are a long way from solving the balance of payments problems of developing countries.

But what distresses me about many of the proposals made which are basically designed to meet other problems, whether the instability of the gold exchange standard with two or more key currencies, or a quantitative shortage of world liquidity, is that they are likely to subvert the balance of payments discipline which is so needed and so hard to provide. More liquidity for all countries created before persistent balance of payments deficits have been corrected is virtually certain to be inflationary and to delay the achievement of responsible policies. Persistent balance of payments difficulties do not arise from lack of liquidity; on the contrary.

III. The Cyclical Balance of Payments Problem

We come now to what is a world problem, rather than separate problems of different countries, and one which I choose to call the Balogh, rather than the Triffin, view of world liquidity. In a series of articles and books,[3] Thomas Balogh of the University of Oxford has held that the major concern in international trade should be to guard against the consequences of a simultaneous and deep depression in industrial countries which would cut imports of primary products and wreck both the balances of payments and the development programmes of a long list of countries. His reason for concern is that he expects depression in one industrial country to communicate itself to others in a deflationary spiral, rather than recession in one industrial country being corrected by buoyancy in others.

Mr. Balogh may well be right for the future, despite the fact that he has been wrong over the period since 1949. Repeated cries of 'wolf' should not blind us to the possibility that real wolves may materialize and do serious damage.

At the present time, however, it is sufficient to note that the question is hypothetical, and there are enough stop-gap measures of real value — the World Bank, the International Monetary Fund, the machinery of the Economic and Social Council of the United Nations and the Organisation for Economic Co-operation and Development — to permit an orderly attack on the problem should it arise. There is no crisis here, whether of liquidity or anything else. To take measures to construct a world central bank now to meet a critical problem which does not exist does not recommend itself.

IV. *The Hot-Money Problem*

Triffin has performed a valuable service in calling attention to the instability of the gold exchange standard with two or three major currency centres. With one centre, or fifty, the system would be stable. But like the balance of power system in political theory, bipolarity breeds instability, except under particular circumstances.

Triffin goes too far, however, and Lamfalussy still further when he says that the gold exchange standard is ridiculous. It may be possible to stabilize it by simple adjustments. It is not totally irrational to hold national currencies in international reserves, as Triffin says.[4] In fact it is hard to imagine a cheaper, more convenient, or more useful form for reserves.

It is possible that the measures about to be suggested may reduce hot-money flows, or render them stabilizing, which would greatly reduce the need for reserves, whether under a fixed, occasionally adjusted, or flexible exchange rate standard — or they might not. There is the respectable view that with all major currencies more or less in line under the fixed exchange standard, and holders of liquid assets relatively indifferent as to which currency they hold, and therefore ready to speculate by taking open positions, the major money markets have become one market, and small differences in interest rates, such as one or another country may wish to support by reason of domestic monetary policy, will lead to large-scale outflows and inflows of liquid funds.

This difference is not critical to the system in operation, though it would be if it became necessary to liquidate it. The device is one which underlay the Tripartite Monetary Agreement of September 1936, which, however, had a fatal flaw which made it ineffectual; it is the essence of Alan Day's scheme in *The Observer* for uniting the dollar and sterling into a single reserve currency —

though he makes his proposal too narrow — and it is the logical extension of the steps taken by the central banks of Europe in supporting the dollar during its troubles of 1959 and 1960, and extended by them to sterling somewhat more formally in February 1961, buying foreign currencies when they were dumped on the market by private speculators and not converting them into gold. The scheme, in short, is that the central banks of the major currencies, with treasury support, undertake to buy and hold each others' currencies during crises of confidence, when they are under speculative attack.[5]

The Tripartite Monetary Agreement was an absurdity because it provided that the Federal Reserve Bank of New York hold sterling for only twenty-four hours before converting it to gold. The Reserve System has the power, as I understand it, to hold foreign currencies longer than twenty-four hours, though it has never done so, and would probably be well advised not to undertake such a step without the precaution of consulting Congressional leaders. It is also desirable to have the Basle Agreement broadened to include the politically responsible treasuries as well as the technically competent and detached central banks. But the essence is simple: as their defence departments collaborate for defence, so should central banks and treasuries of the responsible countries — the key currencies — collaborate on a flexible basis — and without the necessity for spelling out contractually all possible eventualities — to preserve monetary stability in the face of de-stabilizing speculation.

Formal and detailed agreements have an attraction. Suppose the system fails to work, and one country or more gets stuck with a large supply of a currency which is devalued as the Netherlands Bank was with sterling in 1931, and as the Bank of France almost did when it pulled down sterling by converting its holdings into gold in 1930. Such agreements would be desirable if their prices were not too high — a protracted effort to imagine and provide for every possible disastrous contingency, and to write an international set of bankruptcy laws — an unnerving experience for foreign exchange markets. Far better, in my judgement, to have it understood that each country involved would do everything in its power, by appropriate means, to see that other countries did not suffer loss by any steps taken in its aid. In a world where all recognize the interdependence of the trading powers, and the peacetime principle of aid for reconstruction and economic development has been accepted, specific obligations do not seem vital, and a diffuse commitment, while somewhat uncomfortable, is better than any alternative.

It would be possible to insist on exchange or gold guarantees. Such insistence, however, calls for examination of which claims are covered and which not, what happens in the case of a country whose gold and foreign exchange assets were less than its liabilities, whether Congresses and Parliaments can bind their successors to vote such funds, and so on. It is necessary for mortal man to contemplate death and to dispose of his estate with precision and clarity, envisaging all possible contingencies. This is a secret proceeding. The state is presumptively immortal and the deliberation public. The gold clause in its bonds was repudiated by the United States under the claim of *force majeure,* and war debts to the United States by European powers. A diffuse obligation may be as valuable as a contractual one in an historical view, and is much more effectively put into operation.

What countries should join such an informal and loose agreement? Those that experience hot-money movements in and out of their currencies — probably no more, to begin, than Belgium, Canada, France, Germany, Italy, the Netherlands, Switzerland, the United Kingdom and the United States. If hot money began to move in substantial quantities to Stockholm or Tokyo, Sweden and Japan would presumably become members. And the same for other countries. The central banks of these countries would undertake commitments to the international community which extended beyond their national obligations, refraining from acting to save their own skins first, as central banks did, for example, in the events leading to 1931, and again in the gold scare of April 1937. Other smaller central banks and countries would be encouraged to act with moderation and restraint, but, given the limited nature of both their responsibilities and resources, would be forgiven if they acted in their short-run interests.

Even if central banks did not draw gold when their nationals brought home funds from overseas, the system would not be proof against a world run into gold by means of the London gold market — speculators buying first sterling, with dollars, francs, or marks, and then gold, and forcing central banks to provide gold to the sterling authorities to enable them to keep the gold premium down. For the Bank of England to sell gold while acquiring foreign currencies would quickly run its stock through.

This weakness of the system, however, exists under all the other proposals for stabilizing the gold exchange standard or adding to world liquidity. If private speculators have ready access to gold, they are in a position to bring about a substantial shrinkage of the world credit base whether the International Monetary Fund or national central banks provide the metal. In the long run, therefore, it would be desirable to restrict the use of gold to international payments, and to stop feeding supplies to private hoarders through organized facilities like those in London, Canada, or South Africa.

The issue is not an important one, nor pressing, however. Speculation in gold has been a losing game since February 1934, as compared with speculation in foreign exchange, even when the hoarders have not been so foolish as to pay a premium for it. Interest forgone and storage charges make indulgence in the atavistic impulse to hold gold expensive. To the extent that speculators are rational, it seems unlikely that they will continue long to speculate in this medium.

It would none the less tidy up the payments system, and add a bastion of defence against this possible irrationality, gradually to reduce facilities for private gold hoarding. It will probably be impossible to eliminate them: the determined speculator can buy gold in Bombay or other exchange markets off the beaten track, paying a premium and taking substantial risks. But there is no need to hand speculators a weapon with which they can discipline the monetary authorities, in these days when these authorities are fully aware of the importance of appropriate policies; and it is silly to run unnecessary risks.

This view holds that central banks and treasuries of a limited number of countries, working presumably in Basle or Paris (alongside the OECD), are a better method of rendering the gold exchange standard stable than the Triffin plan, M. Bernstein's proposals for reserve stand-by credits at the Fund,[6] a similar scheme of Governor Zolotas of the Bank of Greece,[7] enlarging the Fund quotas for the second time,[8] Alan Day's 'Goldbuckquid'.[9] We cannot give these alternatives the attention they deserve, but a quick summary, in reverse order, can be given.

(i)   The 'Goldbuckquid', linking only gold, dollars, and sterling, is too narrow. The scheme is roughly the same as that above, though perhaps more formal and less flexible. It has the advantage of being limited to only two countries, which might make it easier to operate, but the two countries no longer are the only ones that count.

(ii)   Merely enlarging the Fund again is insufficient, given the Triffin problem, and runs the risk of weakening balance of payments discipline of countries with no interest or concern for hot money by according them enlarged facilities. The International Monetary Fund is best suited to meeting the liquidity needs of individual countries — apart from hot money. Its limited utility for hot money has been fully demonstrated first by the fact that it was unused through every British crisis except for that in 1957; and secondly that no role was found for it in the troubles of the dollar in 1959 or 1960. A key currency cannot effectively turn to the Fund to meet attacks based on confidence. For the dollar to have done so would have been to weaken confidence in it. The pound could do so in the fall of 1957 only as one of a series of measures, including a Reconstruction Finance Corporation loan. The essential difficulty is that the rules of the Fund are designed to meet problems of balance of payments deficits arising from monetary, fiscal, or exchange rate maladjustment, rather than short-run crises of confidence. In fitting it for the first task, its amounts, rules, methods of operations are necessarily made inadequate to the second.

(iii)   The reverse stand-by credit schemes of Bernstein and Zolotas would amend the rules of the Fund by providing that countries requiring extraordinary assistance should obtain it from the Fund, and that the Fund should obtain the funds needed by arranging lines of credit in advance, from surplus countries. This is broadly similar to the central bank proposal, except that operations would go through the Fund, and would be subject to formal guarantees on exchange rates. It is flexible, unlimited in amounts, and would require very little legislation, all of which constitute distinct advances over the Triffin plan. It has the disadvantage of giving the Fund two separate tasks to perform — the financing of individual country deficits and the maintenance of confidence; it involves a number of countries without responsibility in the affairs of the key currencies; and it provides rather more rigid exchange guarantees than the system may be able to withstand in the long run. But it is a major improvement over the Triffin proposal.

(iv) The Triffin plan suffers the weaknesses of the reverse-standby-credit scheme and from the further flaw of muddling up the balance of payments deficits of separate countries with the hot-money problem. Under-developed countries would have no basis for seeing that the credit arrangements needed for hot money should not be extended to their overdrafts to finance persistent deficits. In fact Professor Triffin's book encourages them in this view, by recommending enlargement of the international credit base at a rate of 3 to 5 per cent a year by loans to under-developed countries.[10] The Triffin scheme has the further serious disadvantage as compared with other schemes, that there is no incentive system for correcting persistent balance of payments disequilibrium.

Many questions arise as to how such a system of central bank co-operation would work, and especially what would happen if persistent balance of payments disequilibrium gave rise to a crisis of confidence and a hot-money outflow. This, of course, is the problem that puts any system to the test. All one can say is that the central bank and treasury authorities of the countries concerned — the key currency under attack and the other key currencies — would have to decide what the long-run prospects for the currency were, and whether or not to render short-run support at existing exchange rates. No system can evade such a decision, however. Each merely establishes a locus where it is taken. In my judgement it is for a superior system to decide in principle that the other key currencies will render short-run support if they believe the long-term prospects are strong. If all agree, the burden is distributed among them in accordance with the amount of capital inflow to each. Strong pressure would be exerted to reach a consensus, but if one country did not concur it could withhold compliance, a strong source of pressure for correcting persistent deficits. And group pressure would be exercised against the persistent creditors.

Note how effectively the system has operated in the last two years when many observers claimed we were moving rapidly towards a crisis. Pressure on the United States to correct its deficit was substantial; but while this was being felt, the central banks of Europe held the dollars that private holders dumped on the market.

And pressure was exerted by the group on the German balance of payments surplus.

If large-scale short-term capital movements come about, not because of crises of confidence, but because of attempts to maintain international differences in interest rates when all countries have virtually perfect confidence in each others' rates, central bank support of forward exchange rates might be used to separate international money markets. If New York wants a 2 per cent rate, for example, when Frankfurt has 4, rather than have the Bundesbank hold all the dollars which private holders want to transfer to the market with the higher rate, the Federal Reserve Bank of New York might buy forward dollars at a premium equivalent to 2 per cent per annum. This would enable holders of short-term funds to earn 2 per cent in the New York money market, and 2 per cent through a forward sale, or the same amount as in Frankfurt while holding their spot funds in New York.

I am not enthusiastic about the proposal in the President's balance of payments message of February 6, 1961, to establish special high rates for central bank funds in New York. The policies of central banks of key currencies should not be dictated by considerations of return, in international questions any more than in domestic. For the central banks of smaller countries, the issue does not matter. They will either try to earn the highest possible return in one of a number of currencies of equal safety and utility to them, or they will keep their funds in the currency in which they are needed for normal transactions.

For private holders, however, there may be point in separating the rate of return to foreigners from that accorded to domestic holders, and the use of intervention in the forward market is accordingly worth studying.[11]

V. The Liquidity Problems of Individual Countries

An individual country without a persistent balance of payments deficit may have a liquidity problem in so far as its quick assets are insufficient to enable it to face the future with the confident assurance that it can meet any unlikely short-run variation in its requirement for foreign exchange. This is the problem which the International Monetary Fund and the Anglo-American Financial Agreement of 1946 (the British loan) were designed to solve. This liquidity problem cannot be met so long as a persistent deficit remains in a country's balance of payments — as the experience of both the fund and the British loan prior to the Marshall Plan amply proved. It is a real problem and, for a few countries, particularly Britain, a serious one. It is the sort of problem which used to be solved by stabilization loans — borrowed for adding to liquidity, not for spending. In retrospect, it appears that the United States made a mistake in undertaking the British loan first and the Marshall Plan second, or regarding the British loan as an amount needed for financing deficits.

Apart from Britain, and countries with persistent balance of payments deficits, this problem is in good shape. It may arise as a number of countries with persistent deficits manages to cure them and move towards convertibility and balance around a long-run level. Where IMF quotas are too small, if such cases exist, there may be room for new stabilization loans. This does not mean 'rescue operations' undertaken to provide exchange for current payments in sharp deficit.

The adequacy of reserves of individual countries has been thoroughly discussed in the literature, and I do not wish to summarize that discussion, or extend it. It is useful, however, to indicate opposition to the support of Triffin for a figure of 35 per cent of annual imports, which, however admirably qualified, none the less remains as the conclusion of his discussion. The adequate level for every country differs, depending upon its circumstances, and upon those of the countries with which it trades.

There is one possible device worth considering to rectify a possible shortfall of reserves of *pairs* of countries (or larger numbers) and that is a swap of foreign exchange. In present circumstances, for example, the Bank of England and the Federal Reserve System could strengthen their reserve positions by each establishing a deposit on its books in favour of the other: say $560 million at the Federal Reserve Bank of New York in favour of the Bank of England and £200 million at the Bank of England on behalf of the Federal Reserve System. The net reserve position of neither would be helped; and this would in no way help them *vis-à-vis* the moderate persistent surplus countries of the Continent — Belgium, France, Germany, Italy, and the Netherlands. But it would ease their position against one another. The same device could be used among all key currencies, assuming that all were in broad balance, to correct any alleged shortfall of world liquid resources. In the United States this action would ultimately require legislation to relax the ratio of gold to Federal Reserve liabilities, in preference to a change which would include foreign currencies along with gold. But by such a system, bilaterally or on a wide multilateral basis among key currencies with a fair degree of over-all balance, reserves can be created much more cheaply in terms of real resources than by mining gold.

VI. The World Liquidity Problem

While individual countries have a liquidity problem, I doubt that the world has one, apart from persistent balance of payments deficits and surpluses and hot money. I doubt further that any quantitative statement concerning such a problem can be made, either in terms of the need to expand reserves 3 to 5 per cent a year to take account of the needed expansion in trade; or as a short-fall from new gold production; or in terms of world gold stock (said by Harrod to fall $76 billion short of present needs). The quantity theory of money has no greater validity internationally than domestically, and in the latter connection I regard its validity as small. Moreover, to the extent that it is useful to add to world liquidity, whether for all countries or for key currencies, the methods of an increase in IMF quotas, or a swap of central bank funds can be adopted, without changing the gold price or establishing an international central bank.

I choose not to argue the case against raising the gold price: its arbitrariness, waste of real resources, the political difficulty of favouring South Africa and the Soviet Union, the spur to gold hoarding and speculation. It is hard to see what profound difference it makes in the world, apart from miners and speculators, whether one takes a given amount of gold and adds national moneys to it (appropriately stabilized among each other) or takes the same amount of gold and calls it the sum of the foregoing. The differences for miners and speculators argue strongly against revaluation.

Creation of formal world central banking institutions, or even an international currency as Jean Monnet suggests, is a worthy long-run objective. But effective progress is better made towards it empirically, than by constitution-writing, handling real problems as they emerge, and with the basis of such international consensus as is required and can be mustered, rather than by obtaining agreement in advance to all possible contingent problems. Ultimately if desirable, the rules of the game can be codified and even improved, when there is a sure consensus. To spend time now looking for such a consensus, examining attractive panaceas, seems to me to divert attention from real problems, run the risk of creating new problems where none now exist. A physicist acquaintance has observed that all games break down, as virtuosity in playing and interest in winning (called Gamesmanship by Stephen Potter) triumph over the initial purpose of enjoyment. Beanballs, offside bowling, the two-platoon system or the Queen's Gambit Declined come close to destroying their respective games. To the philosopher this can be generalized into the proposition that all order decays.

There is then little hope for fixing up the international payments mechanism in a way that will be eternally proof against the ravages of time and national gamesmanship, whether with rules of the game that emerge out of evolving practice, or with promulgated statutes of new or revised international organizations. I am disposed to believe, however, that more lasting progress and surer is achieved by solving problems one by one as they emerge, rather than undertaking the grand design of a new system of international payments.

NOTES

[1] There is, of course, the possibility that the monetary authorities will pay attention only to the gross reserve position, and not to the net; but there is no inevitable reason why they should. The question is one of interpretation of fact, and I see no reason to believe that monetary authorities are less sophisticated than, say, small businessmen who have learned to distinguish between, say, income and changes in cash. If, of course, there exists an asymmetry of response to decreases in assets and increases in liabilities, in the nature of human myopia and self-delusion, the case for 100 per cent reserves in domestic banking is irresistible, as many economists, the writer excluded, have convinced themselves.

[2] See Alexandre Lamfalussy, 'La Liquidité du système monétaire internationale', mimeographed paper prepared for the Colloquium of the Société Royale d'Économie Politique de Belgique, held in Brussels, April 22 and 23, 1961. While my paper was outlined and partly written in rough draft before this Colloquium, it has benefited greatly in revision from this paper and its discussion.

[3] The earliest major statement was *The Dollar Crisis* (Oxford, 1949); the most recent is in the *Economic Journal* for June 1960.

[4] Robert Triffin, *Gold and the Dollar Crisis*, New Haven, Yale University Press, 1960, p. 90.

[5] I find somewhat naïve the action (or the account of it in the press of April 28, 1961) of the United States Treasury in taking some of the German pre-payment of debts to the United States in Deutschemarks to hold against possible speculative attack. It does represent, however, a marked change in the United States attitude towards foreign currencies, and permits an increase in world liquidity.

[6] See his paper before the American Economic Association meeting at St. Louis, Dec. 1960.

[7] Letter to Per Jacobsson, Feb. 24, 1961, mimeographed.

[8] As proposed by Managing Director Jacobsson in April 1961.

[9] *The Observer,* Feb. 12, 1961.

[10] See pp. 97, 100, 101, 117.

[11] This proposal assumes, of course, that the number of domestic holders of dollars who will sell dollars forward to earn the premium is limited, or in any event no greater than the number who would be willing to open up accounts earning 4 per cent in Frankfurt — to use the same illustration. If it either is unlimited, or greater than the spot flow of domestic funds, the forward proposal gains nothing, except perhaps the change of an actual liability to a future one, and its nonappearance in the weekly central bank statement.

CHAPTER EIGHT

FLEXIBLE EXCHANGE RATES*

Introduction

This paper is intended to marshall the arguments for and against a flexible exchange rate for the dollar. It undertakes no new investigation of experience or exploration of theory, but reviews existing analytical literature.

It should be noted at the outset that while the subject has produced some polemics, many writers have conceded that the issue is a close one.[1] The disputatious character of the subject is further illustrated by the fact that most of the literature is put forward negatively in the form of rebuttals of arguments of a converse position.

The paper pays no attention to the semantic question whether a flexible rate is more "liberal" in some sense than a fixed-exchange rate, although it may be conceded to be more "liberal" than a fixed-rate system maintained by trade restrictions. As Robbins points out (19, pp. 96–97), the most liberal system would be a single world monetary unit with fixed rates, like that prevailing within a single country. The analysis is confined to functional questions.

The subject is treated under four headings, each of which may encompass a number of subsidiary aspects. These are:

* From *Monetary Management* by Frank M. Tamagna *et al.,* A Series of Research Studies Prepared for the Commission on Money and Credit, Englewood Cliffs, N.J., Prentice-Hall, Inc., 1963, pp. 403–425.

This paper was written in February 1960. It has been revised to a limited extent to take into account the comments of Emile Despres, R. Rhomberg, R. Sammons, and S. C. Tsiang, for which thanks are given. The references include only three subsequent contributions to the literature, Einzig's *A Dynamic Theory of Forward Exchange,* Sohmen's *Flexible Exchange Rates: Theory and Controversy,* and Triffin's *Gold and the Dollar Crisis,* but it has not been possible to deal in detail with the argument of these works, insofar as they extend the authors' earlier positions.

1. The character and role of speculation under flexible exchange rates.
2. The impact on trade (and investment).
3. The impact on domestic stabilization.
4. Special considerations affecting a reserve currency.

As readily imagined, these subjects are interrelated in a number of ways so that any separation is artificial.

I. The Character and Role of Speculation under Flexible Exchange Rates

Before it is possible to discuss the impact of flexible exchange rates on trade and investment, we must know whether rates will fluctuate within narrow limits or widely. If expectations are inelastic, and speculators anticipate that a changed rate will return to its old level, they will buy when the rate falls, and sell when it rises. Under these circumstances speculation is stabilizing and the rate will not vary widely. On the other hand, with elastic expectations, depreciation will be interpreted as a signal that the rate will go lower. Speculators then sell, and the rate will go below the level needed to bring the balance of payments into equilibrium. In these circumstances, speculation is destabilizing, and the rate will fluctuate in wider limits than those needed to balance the accounts over time.

The nature of speculation is of vital importance to the practicality of a system of flexible exchange rates. With speculation stabilizing, the automatic pilot will steer a steady course; if it is destabilizing, the rate will "track" as the expression goes, that is, swing in exaggerated fashion around the long-run path to the detriment of trade and investment.

How does speculation behave under flexible exchange rates? Nurkse (16, pp. 117–122) claimed that it tended to be destabilizing, and was severely criticized for his historical evidence (8, p. 176 note). Friedman says that the speculators were "right" in attacking overvalued exchanges, and that there is as much reason to call their action "stabilizing" as "destabilizing." But this view identified the character of speculation only with the direction of the movement, and not with its extent.

In the case of the French franc in the 1920's, which is the subject of much of Nurkse's discussion and that of subsequent writers

113

(*e.g.*, 26), the rate was 5 cents in May 1925, which was not far above the long-run equilibrium level which later proved to have been about 4.5 cents. It is difficult to be precise about the equilibrium rate, and contemporary purchasing-power-parity calculations by Dulles, Rueff, Quesnay, etc. (5, p. 527; 13, p. vii)[2] supported a lower level. But 4 cents (3.912) at which the franc was stabilized *de facto* in December 1926 and *de jure* in June 1928 was clearly an undervaluation and not only because of the large-scale repatriation of capital. At that rate exports were buoyant and imports stagnant. On balance-of-payments evidence, the equilibrium rate was nearer 4.5 or even 5 cents.

Let us suppose the rate was overvalued in May 1925 at 5 cents. Speculation which sold it was stabilizing so long as the rate was above 4.5 or even 4 cents, but it was clearly destabilizing thereafter, and violently so in producing the rate of 2.0 cents (49.220 to the dollar) on July 20, 1926. Moreover, if the Bank of France had not intervened after August 7, 1926, the rate would have gone much higher as repatriated capital flowed back after the establishment of confidence by the Poincaré cabinet. It is interesting in reading accounts of the period to observe the restlessness of business as the rate appreciated (14, pp. 175, 177–178, 184; 2, p. 370).

Friedman has a powerful theoretical argument that speculation must be stabilizing. Speculators are rational and well-informed people. They will continue in the business only so long as they find it profitable. They can make money by buying cheap and selling dear. To buy cheap and sell dear is to stabilize. Therefore, speculators stabilize.

One can take exception to various steps in this analysis. Eastman and Stykolt (6) tried to test whether the Canadian stabilization fund has stabilized the Canadian exchange rate by seeing whether it had made profits. But of course if the fund had successfully pegged the rate at a fixed price, it would have stabilized to a maximum and, buying and selling at the same price, made no profits at all. There must be some variation about the trend before buying and selling become profitable.

Baumol (1) has pointed out, moreover, that speculators may be divided into two groups, which we can call insiders and outsiders. The insiders can make most money by exaggerating the swings of the rate, driving it well up, and then, when the outsiders begin to buy, selling out and driving it well down. Speculators as a whole will lose money, buying high and selling low. But the inside speculators will make much more money than through stabilizing speculation, largely at the expense of the outside speculators who are neither intelligent nor well informed. On this showing speculation can be on balance destabilizing.

It is sometimes argued that there is more speculation with a pegged adjustable currency than under flexible exchange rates because speculators can't lose when there is pressure on the exchange rate. If the balance of payments is in disequilibrium, the speculator can freely go short of the exchange rate. He has in effect a "one-way option" since the rate can fall but has little chance of rising except perhaps within this narrow range set by the gold points (see Scammell, 20, pp. 99, 184).

MacDougall takes exception to this view (12, pp. 340, 385). In his judgment, crises occur in lumps, rather than in a steady trend, and when such a crisis occurs or an adverse trend is revealed by the sudden removal of temporary favorable factors, the rate is under pressure in one direction only. This gives speculators a one-way option under either system, fixed movable peg or flexible rates, and encourages destabilizing speculation. In a world of instantaneous communication where speculators share the same sources of news, opinion as to the revision of the rate is likely to alter precipitously and to produce sharp unidirectional movements much akin to the movable peg. If the authorities can see the trend more clearly than the market, MacDougall argues, they can adjust the movable peg in advance of the market and prevent the buildup of one-way options. But it should be observed that some of his case, that one-way options will equally occur under flexible exchange rates, rests on the view that the authorities are intervening to prevent short-run changes in the rate, thus delaying recognition of the necessity to change the rate. If they are myopic under this system, there is no reason that they should be less so under a movable peg.

This discussion raises the question of the information of the authorities and their rationality as compared to the market. Friedman concedes that there may be times when the authorities have knowledge which is not available to the market, but on the whole he sees "no reason to expect that government officials will be better judges than private speculators of the likely movements in under-

115

lying conditions of trade." (18, p. 188). On this account he is opposed to intervention to smooth out temporary fluctuations, which he recognizes as performing a socially useful function. An extensive market with stabilizing speculation, he would hold, will do as well or better in the usual case. Most other writers advocating flexible rates expect government intervention to prevent or moderate seasonal, small random structural, and even cyclical fluctuations.

There is much to Friedman's argument here, if it be conceded that speculation is stabilizing. If, on the other hand, there is destabilizing speculation from time to time, government intervention may be necessary to smooth out fluctuations and to prevent exaggerated swings in the rate from having an effect on the economy. In this case, if the authorities have no clear view of the long-term trend, they may inadvertently provide the same kind of one-way option to speculators which is alleged to exist under the movable peg. Friedman's position comes close to the view that there can be no exchange crises under flexible exchange rates with government intervention eliminated, because of the far-sightedness of speculators. If it be conceded that speculators have close to perfect foresight, while government officials have a vested interest in misinterpreting the underlying strengths and weaknesses, the case for flexible exchange rates without government intervention becomes a powerful one. But Friedman's assumptions remain assumptions, not demonstrable facts.

Some writers discuss the significance of forward markets under the heading of speculation, addressing the question whether the addition of facilities for trading in forward exchange converts destabilizing into stabilizing speculation. This matter is dealt with below under the impact of a flexible exchange rate on trade and investment.

But the question of whether speculation is stabilizing or destabilizing or whether flexible exchange rates will track or steer a steady course cannot be settled by recourse to theoretical arguments. At basis it is empirical. And the answer must be that both are possible. With a flexible exchange rate one can have short-term stabilizing speculation, as in the Canadian case, where movements of the rate have been held since early 1952 within a limit for the average monthly quotation of 5½ per cent[3] or one can experience the tracking swings of European currencies during the 1920's.

The Federal Reserve Bank of New York, in a monograph by Holmes, states that "Experience in the exchange market, particularly in the twenties and thirties, has shown, however, that purely speculative influences have tended to be destabilizing more often than not." (7, p. 42.) This is written in the narrower context of the forward exchange market. In addition a distinction is made between "pure speculation" which is said not to have been important for some time, and the speculative pressures arising from the normal participants in the market who sometimes cover and sometimes do not. In this experience, then, the market is either destabilizing or thin.

What determines the nature of the speculation is largely the character of monetary and fiscal policy, not the exchange system. S. C. Tsiang's discussion of the French experience (26) concludes that the difficulty lay not with the fluctuating exchange rate but with excess domestic liquidity which could not be curbed. In Canada, with stable domestic fiscal and monetary policies, short-term capital movements have responded in stabilizing fashion to changes in the rate on New York.[4]

II. The Impact of Flexible Exchange Rates on Trade and Investment

One objection to flexible exchange rates is that trade responds very slowly in the short run to changes in the exchange rate. There is a considerable literature on the elasticities of demand in international trade, much less on supply; but there is really no need to review this literature since most proponents of flexible exchange rates would be willing to stipulate the facts on this point. (See Scammell, 20, p. 88.) Measurements by Rhomberg (18) suggest that the adjustment mechanism in the Canadian mechanism was speculative short-term capital movements, rather than trade which responded only marginally to changes in the rate. But if speculation is stabilizing, and the rate adjusts to the equilibrium level smoothly with the help of short-term capital flows, the time necessary to complete the trade adjustments will be forthcoming.

A more significant question is whether a flexible exchange rate discourages entry into foreign trade, and reduces welfare by reducing international specialization and exchange. Friedman asserts that it does not for a variety of reasons (8, p. 174 ff.): uncertainty

117

can be reduced by the establishment of forward markets; and the certainty provided by fixed exchange rates is illusory, since the maintenance of fixed rates may require sudden changes in the availability of credit or even of the right to import or export. Flexible rates as a deterrent to trade are also dismissed by Scammell who adds the further argument that traders may just as easily gain as lose by flexible exchange rates. This last line of reasoning is unacceptable since what counts is not the mean of the probability distribution as to profits, but the existence or absence of a central tendency about the mean, *i.e.*, the increase of uncertainty with its attendant cost.

Let us first settle the question about the forward market. The addition of a forward market may make it somewhat easier and slightly cheaper for people without established international connections to hedge.[5] But there are those who argue, among them the writer, that the addition of a forward market in no way basically alters the operation of the foreign exchange market. Without these facilities, it is possible to go long by borrowing in one market and lending in the other, and short by reversing the process. This view is not shared by others, notably Tsiang (27), Sohmen (22), and more recently and forcefully, Einzig (6a, especially Chapter IX), who argue that the elasticity of the demand and supply in a newly established forward exchange market is in addition to that previously existing in the spot market, rather than merely transferred from one market to another. New traders are drawn in by the existence of a forward market, whether speculators or incremental exporters and importers attracted by the premium or discount on foreign exchange in the forward market.

The importance of the issue is that the broader the market, and the higher the elasticities of demand and supply, the more stabilizing will be the action of the combined markets. With no increase in speculation, and without trading responses to shifts in the forward rate (such as is implied on balance by the view that elasticity in a new forward market is achieved only at the expense of previously existing elasticity in the spot market), changes in interest rates, for example, will not elicit any greater response with forward rates added than before.

Unhappily there is no way to choose between these positions on theoretical grounds, and no means of devising an effective empirical test. It is a more rational position that the forward market produces no change from the situation in which a speculator or trader can borrow in one market and lend in the other at the gain or cost of the interest differential. But it is easy to adduce an excess of rationality in these matters. Spraos, for example, does so when he asserts that it is irrational to speculate in anything but the cheapest and most convenient way, and that therefore, given the presence of a forward rate there can be no leads and lags in international payments if the authorities peg the forward rate (23). But traders approach the exchange market with exchange or needing exchange, and face decisions whether to speculate by taking no action, or to hedge by acting. It may be irrational from some wider viewpoint to speculate by failing to take action to cover a position in the spot market when one could close out the spot position and open one in the forward market, but from the limited horizon of the trader it is completely understandable, and in this sense rational.

It must be understood that all writers who believe that the addition of a forward market broadens and stabilizes the market for exchange imply that there is interest arbitrage. In the absence of interest arbitrage, or of substantial other capital movement financed, say, by the leads and lags, no net position can be opened up in the forward market, since any buyer or seller of forward exchange must find another party interested in selling or buying. Experience in the 1930's suggests that when interest arbitrage has been cut off, forward markets become extremely thin, and discounts go to rates at which the currency is likely to settle if there is a devaluation, *i.e.*, the forward rate must then represent a level where there is just as much reason to think it is too low as too high. Such forward markets provide little basis for hedging because the cost is too high. The result is that forward markets function effectively only with interest arbitrage, which is the same as saying that they are just a more efficient way of hedging or speculating at the cost of or while earning the interest-rate differential. But it must be admitted that forward markets may attract buyers and sellers who would not otherwise have entered the market.

It is true that interest arbitrage does not function effectively in all markets. In sterling, forward discounts or premia may differ from the interest parity by half of 1 per cent either way without attracting funds into interest arbitrage (7, p. 46). The Federal

Reserve Bank of New York points out that there are numerous obstacles to the movement of funds: the funds available for movement are not unlimited, many money markets lack suitable instruments for short-term investment, or some potential investors face legal or institutional obstacles to international investment. Overhanging the market for many of the lesser international currencies has been the legacy of exchange control and fear of possible future blockage.

On this account, there tends to be more trader arbitrage than speculative arbitrage and this limits the availability of hedging in amount of occasionally in direction. When sterling sold at an abnormal discount, it was profitable for importers of sterling-area products to switch their financing from the United States to London and cover forward at a discount. But this meant that United States exporters extending credit to sterling customers were less and less able to hedge. Accordingly, they tended to shift to a cash basis, with resultant pressure on sterling from the leads and lags.

It might be claimed that a system of flexible exchange rates coupled with freedom of exchange transactions will elicit enough interest arbitrage funds to hold forward rates to the interest differential. But this requires action abroad, as well as in the United States, and a change in attitudes toward the market. There is no assurance that these changes will be forthcoming in the variety and degree requisite to make hedging cheap and widely available. This sort of institution, in my judgment, must evolve slowly from years of experience rather than be created at the stroke of a pen.

Moreover, there is one aspect of trading uncertainty which a perfectly functioning forward exchange market cannot correct. Suppose an importer enters into a contract to buy goods abroad, and covers his exchange risk with a forward contract. He is by no means entirely free of the risks of exchange-rate fluctuation. Such freedom must imply that the exchange rate will not alter before the fruition of his contract and permit a competitor to buy similar goods at a lower price. Fluctuating exchange rates increase the risk of holding inventories of internationally traded goods, whether or not the risk in any particular transaction is covered, and hence tend to reduce the volume of trade.

But assume that a trader can protect himself by hedging for three or six months, *i.e.*, for any given transaction. Is this adequate?

Assuming that rates vary more widely than in the Canadian case, it can be argued that the needed certainty of the exchange rate goes beyond any particular transaction and concerns whether it is worth a trader's while to enter into foreign trade, *i.e.*, to plan to carry out a succession of deals involving selling or buying abroad. Admittedly the world is full of uncertainty — costs may go up in the country where he plans to buy, or credit may be shut off at home, and more certainty on one score, such as the exchange rate, may increase uncertainty in others. But what counts is the effect of a flexible exchange rate on the calculations of the individual trader who will not, because of his limited horizon, take into account every uncertainty or calculate a probability distribution for every possible event. For most traders, operating within a circumscribed boundary of knowledge, flexible rates increase the level of uncertainty over fixed rates, as recorded by them. This may reflect want of rationality, but represents a realistic view. Certainty for three or six months is not enough. Business decisions are not made to sell now in the foreign-trade sector, now at home, with each separate deal calculated afresh. There must be, as MacDougall says, certainty over one or two year's time (12, p. 384) or stabilizing speculation which keeps the rate within a narrow range.

It can be argued in opposition to the foregoing that the certainty for one or two years given by the fixed-rate system is spurious, and illogical. An intelligent foreign trader will know that uncertainty is inevitable whatever the system of exchange in force. Perhaps. But there may be something here which we can call "exchange illusion." Under flexible rates, fluctuation is built into the system and almost guaranteed. Under fixed rates, the authorities have indicated an intention to maintain a given rate, whether or not in the long run they succeed. There would seem to be both a higher chance of stability with fixed rates, and a more widely shared belief in the prospect for stability.

Let us assume that rate adjusts over time to bring trade balances into line without reducing the volume of trade below the levels maintained under a fixed rate. Observe that the adjustment is brought about by shifting resources into and out of the foreign-trade sector — exports and import-competing industry — when the rate depreciates and appreciates respectively. Is this method of adjustment desirable?

Clearly it is desirable when significantly large structural changes occur. If a foreign innovation destroys the market for an important export, balance-of-payment adjustment requires resources to be redirected into new export or import-competing lines.

But not every balance-of-payments disequilibrium should be corrected by stimulating the shift of resources. Such movements are costly, requiring new investment in expanding lines, which may later be stranded, and moving resources occupationally and possibly in space. It is hardly appropriate to move resources at significant cost for seasonal fluctuations of the exchange rate, if these should happen not to be moderated by stabilizing speculation. A more difficult question arises for cyclical movements of the balance of payments around a long-run equilibrium.

The International Monetary Fund, formed in part to forestall competitive exchange depreciation, was established on the theory that for some types of disturbances, it is desirable to finance an imbalance of payments with a change in international reserves rather than attempt to eliminate it. There is no need to discuss whether depreciation goes too far and becomes competitive, and countries attempt to use the international margin to stimulate increases in income. If it be assumed merely that in the absence of action, a cyclical pattern of payments will develop, averaging out over the cycle to zero, the question is whether a country should draw down and build back reserves over the cycle, and the converse, or should it shift resources into and then out of (or out of and then into) the foreign-trade sector? The same question could arise for seasonal fluctuations — though less sharply because of stabilizing speculation, and for the random occurrence of small structural changes.

The Friedman answer to this question is readily imagined. If the cyclical, seasonal, or randomly distributed pattern of small structural changes is clear, speculators will be aware of it, as well as the authorities. They will stabilize the rate and prevent the necessity for the shift of resources. But if the future cannot thus clearly be foreseen, there is no basis for believing that resources will be drawn back into their old occupations, so they had better move anyway.

But this attaches too much importance to the rationality, foresight, and tenacity of speculators. The stock market goes up and down cyclically, rather than remains steady, because speculators play short swings. Their knowledge and rationality inform them that the broad mass of the participants in the market are myopic, and that there is more to be gained from exploiting this myopia than from looking very far ahead. When the cyclical pattern is clear, government's horizon will stretch beyond that of the speculators. In this case there is good reason not to move resources but to draw down or add to reserves.

III. The Impact on Domestic Stabilization

The argument for flexible exchange rates made by Meade (13) is that it is possible to separate domestic from international policy. Monetary and fiscal policy can be made to fit domestic requirements. The flexible exchange rate system takes care of the balance of payments.

Nurkse has taken exception to this sharp dichotomy in Meade's system (17, p. 143). In his *Geometry*, Meade gets a balance-of-payments adjustment from the flexible exchange rate partly by hypothesizing the appropriate change in domestic money spending. Depreciation improves the balance of payments when accompanied by the appropriate reduction in money spending (or what Alexander calls "absorption"). But which plays the leading and which the supporting role is a matter of choice. The balance of payments may just as well be said to have altered because of a deflation of money expenditure with an appropriate change of the exchange rate.

Most students discussing the impact of depreciation on the exchange rate do not go as far as Meade in stipulating the appropriate change in income. Rather they assume income constant. In this condition, however, the improvement in the balance of payments — the increase in exports and the decline in imports — has a multiple impact on national income. Monetary and fiscal policy can be invoked to return national income to its original level, but this is altogether different from saying that monetary and fiscal policy can proceed to cope with domestic needs independently of the balance of payments.

Laursen and Metzler (11) have held that even with a system of flexible exchange which kept the balance of payments in continuous equilibrium there would be domestic effects of international changes

123

because of changes in the terms of trade and real income. These effects, it will be remembered, were thought to be perverse, *i.e.*, depression abroad would be inflationary because the worsening of the terms of trade would lower real income and therefore increase the consumption ratio. The Laursen-Metzler effect is unacceptable for several reasons. It confuses real and money income, and deals with an effect which would, if correctly put, be so small as to be negligible. But their model may require large frictionless reallocations of resources and it is these which throw the most doubt on the possibility of separating the domestic from the international equilibrating process. Suppose, for example, that the terms of trade worsen because of depression abroad. This will bring about an automatic depreciation of the exchange rate which, with favorable elasticities of demand, will maintain the balance of payments. But the mechanism may require substantial shifts of resources. If the elasticity of demand for imports is high, for example, *i.e.*, if the substitution effect between imports and home production is large, the worsening of the terms of trade due to a decline in demand for exports will lead to a balancing of trade at a lower level of exports and imports. Resources must be shifted from exports to import-competing production. How are these shifts of resources to be brought about with a constant money income? If expansion is required in the import-competing industry, can it be financed out of depreciation allowances and normal investment? Large resource reallocations are likely to be inflationary on balance because of an asymmetrical impact of expansion in one industry and contraction in another. Not all economists would subscribe to this asymmetry, and particularly not Professor Friedman who believed in 1942 that the war-induced reallocations of resources could have been carried out in a noninflationary fashion. But the weight of opinion would hold that resource shifts require net expansion.

Professor Friedman wants an automatic device in flexible exchange rates to balance his automatic mechanism of a fixed money supply in domestic policy. This view, it should be noted, is at variance with that of Meade, who wants to use monetary and fiscal measures internally. Robbins objects strongly to locking the domestic monetary mechanism and throwing the key away. He states that there can be no such thing as an automatic money mechanism from which policy is excluded: Even a constant money supply can only be fixed as a result of policy (19, pp. 96 ff.). But the money supply is not inelastic. (If it were, perhaps a case might be made for flexible exchange rates.) Advocacy of flexible exchange rates under present conditions must reckon with the fact that money supplies are elastic. When export and import prices rise because of depreciation, exporters and importers attempt to borrow more. This can be prevented by raising interest rates. But this means that monetary and fiscal policy must be used. In his *Balance of Payments,* Meade attempts to show that the gold standard and flexible exchange rates amount to much the same thing, by introducing monetary policy at the appropriate state (13, p. 192). This is in contradiction to his later separation, assigning monetary and fiscal policy to domestic problems, flexible exchange rates to international.

An important aspect of the discussion concerns the question whether flexible exchange rates accelerate cost-price inflation. The mechanism, set out by Scammell (20, pp. 91–92) runs from depreciation through higher import prices to wage increases. Scammell regards this as a "very powerful argument." Friedman, on the other hand, is not impressed. In his view, inflation is always monetary (8, p. 181). The notion of a wage-price spiral is a fallacy. Wages cannot be raised unless the money supply is expanded to finance the higher level of costs.

The Friedman position is extreme. There is little doubt that for economies poised on the verge of inflation, depreciation provides an inflationary push. If the monetary and fiscal mechanisms are weak, inflation may keep pace with the depreciation as in the experience of the French franc in 1936, 1938, 1946, and the summer, but not December, of 1958.

If depreciation takes place because of a recession abroad, the appreciation of the foreign currency implicit in the depreciation of the local one may accentuate foreign depression. The depreciation of sterling in 1931–1932 intensified deflationary pressures in the United States, particularly through its effect on the prices of farm export products.

The argument connecting depreciation and inflation applies equally to a system with a movable peg and to flexible exchange rates. But a distinction between them is sometimes made in this regard. MacDougall states that flexible exchange rates make it more difficult to resist wage claims (12, p. 341). A fixed rate sets limits to how high costs can be raised without setting off an adverse balance-of-payments reaction. Under flexible exchange rates these limits are removed. If a persistent redistribution of factor shares in favor of wages presents an inflationary problem in an economy, a fixed exchange rate may present one means of forcing a show-down.

This connection between exchange rates and monetary and fiscal policy can be generalized to raise the question of which exchange system puts more pressure on the authorities to adopt policies conducive to stabilization. Under a fixed rate, monetary and fiscal policy must bear the brunt of balance-of-payments adjustment. But a flexible system also lays heavy demands on the authorities if it is to function properly. Leaving aside the question whether they attempt to smooth out short-run fluctuations around the equilibrium rate, in the event that the authorities are under various domestic pressures to relax credit or unbalance the budget, the issue is, which system enables them best, or encourages them most, to resist these pressures.

A related question puts the matter in terms of which system more alarms the public — and presumably encourages it to support the authorities in appropriate stabilization policies. Robbins states that the real issue is whether the public will be more alarmed by a falling rate or dwindling reserves (19, p. 100). Haberler has argued that flexible exchange rates are more inconvenient to inflating governments than fixed rates plus exchange control (10, p. 26), and this may be granted. But exchange control may be invoked by government to halt either the loss of reserves or a falling rate. If exchange control be ruled out, the question remains which system makes more urgent and realistic demands on the authorities properly to discharge their functions in the face of pressures to do otherwise.

It is evidently difficult to generalize about these questions. Much will depend on the recent experience of the market and of the authorities. In Europe in the 1930's, exchange rates were more sensitive than reserves, so sensitive indeed that Germany then, and today many more countries in circumstances similar to the 1930's, would adopt exchange control rather than depreciate. But the reverse can also obtain. On the whole, it seems likely that so long as foreign exchange control is available under either system, the operational question is not whether flexible or fixed exchange rates put more pressure on the authorities, but whether, in any given case, the authorities fear the reaction from either losses of reserves or a falling rate more than from the reimposition of exchange control.

The significant conclusion in this area is that monetary and fiscal policy are more important to stability than the question of the exchange system. If monetary and fiscal policy are competent, a flexible exchange system will work well. Speculation will be stabilizing; rate changes will be limited. Day-to-day, seasonal, cyclical, and small random structural disturbances in the balance of payments will be offset by stabilizing speculation or changes in official reserves. More significant and far-reaching structural changes will produce change in the level of rates. The only difference in this system from that with fixed exchange rates lies in the reaction to these major structural changes. With a fixed rate, large structural changes, if they are recognized by the authorities, may be met by an adjustment of the peg or by monetary and fiscal policy, which may be unsatisfactory in terms of domestic requirements; or by permanent changes in the level of reserves, if these are abundant. Movement of the exchange rate and the reallocation of resources between the domestic and foreign-trade sectors are preferable to domestic deflation or the exhaustion of reserves. The disability of fixed exchange rates is that the rate may not be adjusted when it should be. Against this, however, the disability of the flexible exchange rate is that it may be adjusted when it should not be.

But if monetary and fiscal policy are not strongly and competently managed, flexible exchange rates may compound the difficulties. To assume the appropriate monetary and fiscal policy begs the issue in many cases, particularly when there is a delicate balance between inflationary pressures and the forces trying to contain them. In these conditions, flexible exchange rates may give the marginal push which enables the inflationary pressures to overwhelm the restraints.

For the United States it is true that we can by and large assume monetary and fiscal policies determined independently and without undue pressure from the balance of payments. But for the United States to adopt flexible exchanges raises another question, not perhaps so widely treated in the literature, whether all rates can float at once, or whether there must not be one currency which is the holder of the system's ultimate reserves and the benchmark of stability.

IV. *Maintaining the Value of Reserves Under a System of Flexible Exchange Rates*

It is possible to imagine a system in which every country in the world had a flexible exchange rate and which operated with no reserves at all of gold and foreign exchange; or one where every country in the world save one permitted its rate to float, and all maintained reserves of gold or exchange on the currency with a fixed rate in terms of gold. But it is difficult to see exactly what is implied by a system of universally floating rates with each country possessing reserves in exchange. In particular, this last arrangement raises the question how much central bank cooperation would be necessary to operate it, and whether there would not be strong incentives for the monetary authorities in various countries to protect their balance sheets by shifting reserves out of depreciating and into appreciating currencies, thus injecting destabilizing speculation into the system from an official source.

Robbins makes somewhat the same point in a different context when he states that it is unrealistic to think of flexible exchange rates all around (19, p. 101). Presumably reserves of stable value are maintained within the blocs. Friedman, however, suggests that the sterling area and the European Payments Union posed no insuperable problem for his system of flexible exchange rates. It is not clear (when he wrote in 1953) whether he contemplated that the dollar might also float. He stipulates that countries with gold stocks and a flexible rate would establish an open market for gold, much as Britain did between the 1931 devaluation of sterling and the exchange control of August 1939. He does not state whether the value of gold in central banks would be altered frequently on the basis of cost or market, whichever is lower.

If the United States maintains the price of gold at \$35 an ounce and other countries maintain reserves in dollars, the dollar can appreciate or depreciate as other countries on the average depreciate or appreciate respectively. Other countries' reserves will vary in value in local currency, but not in gold or dollars. The larger the amount of reserves, the larger perhaps the resistance to appreciation because of the "book loss" in local currency. The United States would have no control over the value of its currency in foreign exchange, but it would make it possible for other countries to alter the value of their currencies.

If the United States should adopt a flexible exchange rate too, however, the system is underdetermined. Assume that the authorities intervene in the market in the short run, which is why it is convenient or necessary for them to maintain reserves. An attempt to depreciate the dollar by buying sterling at rising prices could be offset by the British by continuous offerings of sterling against dollars at the old price. To bid up the price of gold in dollars might result in a parallel rise of the gold price in sterling. The exchange value of every currency would depend only partly on national action, but in significant part on international cooperation. There would have to be agreement on what exchange rates ought to be, or a freely flexible rate without intervention. If any but occasional intervention occurred, it would be necessary to evolve an international management of exchange rates.

In addition to the problem posed by short-term rate-making, central banks will be concerned with the value of their reserves. If they forecast a decline in the dollar, they will want to protect the value of their reserves by converting them into gold or into a stronger currency than the dollar. As we have noted, this would constitute destabilizing speculation and would further weaken the currency under pressure.

This is the same problem in a somewhat different setting that Triffin has addressed in his articles on the dollar-exchange standard (24, 25). This is not the place to present an extended analysis of his solution to what he sees to be the inevitable degeneration of the exchange standard based on a national currency: as countries accumulate reserves in a strong currency they ineluctably weaken it by piling up its foreign liabilities until they reach what are suddenly deemed to be alarming heights. But it may be pointed out that Triffin's interesting scheme for internationalizing exchange reserves would not relieve the United States, or other countries whose currencies serve as stores of value for still other countries, from having to pay attention to these liabilities. The heart of the Triffin scheme is to transfer the liabilities from national to international hands, *i.e.*, to the International Monetary Fund. But this substitutes a liability to the Fund for one to various countries, and the former must be covered by an exchange guarantee. Professor Haberler has suggested that the United States offer guarantees to foreign central banks of the gold value of their dollar holdings, and this would do directly what the Triffin scheme accomplishes indirectly (9, p. 9). A third means of lending support to the exchange standard could be developed from Despres' elliptical suggestion (4, p. 1037) for a new "tripartite monetary pact" in which the major central banks undertake to accumulate one another's currency without limit, and possibly with some exchange or gold guarantees, so that a run on the dollar into sterling, say, would merely transfer dollar deposits from the rest of the world to the account of the Bank of England.

This is, as noted, not the place to analyze these various suggestions for buttressing the exchange standard. They are mentioned only to indicate the necessity of international monetary cooperation, of one kind or another, under a reserve standard. So long as countries use reserves as part of the international monetary mechanism, some such cooperation is almost certainly called for, with or without floating exchange rates. If all countries in the world except the dollar have flexible exchange rates, the necessary cooperation is furnished by the United States giving up control over the value of the dollar. But if the United States wants control over its rate, too, there must be cooperation to prevent two countries trying to push a mutual rate in different directions.

The present position illustrates the case very well. The United States has a structural disequilibrium in its balance of payments for which a small measure of exchange depreciation would be helpful in shifting resources into incremental exports and import-competing lines. The same result could be accomplished by a coordinated appreciation of sterling, the mark, the franc, etc. in belated recognition that the 1949 devaluation was excessive. But devaluation of the dollar is not possible in the absence of exchange guarantees to holders of dollar reserves; if the possibilities of such a move could be contemplated in the absence of guarantees, many holders of dollars would convert them into gold or a stronger currency and precipitate a run. Since it is not clear that Britain is prepared to operate an international standard on a world basis — or for that matter any other country such as Germany — even if world acceptance would be forthcoming, the United States is in no position to change its rate. Its responsibilities for maintenance of the world monetary mechanism inhibit it in this respect, just as its responsibilities for the military defense of the free world require it to maintain troops abroad, continue research in missiles, and provide aid to under-developed countries, all at considerable expense and harm to its balance of payments.

It may be worth noting that the British justification for main-taining London as the center of operation of the gold standard before 1914 was an economic one, just as the attack on the sterling area by Day (3) and Shonfield (21) has been based on the conten-tion that it cost too much. The role of New York as the holder of the world's exchange reserves, like that of London of an earlier day, has evolved in practice, rather than been devised. But it has never been rationalized on economic grounds. If there be a rationaliza-tion, it is that the world needs an international monetary mechan-ism, and since the one in use happens to rely on dollar balances, it is up to the United States to make it work as part of the discharge of its world responsibilities.

This same rationale argues strongly against any attempt by the United States unilaterally to depreciate its currency, or unilaterally to adopt a new basis for the dollar such as a flexible exchange rate. There were strong arguments in 1960 for a redistribution of inter-national responsibility for the world monetary mechanism, as for the responsibilities in the defense of the free world and in economic aid to underdeveloped areas. Whether this involves a further trans-formation of the International Monetary Fund — which has served in the past only as a supplement to the dollar exchange standard, not as a substitute for it — or direct central bank cooperation, is not the concern of this paper. But it is hard to see how any change could move in the direction where the United States currency and every other one was free to float without any central bank interven-tion. It seems to me most unlikely that the world could be persuaded to adopt a system where no country used reserves. In this circum-stance, the task is perhaps more effectively to share responsibility for the maintenance of the world exchange standard. Whether this involves broadening the IMF, guarantees on reserve holdings, central-bank agreement to hold one another's currency as re-serves, it probably has to have some agreement about exchange rate

131

management. It is too one-sided for the United States to have no freedom to adjust, and other countries complete liberty of action within the rather loose and widely ignored roles of the Fund. But there seems to be little to be gained, and something to be lost, by having the system one of flexible rates.

V. Widening the Gold Points

If the United States does not adopt a system of flexible exchange rates, is there anything to be said for widening the gold points? In particular, is there a case to be made for widening the area of exchange fluctuation about the mint parity for the sake of giving a further reward to stabilizing speculation and imposing a more substantial penalty on bear speculators when they are proven wrong?

There may be merit in a small step in this direction, perhaps to increase the handling charge from ¼ per cent to ½ or even 1 per cent. The latter figure would give a range of about $2.80 for sterling from $2.828 to $2.772 with no allowance for any of the normal costs which make the gold points diverge from the mint parity, *i.e.,* freight, insurance, and interest, and assuming no spread in the other country. For foreign central banks, however, these costs may not be relevant if they hold gold under earmark in New York, since purchases and sales of gold into and out of earmark incur virtually no other expenses than the Treasury's handling charge.

But the writer is unenthusiastic. A wide spread between the gold points would be a major step toward a flexible exchange rate, and the arguments pro and con have been added up above and found to emerge on the whole with a negative verdict. Secondly, there might be untoward dynamic consequences of such a step even on a limited basis. One might be decision by a number of central banks with large dollar deposits to convert them into gold prior to the entry into effect of the new charges. And if one tried to adopt the system without warning or prior discussion, one might be open to the charge of unilaterally modifying the system of international exchange and disrupting central bank cooperation. Perhaps if the major central banks had been consulted and voiced no objection, it might be appropriate to make the change.

But third, there does not seem to me to be any great benefit to be gained. If the rate is held fixed within limits, stabilizing speculation performs only a limited service in substituting for changes in official reserves, and there is little need to encourage more at the expense of added uncertainty for trade and investment. And destabilizing speculation is not likely to be discouraged significantly by widening the penalty from guessing wrong. Most destabilizing speculation at present is in the leads and lags — *i.e.*, in trader speculation, rather than pure speculation, to use the language of the Federal Reserve Bank of New York. This enters into speculative positions through exports and imports and typically only contributes destabilization when it has the wind up. It may be expensive for the rats to leave the sinking ship, and they may be wrong in paying the price. But rats are rats, not calculators working on a fine margin. There may be some considerable satisfaction to the authorities in punishing them, but their conduct is unlikely to be modified.

VI. Conclusion

Sound domestic and monetary policy are of greater importance for the balance of payments than exchange-rate arrangements. There is no means by which the balance of payments can be isolated from domestic monetary policy, or vice-versa. Central bank cooperation is a vital requirement in the operation of any long-lasting international monetary system. Viewed in this perspective, the case for a flexible exchange rate for any other country may be made but it is not open and shut. In the special case of the dollar, which is the world's reserve currency, there would be a loss for the world international monetary mechanism from the adoption of a flexible exchange rate.

Bibliography

1. W. J. Baumol, "Speculation, Profitability and Stability," *Review of Economics and Statistics* (August 1957), pp. 263–71.
2. L. V. Chandler, *Benjamin Strong,* Washington, D. C.: The Brookings Institution, 1958.
3. A. C. L. Day, *The Future of Sterling,* Oxford: Clarendon, 1954.
4. Emile Despres, "Statement on the Significance of the European Common Market to the American Economy," *Hearings on Employment, Growth and Price Levels* before the Joint Economic Committee of the Congress of the United States, Part 5 — Inter-

national Influences on the American Economy, Washington, D. C., 1959.

5. E. L. Dulles, *The French Franc, 1914–28*, New York: Macmillan Co., 1929.

6. H. C. Eastman and S. Stykolt, "Exchange Stabilization in Canada," *Canadian Journal of Economics and Political Science* (May 1956), pp. 221–33, and "Exchange Stabilization Further Considered," *ibid.* (August 1957), pp. 404–08.

6a. Paul Einzig, *A Dynamic Theory of Forward Exchange,* London: Macmillan Co., 1961.

7. Federal Reserve Bank of New York (Alan R. Holmes), *The New York Foreign Exchange Market,* New York, 1959.

8. Milton Friedman, "The Case for Flexible Exchange Rates," *Essays in Positive Economics,* Chicago: University of Chicago Press, 1953, pp. 157–203.

9. Gottfried Haberler, "The Deficit in the American Balance of Payments and U. S. Foreign Economic Policy," Committee on National Trade Policy, January 1960.

10. Gottfried Haberler, "Currency Convertibility," American Enterprise Association, pamphlet, 1954.

11. S. Laursen and L. A. Metzler, "Flexible Exchange Rates and the Theory of Employment," *Review of Economics and Statistics* (November 1950), pp. 281–99.

12. Donald MacDougall, *The World Dollar Problem,* London: Macmillan Co., 1957.

13. James E. Meade, *The Balance of Payments,* Oxford: Oxford University Press, 1951.

14. E. Moreau, *Souvenirs d'un Gouveneur de la Banque de France.* Paris: Librairie de Medicis, 1954. Preface by J. Rueff.

15. E. V. Morgan, "The Theory of Flexible Exchange Rates," *American Economic Review* (June 1955), pp. 279–95.

16. R. Nurkse, *International Currency Experience,* Princeton, 1946.

17. R. Nurkse, "The Relation between Home Investment and External Balance in the Light of British Experience," *Review of Economics and Statistics* (May 1956), pp. 121–54.

18. R. Rhomberg, *Flexible Exchange Rates and the Process of Short-Run Balance of Payments Adjustment, Canada, 1951–57.* (Thesis, Yale, 1959).

19. Lionel Robbins, *The Economist in the Twentieth Century,* London: Macmillan Co., 1954.

20. W. M. Scammell, *International Monetary Policy,* London: Macmillan Co., 1958.

21. Andrew Shonfield, *British Economic Policy Since the War,* London: Penguin, 1958.
22. Egon Sohmen, *The Economics of Flexible Exchanges,* M.I.T. thesis, 1958; subsequently published in revised form as *Flexible Exchange Rates: Theory and Controversy,* Chicago: The University of Chicago Press, 1961.
23. J. Spraos, "Speculation, Arbitrage and Sterling," *Economic Journal* (March 1959), pp. 1–21.
24, 25. Robert Triffin, *Gold and the Dollar Crisis,* New Haven: Yale University Press, 1960.
26. S. C. Tsiang, "Fluctuating Exchange Rates in Countries with Relatively Stable Economies: Some European Experiences after World War." *Staff Papers,* International Monetary Fund, October 1959, pp. 244–73.
27. S. C. Tsiang, "The Theory of Forward Exchange and Effects of Government Intervention on the Forward Exchange Market." *Staff Papers,* International Monetary Fund, April 1959, pp. 75–106.

NOTES

[1] "The question is a difficult one; and . . . one about which reasonable men may take very different views." (Robbins, 19, pp. 99–100.) "The arguments for and against a system of flexible, exchange rates are . . . finely balanced." (Scammell, 20, pp. 194–195.) "There are clearly arguments on both sides. There is no absolute truth in this matter." (MacDougall, 12, p. 387.) Contrast Friedman (8, pp. 202–203) who states that so long as flexible exchange rates are not adopted, it will be impossible to achieve multilateral trade free of extensive and complex restrictions.

Note: Numbers in parentheses refer to publications cited in the Bibliography at the end of this Research Study.

[2] Note that S. C. Tsiang (26, p. 249) adopts as an indirect indication of destabilizing speculation a cumulative and widening deviation of the exchange rate from the purchasing-power parity. This has grave dangers because of the importance of internationally-traded commodities in wholesale-price indexes, normally used for these comparisons. *In extremis,* of course, as Tsiang recognizes (*ibid.,* note 4), domestic goods are priced in foreign exchange so that the purchasing-power parity is equivalent to the exchange rate and no destabilizing speculation can be indicated. The Dulles table (5, p. 527) shows how the purchasing-power parity, which is not independently determined, follows the course of the exchange rate.

[3] It may be useful to include a table of average monthly quotations for the Canadian dollar from the *Federal Reserve Bulletin.* The months in which the highs and lows are recorded are noted to indicate the absence of a seasonal change and to furnish an impression of the movement. Recorded daily quotations would move, of course, within a somewhat wider range.

Monthly Average Highs and Lows for Quotation of Canadian Dollar
in New York (in U.S. Cents per Canadian Dollar)

	High		Low	
1951	97.41	Dec.	93.48	June
1952	104.17	Sept.	99.49	Jan.
1953	103.01	Jan.	100.55	June
1954	103.44	Feb.	101.58	May
1955	103.50	Jan.	100.05	Nov.
1956	104.10	Dec.	100.08	Feb.
1957	105.47	July	102.30	Dec.
1958	104.16	July	101.54	Jan.
1959	105.51	Oct.	102.58	Feb.

Source: *Federal Reserve Bulletin,* January issues.

[4] It is interesting to observe that long-term capital investments have sometimes been destabilizing — *i.e.,* the movement of investment into Canada has continued fairly steadily without regard to the exchange rate — both when the rate is falling, which is stabilizing in the short-run sense, and when it is rising — which would be destabilizing in the short run. This speculation, however, which ignores the question of the rate altogether, is clearly stabilizing in the long run. It assumes that the Canadian dollar is going to be worth about a dollar U.S., and that the short-run deviations around this level are too unimportant to take into account over a long period.

[5] The New York Federal Reserve Bank, however, points out that it is necessary to have a good credit rating to enter into forward contracts (7, p. 39).

CHAPTER NINE

THE CAUSE AND CURE OF DISEQUILIBRIUM IN THE BALANCE OF PAYMENTS OF THE UNITED STATES, JANUARY 1960*

Introduction

So much of a general nature has been written on the present weakness of the balance of payments of the United States that it seems useful to confine the present paper narrowly to a limited number of analytical and policy issues. The analytical questions are two: (1) to what extent has the disequilibrium been caused by inflation in costs and prices, or by structural change; and (2) to what extent will the disequilibrium cure itself? These questions are evidently interrelated. The policy issues in turn depend on the analysis, and arise if the disequilibrium is not self-correcting. If the disequilibrium is caused by inflation, the best therapy, though not the only conceivable one, is disinflation. If, on the other hand, the disequilibrium is structural in origin, the range of possible action is not very greatly narrowed, nor is disinflation deprived of all possible role. Offsetting structural action is possible in a wide variety of policies with widely differing side effects; or if the market has moved to correct the disequilibrium in a desired direction part, but not all the way, it may be possible to assist it in completing the new equilibrium.

If one measures the "deficit" in the balance of payments by the

* A paper presented at a Conference on Trade Policy organized by the Committee for a National Trade Policy, Inc., January 27, 28, 1960 in Washington, D. C.

net loss in gold and dollars, and the change which is to be explained is the rise in this deficit from an average close to $1.5 billions from 1950 to 1956 to an average of $3.5 in 1958 and 1959, it is clear that major changes have occurred in exports and imports. Some increase has taken place in United States private capital exports, both direct and portfolio. And military expenditure abroad has risen slightly since 1955, after a sharp rise between 1950 and 1953. But the largest changes have occurred in the current account, particularly in merchandise exports and imports, and more especially in net exports of manufactured products. Leaving out the peak surplus of 1957, the current account, including transfers, has gone from a deficit of less than $1 billion a year to a deficit of $2.5 billion. The merchandise exports surplus has declined from an average of $2.5 billion between 1950 and 1956 to an annual rate of $0.8 billion for the first nine months of 1959; and net exports of finished manufactures have fallen from a surplus of $5.2 billions in 1953 and $6.0 billions in 1956 to $5.4 billions in 1958 and $4.4 billions in the 12 months ended September 1959. The size of these swings has led to the view that the United States has priced itself out of world markets through inflationary cost and wage pushes.

Inflationary Disequilibrium

The evidence furnished by price indexes in support of this position is weak. Table 1 presents series for eight foreign industrial countries and the United States on wholesale prices, and within them prices of finished goods, plus cost-of-living indexes and hourly earnings, for 1957 and for the latest available month in 1959, with 1953 as 100. While no single base year is free from distortion, 1953 is not a bad base, coming as it did after the end of the Korean War and its inflationary boomlet.

The figures present evidence for and against the inflation thesis. In September 1959 United States wholesale prices were higher than those of any other industrial country; but the cost-of-living index, apart from the French index where the 1953 base was seriously overvalued and a successful devaluation has reduced French dollar prices, the lowest. Finished-goods prices, which are all that are available for the United Kingdom, show that United States prices were not out of line in 1957 but may be said to be so, particularly vis-à-vis Japan and Italy, in September 1959. And while hourly earnings,

Table 1. Price and Wage Comparisons, Industrial Countries, 1957 and Latest Month 1959 (1953 = 100)

Country	Wholesale Prices		Finished Goods Prices		Cost of Living		Hourly Earnings	
	1957	Sep. 1959	1957	Sep. 1959	1957	Sep. 1959	1957	Sep. 1959
Belgium	106	102	—	—	107	110 (Oct.)	125	132 (June)
Canada	103	105	104	106	106	110	118	125 (July)
France (in $)	100	91	98	86	98	92	122	113 (June)
Germany	105	105	106*	106*	106	114 (Oct.)	130	146 (May)
Italy	103	98	106*	100*	110	113	120	126 (July)
Japan	105	100	107*	99*	109	111 (Aug.)	—	—
Netherlands	107	106	107	105 (Aug.)	115	120 (Oct.)	133	145
United Kingdom	—	—	110	112	116	120 (Oct.)	135	139 (Apr.)
United States	107	108	107	109	105	109	115	125 (Oct.)

*Producers' Goods

Source: Derived from United Nations Monthly Bulletin of Statistics, December 1959.

itself not a perfect index of wages, rose less in this country than in any other except Canada (and France), it should be borne in mind that a smaller percentage increase was a larger absolute one because of the much higher U.S. level of hourly wage rates in the base year.

A comparison of the latest monthly figure with 1957 lends some support to the inflation thesis, especially in earnings. The percentage increase in U.S. earnings is higher than for any other country — though not much above that of Germany, while that in the cost of living is higher than any save the German. Moreover, while the wholesale-price increase was small and exceeded by the Canadian, a number of other countries actually experienced declines in whole-sale prices.

But the total impression left by the table is one of disbelief. The indexes are not so accurate that the differences between the behavior of those here and abroad are significant. The price behavior of all the industrial countries, apart from the correction of French overvaluation, and with possible exceptions for the recent decline in Italian and Japanese prices, has been broadly similar. Whether one regards a rate of price increase of 1 to 1½ per cent a year as seriously inflationary or not — and I confess I do not think a monthly rise of 1/10 of one percentage point is front-page news — broadly the same rate has occurred in each competing country. In the British expression, there isn't anything in it, meaning that there is not much difference among them.

This does not mean that there are not a number of lines where European and Japanese goods do not outsell American exports based on price, or that the competitive positions of Western Europe and Japan vis-à-vis the United States have not improved. They do and they have. What seems to have happened, however, is that the supply of competitive exports has increased in a number of lines at previously existing prices which were already below those prevailing in the United States, but which were not effective because of limited supplies. In other instances, new industries have come into operation in Europe and Japan and competed effectively with those in the United States without involving relative price changes.

Another way of testing the inflation thesis is to see how general or how specialized is the change in the import surplus. This again requires a choice of dates for comparison, with all the risks thereby entailed. Table 2, however, compares the change in net exports (or

Table 2. Change in Net Exports (Exports — Imports) of Selected
Categories of U. S. International Trade: 1956 — 12
Months Ended September 1959 (in millions of dollars)

Finished manufactures — total		−1,665
Machinery and related items		−155
Construction, excavating and mining machinery	−85	
Electrical machinery	−56	
Engines, turbines, and parts	+25	
Machine tools	+11	
Office machinery	+ 4	
Agricultural machinery	−38	
Tractors, parts, and accessories	−86	
Automobiles and parts		−871
Civilian aircraft		− 34
Railway equipment		+ 17
Textiles		−123
Other nonfood consumers' goods		−145
Steel mill products		−195
Petroleum products		−117
Paper and paper products		+ 64
Medicinals and pharmaceuticals		+ 28
Crude and semimanufactured materials — total		−1,108
Iron and steel mill products		−356
Steel scrap and pig iron		−192
Coal and related products		−324
Petroleum, crude		−138
Fuel oil		−210
Copper, unwrought		+191
Cotton, unmanufactured		−380
Other textile fibers and semimanufactures		− 3
Industrial chemicals		+123
Rubber		+112
Sawmill products		+ 33
Paper base stock		+ 16
Tobacco, unmanufactured		+ 14
Oilseeds and inedible vegetable oils		+ 53
Hides and skins		− 17

Source: Survey of Current Business, December 1959, pp. 12, 14.

net imports) of leading categories of finished manufactures and
crude and semimanufactured materials between 1956, before the
Suez bulge of United States exports, and the latest 12-month figures,
ended September 1959. The figures are from a useful article in the
December 1959 *Survey of Current Business.* Net exports of crude
and finished foodstuffs are omitted from consideration as they held
up well over the period.

The major changes revealed by Table 2 occur in automobiles ($871 millions), various categories of iron and steel products aggregating $743 millions, petroleum and products ($465 millions), cotton ($380 millions), and coal ($324 millions). The sum of net changes in these categories aggregates to $2.8 billion or the same magnitude as the net total change indicated. All other changes therefore offset one another. Cotton and coal are clearly special situations. In the former, such pricing out of the market as has taken place was the result of farm price supports, not inflation. In coal, exports fell as a result of import restrictions in Europe in response to oversupply and despite the fact that United States supplies are competitive with those in Europe.

Automobiles, steel, and petroleum products may be said to contain elements of pricing ourselves out of the market, but hardly of a generally inflationary sort. In petroleum, rising costs of exploration and continued depletion of domestic resources in this country have led to higher marginal costs of new supplies. Imports would have been much larger had it not been for restrictions adopted in the name of national defense.

The sharp decline in net exports of steel mill manufactures, iron and steel mill semimanufactures and crude materials, and pig iron and steel scrap is partly attributable to price changes, perhaps, but mainly a result of the steel strike, prospectively and in actuality. International comparison of steel prices presents serious problems of comparability of product, and resort to index numbers encounters the difficulty that not all product prices move in the same direction. Moreover, a certain amount of price administration and discrimination prevail. For the limited extent to which they can be meaningful, however, it may be useful to present a selection of price relatives shown in Table 3. Pricing out of the market may have occurred in plates if the figures are to be believed, and especially vis-à-vis Japan, but major importance must be attached to the strike.

Finally the drastic reduction in the value of automobile and part net exports seems to be due to changes in supply abroad, and in taste in this market, rather than to consideration of price, but the role of the latter is impossible to disentangle.

Some decline in exports of capital equipment has been caused by the 1958 recession, especially as concerns Canada and Latin Amer-

Table 3. Prices of Iron and Steel Products, Index Numbers September or October 1959 (1953 = 100)

	Pig Iron	Steel Products
Belgium	103	120 (billets)
France (in dollars)	116	102 (heavy sections)
Germany	115	109 (Bessemer bars)
Japan	—	92.5 export price, plates 85 e.p. tinplate
United Kingdom	138	90 export price, plates 110 e.p. tinplate
United States	119	125 export price, plates 110 e.p. tinplate

Source: Derived from United Nations *Monthly Bulletin of Statistics,* December 1959, pp. 144, 145.

ica. Against this, however, can be set the decline in net imports of raw materials such as copper and rubber, the latter also affected by the expansion of synthetic production which expands exports and replaces imports of the natural product.

Finally, it is useful to take a look at the evidence of the United States competitive position derived from data on percentage shares in world markets for manufactured goods. A difficulty is presented by the fact that British and United States authorities handle the data differently, and emerge with slightly different results. The British comparison of market shares is based on totals which include Canada and Switzerland, which have been excluded from the Department of Commerce calculation. In both cases, manufactures comprise goods shown in sections 5 to 8 of the Standard International Trade Classification, but exclude special category goods. The British data are more up-to-date. The United States figures are limited to exports to the free world and offer a more complete breakdown.

Table 4 is the British presentation. The United States figures for a

Table 4. Industrial Country Shares of World Manufactures, Selected Periods, 1953 — First Half 1959 (in per cent of dollar totals)

	U.S.	U.K.	Germany	France	Japan	Others[1]
1953	25.9	21.3	13.3	9.0	3.8	26.8
1956	25.2	19.1	16.4	7.8	5.7	25.8
1957	25.4	18.1	17.5	8.0	5.9	25.1
1958	23.2	18.0	18.6	8.5	6.0	25.7
Jan.-June 1959	22.5	18.1	18.5	9.0	6.3	25.6

[1] Belgium, Canada, Italy, Netherlands, Sweden, and Switzerland.
Source: British Information Service, *British Record,* October 30, 1959 and previous issues.

somewhat smaller total show different figures for the separate market shares, as given in Table 5.

Table 5. Exports of Manufactured Goods From United States, Japan and Western Europe to the Free World (in per cent of dollar totals)

| | United States | Japan | OEEC Countries of Western Europe | | | | |
			Germany	United Kingdom	France	Italy	Other[1]
1953	29	4	14	23	10	3	17
1956	28	6	17	20	8	3	18
1957	28	6	18	19	8	4	17
1958	25	6	19	19	9	4	17

[1] Except Switzerland.

Source: U.S. Department of Commerce, *Survey of Current Business,* December 1959, p. 17.

They provide, however, a breakdown by categories, given in Table 6. This seems to show a more general tendency to decline — in tractors, agricultural machinery, office machinery, and other items not mentioned in the earlier discussion of absolute changes in the net merchandise surplus. Nonetheless, the importance of the decline in automobile exports is underlined, and it is clear that there are significant groups of manufactures which were still expanding up to 1958 — chemicals, paper, textile yarns, etc. The allegation of inflationary disequilibrium is not disproved; but the burden of the evidence is against it.

Structural Disequilibrium

A structural disequilibrium has been defined as having occurred when "a change in demand or supply of exports or imports alters a previously existing equilibrium or when a change occurs in the basic circumstances under which income is earned or spent abroad, in both cases without the requisite parallel changes elsewhere in the economy."[1] The seriousness of the disequilibrium depends, evidently, on the size of the initial shock and on the speed and extent of the automatic adjustment to it. If there is a reduction in the demand for an export, there may be no structural disequilibrium if deflation at home, expansion abroad, an adjustment of the exchange rate, or an automatic reallocation of resources into new export lines or marginally attractive import-competing lines restores the balance.

Table 6. Exports of Manufactured Goods From United States, Japan and Western Europe to the Free World: Percentage Share From United States

	1953	1956	1957	1958
Total manufactured goods	29	28	28	25
Chemicals	31	33	33	32
Machinery and transport equipment	38	35	34	30
Other manufactures	20	20	20	19
Selected machinery and transport equipment:				
Construction, excavating, and mining machinery	64	70	70	63
Metalworking machinery and machine tools	43	36	37	39
Power generating machinery	29	27	27	25
Other industrial machinery	33	33	33	31
Electrical machinery and appliances	33	28	28	26
Office machinery	46	39	37	36
Agricultural machinery	57	47	46	43
Tractors	63	59	55	48
Commercial aircraft	46	45	49	36
Railway vehicles	26	26	32	35
Commercial motor vehicles (trucks, etc.)	50	50	48	42
Passenger cars	34	26	20	14
Ships and boats	7	5	8	6
Selected other manufactures:				
Paper and paperboard	19	21	22	23
Iron and steel	20	21	23	16
Miscellaneous metal manufactures	24	23	23	22
Textile yarn and thread	9	8	8	10
Cotton fabrics	19	17	17	17
Other fabrics	12	10	9	8

Source: U.S. Department of Commerce, *Survey of Current Business,* December 1959, p. 18.

In my judgment, the structural changes which have taken place since about 1953, and to which the balance of payments of the United States has not adjusted, consist mainly of

1. An increase in the supply of United States imports as a consequence of industrial reconstruction in Western Europe and Japan, and a rapid closing of the technological gap which previously separated these countries from the United States.

2. By the same token, an increased supply of competing exports.

3. An increased demand in the United States for imports from Western Europe and Japan, especially of consumers' goods which are differentiated from United States products.

145

4. An increased awareness of and interest in the possibilities of producing goods abroad at costs below those in the United States, with a resulting expansion of direct investment in lines beyond resource products.

5. Increased awareness of and interest in foreign securities.

These changes came subsequent to the important structural changes of the late 1940's and early 1950's by which the United States undertook to assist the recovery and economic development of the rest of the world, and to take leadership in the defense of the free world, including the leadership in expenditures abroad for defense purposes. These policies were originally justified partly on balance-of-payments grounds; but by 1953 or so, foreign military expenditures and governmental transfers by the United States can be said to have changed from "compensatory" to "exogenous" items in the balance.

The first two changes enumerated, which are in reality two aspects of a single change, are the consequence of the success of United States policies to assist the recovery of industrial nations. The next three are all related to a fundamental change which has occurred in international economic relations, and which involves this country lifting the horizon of its economic vision more completely to the world level. The United States consumer today has to decide not what car from Detroit he wants to buy, but what car, wherever made in the world. The United States manufacturer contemplating a new production process has lately moved from a regional horizon to a national one, but now, in many instances, considers where in the world is the most economical place to undertake production. When New York stock market prices seem high, the investor has recently come to look at quotations in London, Amsterdam, Zurich, Frankfurt, and in some cases Tokyo.

This change is the result of the increase in international communications since before the war, stimulated after the recovery of Western Europe and Japan, by a few phenomena such as the establishment of the Common Market in 1957 with its threat to United States exports. The consumer's interest in imports may be partly faddist, but it seems evident that the war, plus postwar military service abroad, have accustomed great numbers of the consumers of the United States to think in global terms for the first

146

time. Imported goods previously thought inferior are now judged on their merits if not accorded a preference because of an origin deemed exotic or special.

This very general explanation of broad structural change — increased productivity and technological capacity abroad, plus increased awareness of foreign products, productive capacity, and financial investment potential — cannot be proved or disproved. Moreover, it ignores the narrower structural changes which seem to have bunched up in 1958 and 1959 to produce an especially large deficit — the particular circumstances affecting steel, cotton, coal. It further omits the earlier structural changes involved in the depletion of United States mineral resources and the need to go abroad for increased supplies of iron, petroleum, lead, copper, etc., and in the relative reduction of transport costs for bulk supplies. But it has the merit, in my judgment, of underlining what are likely to be basic changes in the short-run behavior of the United States balance of payments — a change in cyclical behavior discussed immediately below, but also a greater sensitivity of American production, consumption, investment to foreign influences. The United States can no longer experience the relative economic isolation which it enjoyed over a wide range of economic activity because of the myopia of its businessmen and consumers. With the narrowing of its technological leadership in many lines, moreover, the United States is as likely to be affected by economic developments abroad as to affect them. This is a very basic change which will mean that this country can no longer ignore the world economy.

Cyclical Behavior of the United States Balance of Payments

In his testimony before the Joint Economic Committee of the Congress on June 30, 1959, R. E. Baldwin suggested that the 1957–1958 recession has revealed a different behavior of the U.S. balance of payments from the recessions in 1937–1938, 1948–1949, and 1953–1954. On the earlier occasion, the balance of payments showed a surplus in recession as imports of raw materials dropped sharply and exports of consumers goods to countries whose incomes were steadier than that here were sustained. In 1957–1958, there was no speculative activity in imports of raw materials: prices had already fallen to relatively low levels, and there were no substantial inventories to be run down. It is true, as already mentioned, that

147

the merchandise trade surplus improved to a degree because of reductions in net imports of copper and rubber shown in Table 2, though the latter involved a partial structural shift from natural to synthetic rubber.

In 1957–1958, however, United States imports were better sustained than exports because of the growing importance of consumers' goods among imports, and because of the success achieved in maintaining consumer incomes; while exports increasingly consisted of capital goods — the machinery and related items in Table 2 — net exports of which declined because of depression abroad.

It is true that in a world recession, other things equal, the country which experiences the deepest recession will have the most favorable balance of payments, and that this could be regarded as support for the inflation explanation for the United States balance of payments if the United States had suffered a lesser recession in 1957–1958, relative to other countries, than in earlier periods. But this was not the case. The recession may have been deeper in Belgium than in the United States, especially in 1957, but in all other industrial countries industrial production was affected less. The different cyclical behavior of the balance of payments in 1957–1958 than in earlier periods must then be ascribed to structural changes in the composition of exports and imports.

Automatic Adjustment Mechanism

It is concluded that the structural explanation carries more conviction than the inflationary one. The question then arises as to how far the structural disequilibrium of the U.S. balance of payments — and the corresponding disequilibrium in the direction of surplus of our trading partners — is likely to correct itself, with or without the support of the normal measures of monetary policy associated with balance-of-payments deficits and surpluses, and how far special balance-of-payments action is necessary.

The full automatic mechanism may be divided for analytical purposes into several stages: (1) the response of the resources directly affected; (2) the inflationary impact of balance-of-payments surpluses and the deflationary effect of deficits through the changes in income on the one hand and changes in the money supply on the other; and (3) the additional impact of supporting monetary measures such as changes in interest rates. In addition,

148

one can discuss this mechanism for the deficit in the United States, and for the surpluses in the industrial countries in Western Europe and Japan.

It is probably unnecessary to trace each of the three stages through in the United States but there is reason to believe that, over-all, the automatic mechanism will not carry the adjustment far. Foreign trade is such a small proportion of total output that resources in export- or import-competing lines which are displaced in the course of balance-of-payments changes are likely to end up working for domestic production rather than to shift into new export- or new import-competing occupations. It is true that the introduction of the compact car is a market response of the automobile industry, which may stem the increase in imports. Expert opinion, however, is reported to believe that it will not reverse it by opening up new export lines or cutting imports very far back. The total deflationary impact of the deficit has been small, particularly when built-in fiscal stabilizers — the automatically unbalanced budget during the recession — checked the decline in income. The rise in interest rates in the United States, permitted or encouraged for reasons of domestic monetary policy rather than the international position — though the two objectives coincided — has led to a reduction in foreign bond issues, and slowed down the withdrawal of foreign balances. At the time of this writing, however, it had produced no positive deflation.

Much more would normally be expected in automatic adjustment abroad, especially from rising wage rates, and the expansionary effect of balance-of-payments surpluses. Brimful employment in every country in Western Europe except Italy (with its structural unemployment) has led in recent months to rising wages and discouraged new direct investment in the most accessible areas of Paris, the line from Brussels to Amsterdam, and the Ruhr. Labor is available only in more rural locations, less suitable from the viewpoint of transport, or in distressed and development areas such as southern Belgium and southern Italy.

But it is surprising to expert analysts how slowly imports have risen in Japan and Italy where in previous periods the marginal propensity to save has been low and has meant that infusions of purchasing power quickly spilled over into external expenditure. The 1955 Japanese export surplus quickly melted under inflationary pressure, but that of 1958 and 1959, despite a record rise in industrial production since July 1958, seems far more resistant.

Part of the explanation is that a number of these countries have taken deflationary monetary action in anticipation of an automatic reversal rather than the expansionary action called for by rising international reserves. Thus Germany raised interest rates in September 1959 and again in November, despite abundant reserves, and in the latter case stimulated a new inflow of short-term capital and a renewed increase in reserves. Japanese interest rates, already high, have recently been further raised despite the long string of successive months of export surplus.

In short, the automatic mechanism would not be expected to work very effectively or quickly in the United States, and is not functioning as rapidly as anticipated in Western Europe and Japan. To halt the balance-of-payments deficit or to bring it down to manageable proportions therefore requires policy action going beyond mere support for the automatic mechanism.

It seems likely, however, that the automatic adjustment mechanism will very shortly take over and apply corrective expansion in Western Europe and Japan. Mass interest in consumption has been stimulated in these countries, and defense expenditures in Germany seem likely to offset the budgetary surpluses which have been the counterpart of past payments surpluses. On this score, the policy action required in the United States need not be very far-reaching or fundamental.

The Role of Deflation

Monetary and fiscal measures — tight money and budgetary surpluses — can correct a structural disequilibrium. How quickly they do so depends on how mobile resources are between occupations, or how readily resources respond to small differences in the return between one industry and another. If resources are relatively immobile, it may be necessary to reduce national income by $100 millions to effect a reduction of $4 millions in the balance of payments, where 4 per cent of every change in income is spent on or withdrawn from imports. The reduction in income by the other $96 millions will reduce incomes in existing occupations or result in unemployment without stimulating new exports or entry into new import-competing occupations. But where mobility is high, a much smaller decline in income will produce the same change in the balance, as resources will quit those occupations which experience a decline in income and shift into export lines or into occupations competing with imports.

Most economists believe that U.S. resource mobility is not very high in the short run, and that deflation has a supporting rather than a leading role to play in correcting structural disequilibrium of any substantial size with any degree of alacrity.[2] Tight money can restrain capital exports; and general monetary and fiscal orthodoxy are useful in preventing an initial correction in the balance itself from having an inflationary effect. Moreover, high interest rates hold foreign capital which might otherwise be withdrawn in gold, and possibly can attract new deposits. But it is not likely that the maintenance or reduction in incomes in this country would stimulate through market forces a sizeable and relatively rapid movement into exports or into import-competing lines. Though tight money and balanced budgets or budgetary surpluses are needed in support, more positive measures are required.

Devaluation

In the ordinary case of a single country which does not serve as a major center for world reserves, the most effective cure for structural disequilibrium of some seriousness is devaluation while preventing any increase in money income.[3] Raising the price of foreign-trade goods relative to domestic stimulates the necessary reallocation of resource into export- and import-competing industries. The difficulty is that this device is not open to this country.

Two reasons account for this limitation. In the first place, devaluation would have to proceed by changing the price of gold, leaving it open to other countries to change their price of gold. It is virtually certain that other countries would do so. The result would be a change in the price of gold, with whatever effects follow from that on our liquidity position, and on the output of new reserves, but no stimulus to correction for the balance of payments. Second, for a world reserve center to devalue without having guaranteed the value of its foreign-exchange liabilities would cause losses to its creditors (holders of dollar balances); and the anticipation of this possibility would lead to runs on the dollar. (In this connection it should be noted that when Britain devalued in 1949 all of its creditors, except for a while Pakistan, devalued with it. Thus holders of sterling suffered no loss in the local-currency value of their reserves, but Britain could not improve its balance of payments through devaluation against them.) I believe that it is important to work out simple means of guaranteeing the exchange value of dollar reserves, but until such a means is available, devaluation is out of the question for the dollar.

Import Restrictions, Export Subsidies, Cuts in Foreign Expenditure

If the disequilibrium is structural, one way to correct it might be to institute other changes in imports, exports, and foreign lending. Devaluation is a method of restricting imports and expanding exports, but this can also be done through direct measures of tariffs or quotas on imports, and subsidies of one kind or another to exports. Foreign lending can be limited by restrictions on capital exports. One form of subsidy to exports and restriction on capital exports is to require foreign borrowers to spend the proceeds of loans in the United States.

It is hardly necessary to argue that these methods of discriminatory and administrative restriction and subsidy are undesirable, and subversive of United States efforts to build an expanding basis of world trade. They cannot be argued against on the ground that they will not meet the need. But it is persuasive, in my judgment, that their side effects, and long-run ineffectiveness, much more than make up for the short-run help they produce for the balance of payments. In particular, as the farm-surplus problem demonstrates, short-run measures which operate at variance with market forces lead to more and more controls and away from an appropriate long-run solution to the allocation problem.

The short-run effectiveness of these means and the interest of less competitive export and import-competing interests in maintaining their market position ensure that there will be great pressure for these actions. The task of government is not merely to refrain from restricting imports and subsidizing exports but to resist pressures to these ends. Similarly, the opposition to military expenditure abroad and to foreign aid will press for reductions in these items which will be difficult to resist. Foreign-aid cuts will not improve the balance of payments dollar for dollar, as cuts in military expenditure

152

abroad would do, since much of the foreign aid is already tied to exports which would fall with the aid. But here again, the immediate balance-of-payments impact is undeniable, and resistance to reductions must be made on the basis that the side effects are worse than the balance-of-payments deficit, which is in any event curable by other more benign means.

Expanding Exports and Redistributing Foreign Expenditure

If devaluation, discriminatory measures to reduce imports and expand exports, and unilateral cuts in foreign military expenditure and economic aid are ruled out, few means are left to correct the residual structural disequilibrium remaining while the automatic mechanism is coming into operation and after it has gone as far as it can. Disinflation is important in a supporting role, but more positive action is desirable.

The two major lines of government endeavor which fit the prescription are removal of foreign restrictions on dollar imports remaining from the long period of persistent dollar shortage, and redistribution of foreign military expenditure and economic assistance to shift the burden away from the United States and to Western Europe. Neither step can be taken unilaterally by the United States, and the former requires action exclusively by foreign countries. But there is reason to believe that they are likely to be sufficient to reduce the long-term deficit to the $500 million to $1 billion figure which can be supported over a long period with benefit to world trade from the expansion of reserves.

The removal of import restrictions has gone some distance in Germany, the Netherlands, and Britain and is slowly getting under way in France, Italy, and Japan. Pressure for a faster rate in the latter countries is desirable, and there is in addition reason to urge on countries like Germany, which have removed all balance-of-payment quota restrictions, to contemplate removing those which have a protective importance, and to refrain from putting on others. With full employment, high foreign reserves and a favorable balance of payments, there is every reason for such a country as Germany to reallocate resources out of low productivity lines, such as agriculture and high-cost coal mines. If this were done, the incremental exports of United States farm products and coal, and the additional sales of oil by U.S. oil companies abroad, would benefit the United States balance of payments at the same time that they brought about a more efficient allocation of world resources. The efficiency and balance-of-payments arguments for reductions in trade barriers are theoretically distinct, but a favorable balance of payments should encourage the reduction of barriers on efficiency grounds. United States leadership in the reduction of trade barriers has petered out under various influences, political and economic. If world trade and prosperity are to continue to expand, it would be useful to have other countries spell us for a time. I do not believe that there has been a change as fundamental as that which toppled Great Britain from her free-trade leadership in the 1850's and 1860's; but the narrowing of the technological advantage of this country calls for at least a temporary sharing of our responsibility to set a world example in reducing trade barriers.

A redistribution of the burdens of foreign military expenditure and economic assistance, while total expenditure and aid are maintained or even increased, has been recognized in Western Europe as desirable. When the United States had a persistent surplus in the balance of payments on current merchandise and service account, it was appropriate for it to have a tendency to overspend relative to the rest of the world in military and economic defense. But when the merchandise and service leadership has been lost, the spending lead can appropriately be adjusted.

An academic outsider may comment on strategy, but hardly on tactics. It has, however, been suggested that the action of the United States in tying loans from the Development Loan Fund to exports of United States origin — itself a backward and discriminatory step — was undertaken to impress foreign countries with the seriousness with which we regarded the payments position, and to apply indirect pressure on foreign countries to play their role in meeting it. If so, it is unfortunate that in making an impression on Western Europe and Japan, it was necessary to reduce economic aid to the underdeveloped countries.

Apart from negotiations to reduce barriers to dollar exports, and to redistribute the burden of foreign defense and aid, government can do little. The important task of competing more effectively in foreign markets and with imports into this country is one for industry. There may be steps which the government can take to this end, such as encouragement of research and new investment.

It has often been suggested that exhortation be undertaken. Basically, however, the task is one for private industry in the climate of disinflation which makes foreign markets attractive.

Other negative action is probably called for, such as not stimulating private foreign investment — at least not for Western Europe and Japan.

Adequacy of These Policies

The removal of export barriers and redistribution of the burden of international expenditures for defense and economic development, against a background of disinflation, may be thought to be rather puny measures. They require cooperation of foreign countries, rather than action by this country alone; and it is hard to see large quantitative results from them, reckoned in terms of billions of dollars.

But the structural disequilibrium in the balance of payments of this country, in my judgment, is not nearly so profound, nor does it call for such heroic measures as those which confronted Western Europe and Japan 12 years ago. The cyclical aspects of the imbalance have lost their force; the random elements which peaked up the deficit in the second quarter of 1959 have been averaged out by time; research and development expenditures here remain on a high level and will produce new export resilience in new industries; and the automatic response to balance-of-payments surpluses abroad, which has been surprisingly slow, is inevitably going to catch up.

Balance-of-payments deficits can persist, and they have done so in the past. But there is nothing in economic or historical analysis which suggests that correction of a balance-of-payments persistent disequilibrium by structural changes — or overcorrection — is likely to open up a persistent disequilibrium in the other direction. The United States can no longer ignore the implications of domestic action for its international transactions and for foreign confidence in the dollar. But there is nothing in the record to suggest that there is any new asymmetry in international balances to replace that which has been overcome, that the United States now has a vastly greater tendency to inflation than other countries, or that further disturbances to equilibrium of a cyclical, technological, or other variety will not be random in their occurrence and incidence.

Until it becomes clear that United States industry, and the adjustment process abroad, are not responding — and the recent evidence on trade suggests that they are — it is safe to rely on these methods of negotiation, plus the automatic mechanism, operating against the background of disinflation, to correct the structural disequilibrium.

Notes

[1] See my *International Economics,* Homewood, Ill., Richard D. Irwin, Inc., 1958, p. 534. It should be pointed out to the reader that my usage of the term structural disequilibrium has been attacked in one of F. Machlup's semantic disquisitions. See F. Machlup, "Structure and Structural Change: Weaselwords and Jargon," *Zeitschrift fuer Nationaloekonomie,* Heft 3, 1958, pp. 280–298, and esp. p. 290. I can hardly think, however, that Professor Machlup has read the chapter on "Structural Disequilibrium" in my textbook beyond the Summary from which he quotes.

[2] E. L. Dale, Jr., writing in *The New York Times* of December 26, 1959, expresses the view of European bankers that tight money and budgetary balance will correct the balance of payments of the United States even though they work more slowly in this country than in Europe. He goes on to say, "Bankers generally do not believe that the United States has a serious 'structural' problem that will give it a 'chronic' payments deficit of serious proportions. In particular they do not believe that the United States is 'pricing itself out of world markets.'" This use of the term "structural" differs from that employed in this paper and approaches the standard attacked by Machlup.

[3] See my *International Economics, op. cit.,* p. 539. Machlup believes that the word "structural" is used in "crypto-apologetic" meanings as a plea for foreign-exchange restrictions, a plea for import barriers, or an excuse for rejecting diagnoses, prognoses, or therapies which apply elsewhere (*op. cit.,* p. 297). Restrictions may be required, to be sure, when the structural disequilibrium is of the size encountered by Europe in 1946.

CHAPTER TEN

*THE UNITED STATES BALANCE OF PAYMENTS AND THE LOSS OF GOLD**

I wish to comment at some length on the recent outflow of gold from the United States and its implications for U.S. domestic economic policy and over-all foreign policy.

Three months ago the American press woke up with a start to the loss of gold through the balance of international payments in 1958 and the first quarter of 1959 and jumped to the conclusion that inflation in this country had outstripped that in the rest of the world with the result that we were "pricing ourselves out of world markets." Today, happily, there is a much better understanding of the real position. It is recognized that over-all prices have risen in the United States just about as much as in European countries and that wage rates have risen, on the whole, a smaller percentage here than there. It is true that the absolute rise in money wages in this country has been higher than in Europe — a 20 per cent rise in U.S. hourly earnings since 1953 is larger than a 40 per cent increase in German wages, when the 1953 rates were $2 an hour in this country and 50 cents in Germany. Moreover, though there is difficulty in getting exactly comparable series, there are indications that steel prices in this country have risen more than those abroad, particularly more than Japanese, probably more than British, and possibly more than German and Belgian. On the whole, however, the view that the U.S. balance of payments has turned adverse because of inflation is widely recognized as largely wrong and entirely oversimplified.

* Statement before the Joint Economic Committee, Congress of the United States, Eighty-sixth Congress, First Session Pursuant to S. Con. Res. 13 on Employment Growth and Price Levels, Part 5 on International Influences on the American Economy, June 30, 1959, pp. 954–958.

157

Let me first review what has happened to our balance of payments, list some of the lesser causes which have contributed to this result, and finally, before going on to discuss their implications for policy, pinpoint the main underlying changes in the position.

The gold outflows of 1958 and the spring of 1959 come on top of a substantial acquisition by foreigners of balances in the United States which goes back, with interruptions on such occasions as Suez, all the way to 1950. It is inaccurate to say that change in one item in the balance of payments has brought about the change in another; all the items are interdependent and mutually determine one another. But loosely speaking, one can say that the foreign acquisition of approximately $12 billion which has brought our present short-term liabilities to foreigners to $16.6 billion has been the result of governmental grants and private investment abroad substantially in excess of our net export surplus of goods and services. For the 9 years from 1950 to 1958, inclusive, and excluding military supplies and services transferred abroad under grants, the annual average export surplus of goods and services has amounted to $2.7 billion, against which there have been unilateral transfers, largely governmental grants other than military, of $2.7 billion, a private capital outflow of $1.8 billion, and a governmental capital outflow of $0.4 billion. The result has been, ignoring errors in estimating, that foreigners have added to their gold at the rate of $400 million and to their balances at $1.3 billion annually.

Changes have occurred in the proportions in which foreigners have acquired dollar balances and gold, and 1958 marked a substantial increase in the outflow of gold, which amounted to $2.3 billion for the year. But this did not reflect any loss of confidence in the dollar by foreigners, whether foreign governmental authorities or speculators in foreign banking centers. Short-term interest rates were low in 1958 and working balances high. In consequence, new claims on the dollar were converted into gold. But foreign balances were not drawn down: U.S. liabilities to foreigners in fact rose by $1 billion during the year. And as short-term money rates tightened in 1959, these deposits continued to build up at a faster rate.

While the United States has been losing gold and dollars, then, for 9½ years, it is important to observe that between 1957 and 1958 there has been a sharp change. Foreigners lost net gold and dollars by $200 million in 1957 and gained $3.4 billion in 1958. The heavy losses by the United States in 1958 have continued into 1959 as exports declined during the first quarter from the 1958 level and imports rose even more. Underlying these short-run changes, and hidden by the average figures cited, have been a steady rise in U.S. military expenditure abroad, a sharp upward movement of U.S. private investment since 1955, and an increased outflow of governmental capital.

Some of the short-run changes exaggerate the position. In the first place, the 1957 exports were inordinately large as a result of the export of substantial quantities of oil to Europe at high prices because of Suez.

Another important influence of the last few months, but one which cannot be measured accurately, is the accumulation of steel inventories against the possibility of a steel strike beginning tomorrow. European producers state that orders from the United States have tripled currently over normal levels. Some of these purchases intended for inventory have in fact been consumed with the upturn of business this spring, but some of the imports of the last few months are borrowed from the future. In 1936 and 1949 inventory accumulation raised the levels of imports above those that could be sustained and narrowed the current-account surplus below its long-term level. That uncertain proportion of present imports which represents accretions to inventories may be regarded as exchanged for gold. It is a common phenomenon in European economies that foreign-exchange reserves fluctuate inversely with inventories of internationally traded goods. That steel has become an internationally traded commodity between Europe and the United States is ascribable to the fact that commodity prices have risen much more than ocean freight rates since 1939. This has expanded the international markets for many bulky products — oil, coal, and steel. This trend, and the reduction in tariffs to which it is similar, have exposed U.S. prices to international competition on a wider front.

A further small transitory influence has been the slight lag of recovery in Europe behind that in the United States. The European recession did not go so deep as did ours, but the low in October 1958 came after that in this country, which was in April 1958. By the first quarter of 1959, the momentum of upturn was higher in the United States than in Europe, and this, even apart from steel inventories, meant that our imports expanded faster than European. As recovery levels off in the United States and continues upward in Europe, this effect will reverse itself. The European recession was particularly serious for coal exports, though these may not recover to previous levels because of the continued inroads in Europe of oil and natural gas. This recession may also be part of the explanation of the decline in sales of cotton by the United States. These fell in the first 3 months of 1959 $125 million below the level of 1958 and accounted for three-eighths of the total loss of exports.

A small part of the U.S. loss of gold and dollars since 1950 is ascribable to the difficulties faced by Germany in regulating its balance of payments, difficulties of an opposite sort to those this country is now experiencing. The German export surplus has continuously been in excess of any amount of long-term lending or investment which the German economy has been willing to undertake, with the result that Germany piles up gold and dollars. Ad hoc measures of lending to the International Bank for Reconstruction and Development and governmental financing of long-term exports have been used, but the problem, similar to that which this country experienced before 1950, persists. A change in the German international position is expected as the country takes a larger share in European defense, but up to now taxation for defense has outstripped expenditures, and accumulated treasury surpluses have been the domestic counterpart of the gain of foreign-exchange reserves.

A final small contributing force has been the recent increase in interest on the part of American investors in foreign securities. The present height of the New York stock market has reduced bond yields and the prospect for growth of American equities below the level of many European and even Japanese securities, despite the difficulties of dealing in the latter. This movement, which is one aspect of the greater awareness of foreign opportunities of which I shall speak presently, has been partly offset by the decline in the U.S. bond market in recent months, cutting off what appeared in 1958 to be a revival of interest in foreign sale of dollar bonds in this market. Compared to foreign transactions in U.S. securities, which have been substantial since the 1920's, U.S. investor interest in foreign securities is limited. But it has been growing.

The reversal of the Suez burst of exports, the accumulation of steel inventories, the German balance of payments surplus, and the new interest in Royal Dutch, Lever Bros., KLM, and Philips on the part of American investors are of small moment compared to two basic changes in the American position since about 1953. These are the widening of the horizon of U.S. producers and consumers to the world scene and the narrowing of the technological gap between the United States and the rest of the world. These factors are related. But the increased awareness of foreign opportunities has expanded U.S. investment abroad and imports, while the technological gain in European and Japanese capacity has worked in this same direction, further cutting down U.S. exports in these and third markets.

This country has always had an interest in selling in foreign markets. Since the war, however, more and more companies and consumers have become aware, in many cases for the first time, of the opportunities that exist to buy abroad or to acquire production there. Depletion of minerals and timber turned consumers of raw materials abroad in increasing number, and in particular oil and steel companies. But more and more manufacturing companies that had previously thought of themselves as limited to this country, except perhaps for sales, have begun to scan a wider area. A typical example would be the motion picture industry, which got into foreign production largely in an effort to use up blocked exchange. It found that for many purposes foreign locations were cheaper than Hollywood, and that United States and foreign audiences liked foreign locales. A business-machine manufacturer going abroad to escape a foreign tariff found that foreign plants could outproduce those in the United States and supplied this market from abroad. Truly international companies domiciled in the United States began to contemplate where, in the whole world, this or that transportable component could be most cheaply made.

The increase in consumer interest in foreign goods is a familiar story, best illustrated by the success of the sports car and small automobile. It is sometimes suggested that foreign goods have a snob appeal, as if this made them less worthy than American merchandise. This comes with ill grace from industry geared through advertising to cultivate associations between particular products and particular images, whether of aristocratic or sturdy commoner variety.

The widening of the American consumer and business horizon to a world view is expanding direct foreign investment on the one hand, and changing the relationship between national income and imports on the other. Direct foreign investment is being undertaken by an increasing number of companies, partly as a response to particular developments, such as the European Common Market, now underway, but partly simply as a reaction to profitable business opportunities wherever they take place. Manufacturing abroad will increasingly substitute for exports, and may give rise, along with foreign mining and drilling, to increased imports. Earnings on foreign investment will partly displace lost exports and offset increased imports. Since trade figures are published monthly on a fairly up-to-date basis, while figures for earnings on foreign investments are estimated only quarterly and with a long delay, there is the possibility that the public will pay undue attention to the changes in merchandise trade to the neglect of the partially offsetting gains in foreign earnings.

Economists have long been predicting an increase in the percentage of national income spent on imports from the 3½ per cent figure to which it had fallen in the early 1950's from 7 per cent at the end of the last century. The expected force was the increased need to go abroad for raw materials. But if the American consumer becomes more cosmopolitan, and more interested in foreign goods, whether cheaper or different, this increase in the propensity to import may work out in considerable degree through manufactures.

The closing of the technological gap between the rest of the world and the United States also produces a fundamental change. For the last 80 years much of the buoyancy in American exports was due to technological innovations, whether in farm machinery and electrical equipment in the first decade of the century, automobiles and radio in the 1920's, high-speed printing and construction machinery in the 1930's and 1940's, or chemical specialties, pharmaceuticals, and air-conditioning equipment, currently. Inventions occurred everywhere but many of them, like radio and automobiles, were brought to quantity production first in this country. Foreign consumers bought them eagerly, and were prepared to

162

spend in excess of their income. A considerable part of the so-called dollar shortage seems to have been due to continuous innovation on the part of American industry. As foreign countries learned to imitate one product, a new technological gap was opened up in another.

This technological gap is no longer so one-sidedly in favor of the United States. It continues in some fields — chemical specialties as just mentioned, certain branches of electronic and computation machinery. But in other fields, it has been closed or even opened up in reverse. In heavy electrical equipment, airplane engines, automobile design, European innovation proceeds faster than American, and U.S. producers seem ponderous — slow to make decisions, and far from daring — in their attempts at imitation. Japanese imitation of the transistor radio, on the other hand, was of lightning speed.

These two factors — the widening of the U.S. consumer and producer horizon to the world level, and the closing of the technological gap between the United States and foreign producers — portend a fundamental change in the long-term balance of payments position of the United States, on top of the short-run factors which have made for the recent loss of gold and dollars to foreigners. Let me now consider their implications for U.S. policies, domestic and foreign.

In the first place, it is important to emphasize that much of what has taken place so far is highly satisfactory. The superficial redistribution of world gold and dollar reserves places the international financial and trading position in much better balance; and the underlying changes in world reconstruction, U.S. interest in foreign production, and sharing of technological leadership in Europe make it less likely that serious imbalances will occur vis-à-vis Europe and Japan. (The position is not so satisfactory with regard to the producers of primary products.) The initial gloomy forebodings about the dollar and the speculative attacks on it from Zurich, Frankfurt, and Hamburg have given way to a realistic appraisal of the position in most quarters. A mild readjustment is required in the position of the dollar, and the United States can no longer order its policies in complete disregard of their effects on its international economic position. But while the readjustment needed is in process, it is important not to push the panic button, or to alter fundamental policies in the U.S. interest. In particular, negatively:

> There is no need to contemplate devaluation of the dollar, or, along with other countries, an increase in the price of gold.
>
> The position is not so serious that the United States should alter its position on foreign aid, beyond attempting to redistribute a part of the burden to Europe and Japan.
>
> While it is important to restrain inflation for its own sake and for the balance of payments position, there is no need to adopt strongly deflationary policies which would inhibit economic expansion or create unemployment.

Much of the present weakness of the dollar is self-correcting. Insofar as imports represent inventory accumulations, they are borrowed from the future and will decline. Balance-of-payments buoyancy in Europe is leading to continued relaxation of import restrictions against U.S. manufactures. Continued recovery in Europe will lift U.S. exports and limit the supplies of goods available for sale here. Moreover, on a longer run basis, the "natural" remedy of higher wages and costs in Europe can be relied upon to work in the right direction. American investors attempting to construct facilities in Europe are finding it difficult to obtain labor in the best locations in the Low Countries, France, and Britain. Employment is full, and expansion can only come about with higher wages designed to move workers from, say, southern France to Paris (where housing is lacking), or from the textile regions of western Belgium to the favored locations between Brussels and Antwerp. In the last several years much of the increase in income from increased technological efficiency, on the Continent, has gone into further investment. But tight employment conditions, except perhaps in Italy, seem likely to correct this in favor of consumption.

Another change which will automatically redress the position is the higher interest rates. These have already cut down the floating of new bonds for foreign account, and renewed foreign interest in New York balances. Tight money may also cut down the availability of funds for foreign direct investment and make the remission of foreign earnings home as dividends more attractive.

There is very little danger from a withdrawal of foreign funds in the United States. It makes no sense to net the $16 billion of foreign funds in this country against the $20 billion gold stock. No other country calculates its reserves net of liabilities, rather than gross, nor does any bank. There is no problem if private owners of funds wish to withdraw them. These have $8 billion, and even if the present rate of loss were to continue for 3 or more years, as I do not think it will, this drain could be met. Foreign central banks which own balances in this country are presumably immune from panic. They have a responsibility to world financial stability as well as to their national interest, and they can hardly fail to bear in mind the action taken by the United States in such measures as the Marshall plan to the ends of international reconstruction and stability. Nevertheless, the Netherlands Bank lost heavily in the devaluation of sterling in 1931; and there were other central banks which speculated against gold in the "gold scare" of April 1937. No public discussions should take place on these issues, but I assume that the Federal Reserve System has reassured itself of the steadiness of its central-bank depositors. It is entirely appropriate for them to convert further additions of reserves into gold, but it would seem undesirable for them to go far suddenly to convert existing balances. To limit their risk, I would think it appropriate for the Treasury to issue them informally exchange guarantees against any loss from devaluation. These would ultimately have to be made good by Congressional action, which could not be guaranteed in advance and should not be the subject of a long debate now.

Over the longer run, the distribution of the burdens of the leadership between the United States and the rest of the free world may have to shift. European countries are beginning to talk about embarking on programs of aid to underdeveloped countries. So long as U.S. aid and investment substantially exceed the current-account surplus of this country, and the current-account surplus of European countries is larger than their investment and aid, there is a case for shifting the present distribution of aid before undertaking any enlargement of it. The same holds true in the military field, both in NATO and in non-European parts of the world where this country has been bearing a disproportionate share of defense costs. It is beginning to be time to reverse the movement of piling financial responsibility for the foreign policies of the free world largely on the United States.

The United States must continue to exercise leadership in foreign affairs. I am not urging a withdrawal to isolationism, nor an attack on foreign aid. Moreover, we can adopt any level of foreign aid

165

we need for the sake of foreign policy, so long as we recognize the implications of such a level for taxes or other expenditure. It is not true that foreign aid, or any other policy, will make this country bankrupt. A narrower international margin means only that we can no longer will the ends and pay for them out of our reserves. If we will the ends, we must likewise will the means.

There is an important implication of our new international position for wages and price policy. Competition in transport and a low tariff policy imply that there are limits to which a particular industry can raise wages and prices. In steel, this limit has pretty well been reached under conditions where Europe has excess capacity. But this does not lead to the conclusion that wages cannot go higher. The implication is that wages must be geared to productivity, and to wages and production in other countries. In the matter of productivity, management has a responsibility for maintaining investment in cost-reducing equipment, and innovation in new products. I hesitate to speak to the complex steel situation because of lack of information. But generally speaking, it seems inappropriate for management to blame imports on wages, or labor to ascribe them to administered pricing or a loss of innovational leadership. Either or both may be true, but to focus attention on the "blame" for imports is likely to lead quickly to the remedy of higher tariffs or quotas. The appropriate answer is rather more productivity, including new cost reductions and new useful products.

It is impossible then to ignore the international implications of U.S. domestic economic policy, and there are a few steps which we ought to take in the more equitable sharing with Europe of the burdens of military defense and aid for economic development. There is no hurry to take action along these lines, but a prudent administration would not put them off. At the same time the international position of the United States is no excuse for failing to take any action which is important in its own right — action to correct internal inequities, to insure growth or limit unemployment. It means rather that in taking such action we must now for the first time bear in mind the position abroad, and possibly, where this sets limits to unilateral, one-sided action, we must take complementary steps to protect the balance of payments at the same time that we carry out those things needed to preserve this country as a vigorous and growing nation.

166

CHAPTER ELEVEN

*INTERNATIONAL LIQUIDITY**

Emphasis on Need to Aid Foreign Exchange Reserves Queried

To the Editor of The New York Times:

Permit me to express a minority view regarding the almost universally recognized need to increase international monetary liquidity.

This need was expressed this year initially in January by Sir Oliver Franks, the former British Ambassador to the United States and now chairman of Lloyds Bank in London. Since then it has been discussed by *The Economist* of May 3, indecisively in the June *Fortune,* and in commencement speeches by Dean Acheson, Adlai Stevenson, and Deputy Under Secretary of State Dillon. Most recently it was brought up by Prime Minister Macmillan in his talks with President Eisenhower.

According to your news columns, the result of these talks has been agreement to present specific proposals to the September meeting of the governors of the International Bank and the International Monetary Fund.

The requirement for increased international liquidity is found in a comparison of the present position with that of 1937. World monetary gold then amounted to $25 billion; world trade for that year to $27 billion. Today monetary gold has increased to $38 billion, but world trade for 1957 ran at $107 billion.

Lendable Funds

The picture is somewhat altered for the better if one takes dollars and sterling held in central-bank reserves in addition to gold, but worsened if one excludes Germany and the United States, which own $27.5 billion of the world's total. Another indication of tight-

* Letter to *The New York Times*, June 25, 1958.

ness is found in the fact that the lendable funds of the International Monetary Fund, established at Bretton Woods, amounted in early 1958 to only $750 million.

These figures, however, are misleading. Comparison should run not to 1937, when world trade was deeply depressed, but to a period of prosperity.

The liquidity ratio is higher today than in 1928, and much higher than in 1913. More important, it has improved every year since the devaluation of sterling, except for the period from September, 1956, to September, 1957. Since September, 1957, moreover, British reserves have gained $1.2 billion. Proportional gains have been registered by every other country in Europe except France and Sweden. When Britain releases her stand-by credit at the fund, $750 million more will be available in this organization.

Underdeveloped countries need resources for investment, not liquid resources to be held idle as reserves. There are, to be sure, some problems of distribution in reserves, particularly affecting the United States and Germany, although United States gold reserves have declined $1.2 billion since January.

Economic Development

The current surge of interest in increasing world liquidity is the result in my judgment largely of frustration. The important international economic problems — to make more resources available to developing countries in ways which insure their effective use, and the stabilization of commodity prices — are making slow or no progress. The task of holding the line on the renewal of the Reciprocal Trade Agreements Act is a largely negative operation.

Nor is the frustration entirely economic. Statesmen have turned to economic problems largely in desperation. Baffled in their attempts to devise a constructive approach directly to their political difficulties, they seek refuge in economic solutions even for synthetic problems. The shoe should be on the other foot — finding political solutions to economic problems.

There are, then, enough international economic problems — the development of underdeveloped areas, the stabilization of primary product prices, correction of the French balance of payments, funding of the German surplus, etc. — without creating more. The world has coped effectively with the exchange crises of 1956 and

168

1957. It would be moderately useful to expand the lending powers of the International Monetary Fund, but this should not be elevated into a major international concern.

Cambridge, Mass., June 19, 1958.

CHAPTER TWELVE

A SUPERABUNDANCE OF
INTERNATIONAL CYCLICAL MODELS*

It is healthy at this moment of comparative world economic stability to investigate the international business cycle. "In time of peace, prepare for war." Moreover, the mystery of 1953–1954 — why Europe's balance of payments was unaffected by the 1953 business recession in the United States after responding so convulsively to 1948–1949 and 1937–1938, to say nothing of 1929–1932 — cannot be regarded as completely solved.

Yet reflection suggests that much attention to international-business-cycle problems would be wasted. Even if we thought that the international-business-cycle problem were pressing, and understood 1953–1954, one could do little to prepare for the future. There are too many possibilities.

This paper may perhaps make a modest contribution to the subject if it catalogues the superabundance of international cyclical models to demonstrate what there is to choose from. The diagnosis, when the time comes, evidently depends upon then-existing circumstances. In advance, all one can say is that anything can happen.

The emphasis is on the impact of the business cycle in one country, on the balance of payments of others. This is not the only possible object of examination. One could focus on the effect of one country's business fluctuations on activity abroad, which is not quite the same thing. But most of the impact goes through the balance of payments, on which significant questions of policy hang.

* The English original of "Une Surabondance des Modèles des Fluctuations Cycliques Internationales," *Revue Economique*, No. 6, November 1957, pp. 927–938 (submitted June, 1957).

The writer acknowledges with thanks the assistance of R. C. Malley, who plowed a much wider statistical field than was ultimately planted.

The balance of payments is the first question for study. It may be further than it is possible to go.

Income and Income Elasticity of Demand for Imports

We start with simple assumptions under which prices are constant and there are no autonomous movements of capital. In these conditions, business cycles produce balance-of-payments disturbance because of differences in amplitude of the domestic movement of income, because of lack of synchronization of cycles internationally, or because of differing income elasticities of demand for imports. Let us assume two countries, A which generally experiences the balance-of-payments surplus, and B with the deficit. In depression, A's surplus may be explained by the fact that its fall in business occurred before B's or went deeper; or, if the movements of business were synchronous and of equal amplitude, because it had a higher income elasticity of demand for imports. The balance-of-payments surplus (and deficit), it need not be stated, is financed by induced capital movements. In prosperity, A has a surplus because its improvement in business is slower, or less extensive, or because its income elasticity of demand for imports is smaller than B's.

The autonomous change in spending in A or B is communicated to the other through the multiplier. Leaving out accelerators and governmental countercyclical stabilizers, the effect of a decrease in income in A will be to lower income in B. The higher the marginal propensity to save in B in response to a given decrease in A's income, the smaller the multiplier, the smaller B's income change, and the larger B's balance-of-payments deficit. Given accelerators, an increase in income in A can result in a larger increase in B, and hence a deficit; or a decrease in B can be communicated in a wider range to A and produce A's surplus because of its depth of amplitude of income in depression.

The accelerator is not the only possible asymmetry in this simplified model. Income elasticities of demand for imports may be higher in A for decreases in income than for increases, and accentuate the surplus; or higher in prosperity than in depression (demonstration effect) and enhance B's deficit. Or the movement of income may be asymmetrical: A may be deflation-prone and tend to go deeper into depressions but to expand less in periods of prosperity,

171

while B is inflation-prone and hence has a wider amplitude of income change in prosperity and a smaller one in recession. The conditions which could produce these types of behavior would include, for A, a high level of accumulated capital, permitting substantial dissaving and limiting the demand for new capital; and for B, little accumulated capital plus a determination to close the technological gap between the rest of the world and itself.

Even without price change or autonomous capital movement, a variety of possible circumstances can produce balance-of-payments disequilibrium from a change in income in one country or another.

Autonomous Capital Movements

Before introducing prices, it may be useful to permit autonomous movements of capital. Here, rather than ring the changes on possible permutations and combinations, it suffices to indicate two major historical patterns, which are exact opposites.

In the period up to 1913, movements of long-term capital from Britain were negatively correlated with the business cycle at home. The matter is complex, and some nice distinctions turn on fine questions such as whether ships are included with domestic or foreign investment, but in general, according to Cairncross, foreign investment picked up when domestic investment declined, and vice versa.

There was, however, some positive correlation at the turning points. Revival would start in both foreign and domestic investment, or both would turn down together. Over longer periods of the cycle, however, foreign and domestic investment were linked through supply: more for one meant less for the other.

In the interwar period, on the contrary, foreign and domestic investment were positively correlated during the cycle as a whole, although at some turning points such as 1928 and 1930, they moved in opposite directions. Investment prospects for overseas countries improved as income in the United States rose and with it United States demand for raw-material imports. The demand for foreign loans then moved with domestic investment. Foreign and domestic investment were connected through demand.

No clear pattern of long-term international investment has emerged in the postwar period. For one thing, business cycles have

172

been limited, with little fluctuation taking place about the rising trend in long-term investment. For another, foreign investment itself has been subject to few systematic forces of a business-cycle nature.

Terms of Trade

When we introduce prices into the analysis, the degrees of freedom increase manifold. We can run the main connections between prices and the cycle through domestic business activity: autonomous changes in domestic spending give rise to price changes which, along with income, produce an impact on the balance of payments. Or the price changes can connect to the balance of payments through capital movements. Or the business cycle can be started by movements of international prices.

Let us start with links between the balance of payments and price changes. Several writers dealing with the period prior to 1914 have concluded that cyclical capital movements brought about cyclical changes in the terms of trade. These may have been caused by the exigencies of the transfer process. A capital outflow from A turned A's terms of trade adverse to enable it to develop the necessary balance-of-payments surplus to achieve effective capital transfer. Or the same phenomena can be explained on other grounds: the capital transfer led to an increase in investment in the borrowing country, B, which, given its relative supply inelasticity, gave rise to a movement of prices adverse to A. Or instead of the capital movement causing the price change, the causation may have run the other way: periods of intensive investment activity in overseas countries which brought about price increases uncovered profit opportunities which capital movements rushed in to take advantage of. The change in terms of trade caused the capital movement, not the other way.

Or still the third possibility: the change in the terms of trade may cause the business cycle. Hilgerdt has suggested that improvements in the United States terms of trade in 1924 and 1927 lowered costs without changing prices, widened profit margins, and hence led to increased investment and expansion of income.

Changing Prices

Given the change in the terms of trade, however stimulated, changing prices associated with the business cycle can produce a variety of balance-of-payments effects, depending upon differences in the amplitude of the price movements, differences in timing, or differences in price elasticity. It is tempting to suggest that this is exactly analogous to changes in income where the balance-of-payments result is related to amplitude and synchronization of income and income elasticity. But the analogy is misleading. Price elasticities are more complex than income elasticities. It is easier to allow incomes to change with prices unaltered, than the reverse. Every substantial price change has an income effect felt in the balance of payments, as well as its impact through substitution of domestic for foreign purchases and vice versa. And the nature of the income effect, with its appropriate elasticities of demand for imports and savings, cannot be inferred from the partial-equilibrium price elasticities.

Suppose A's price rises in prosperity because of rising world income and relative short-run elasticity of supply for A's products. One needs to know first whether the price rise was caused by a shift in demand or in the supply schedule. The pre-1913 model presupposed that cycles in Britain and outlying parts of the world economy were either opposed, or that the amplitude was wider in the outlying areas than in Britain. The interwar model supposed wider fluctuations in developed countries than in primary producers, at least during depression.

Suppose that the rise in A's prices is due to a shift in the supply schedule, i.e., an increase in costs, or domestic inflation. The impact on the balance of payments turns, in the first instance, on the elasticity of demand. If demand is inelastic, exports rise; if unit-elastic, exports are unchanged; if elastic, exports decline. With relatively full employment in developed countries, the demand for primary products is apt to be inelastic with respect to price increases, though not necessarily to decreases. Let us assume that this will improve A's balance of payments. The income effect of the expansion of exports operates in the opposite direction; so does the increase in money expenditure which led to the rise in prices. If the rise in income in the export sector leads to increased profits and hence investment, and increased tax receipts and hence government spending, as Wallich has suggested, the net long-run effect may turn the balance of payments adverse.

Where price changes come about through changes in domestic

investment, the income and the price changes will worsen the balance of payments if foreign demands are elastic with respect to price, but work in opposite directions if inelastic. Where the initial change leading to the price increase is a shift in foreign spending, there is a further beneficial effect, but the net outcome is still uncertain.

Complaint has been heard from underdeveloped countries that they lose from adverse terms of trade in depression, and are prevented from retaining the benefits of rising prices in prosperity because of the inflationary bias to their economies set off by profits.

The contrary complaint has been voiced by representatives of developed countries: that they lose from the terms-of-trade effect in prosperity and from the loss of their customers' incomes in depression.

But there are many other possible combinations. Suppose a demand for imports (such as food) highly inelastic with respect both to income and price. World depression may so improve the terms of trade for such a country that its spending spills over into domestic investment and enables it to fend off depression through a domestic boom. This is the British 1932 to 1938 pattern: big terms of trade effect helping; smaller income-effect hindering to a lesser degree.

Types of Booms

I am not yet content. It is insufficient to combine incomes, prices, capital movements, income elasticities, price elasticities, and amplitudes, even permitting a difference between their values in prosperity and depression, as if these parameters were immutable and fixed. The income elasticities, in particular, will differ from boom to boom, depending upon its nature and in particular upon the nature of the underlying investment cycle. A related factor of vital significance is the character of commodity speculation, if any, together with speculation in foreign exchange.

For model building purposes, let us suppose that there are four main types of investment cycles — in housing, with a duration of 18 years; in industrial construction and equipment, 8 or 9 years; in inventories, 39 months; and consumer purchasing (arbitrary and depending upon innovations, quixotic taste changes, demonstration effect, and replacement cycles). The differences in timing we have

175

already discussed. But in any one period of time, a 10 per cent increase in income produced by an expansion of each type of investment, taken separately, will have a different size of impact on the balance of payments.

In the United States, the income elasticity of demand for imports may be taken to be low for housing booms and slumps, low for industrial construction and equipment cycles, very high for inventory cycles in raw materials, low for cycles led by consumption.

These values will not be identical for every type of country. In Britain, for example, housing is closely geared to imports through timber; in France, imports respond rather sharply to changes in industrial investment; in Germany, a consumer-led cycle, if one can imagine it there, would probably produce a high-income elasticity.

It may be argued that these distinctions are overdrawn, and that the distinction in the income elasticity of the initial round of spending is quickly lost to view as the injections of new spending spread through the economy. The point can undoubtedly be overstressed. But where there are high marginal propensities to import and to save, multipliers are low and a substantial amount of the total effect is produced by the first round of spending.

The 1929–1932 depression in the United States involved sharp simultaneous declines in all forms of investment. By 1936–1937 long-term investment in housing and business equipment had not recovered very far and could not therefore relapse. The period 1935 to September 1937 produced an inventory boom, as stocks were accumulated in fear of higher costs. This was voluntary inventory investment, with a high-income elasticity of demand for imports in the United States. Involuntary inventory accumulation in finished goods in the depression phase of a cycle, when consumers stop buying as in durable goods in 1956, presents, of course, a different picture. Imports, if anything, fall, as production slows down. But unless the consumer cutback induces speculative fears of a decline of commodity prices, the income elasticity of demand for imports will be lower than in periods of positive inventory accumulation and decumulation.

It is difficult to demonstrate these points. The data on inventories in the United States are just beginning to reach a useful state

176

and do not extend to the early period. National-income data are hardly comparable for all the periods, and so on. But it may be suggestive if we furnish one statistical insight in a table which sets out the percentage declines in index numbers of quantity, unit value, and value of imports for consumption in the United States by economic classes, for the three recessions, 1937–1938, 1948–1949 and 1953–1954, measuring in all cases from the highest quarterly average to the subsequent lowest. Wider, but more erratic, declines would be obtained with the monthly data.

These declines in trade may be compared with the change in income and production similarly calculated.

A number of striking differences in behavior of imports by classes are apparent. In 1937–1938 and again in 1948–1949 all classes fell roughly in the same order of magnitude in quantity, although divergent behavior in prices (unit value) resulted in differing changes in value relatives. In 1953–1954, however, the decline in crude materials was far smaller relative to the other classes of materials, in quantity and value. In 1937–1938 the quantity changes in crude materials were the same as in semi-manufactures; in 1948–1949, they were double; in 1953–1954, half.

Perhaps the major aberration, however, is in crude foodstuffs in 1953–1954. This was mainly influenced by coffee, and is hardly related to the business cycle at all. The decline occurred not in 1953 but entirely in 1954. Unit values rose 32 per cent between the first quarter of 1948 and the second quarter of 1949, and quantities finally responded to price, not income, by declining. After the fall of price in the second half of 1954, quantity rose. The substantial decline in the value of coffee imports, which had a large impact on the total value of imports, was principally unrelated to the cycle.

The interaction of quarterly averages of quantity, unit value, and value can be seen more clearly from a final table which indicates timing. Table 3 specifies the quarters of the separate two-year periods in which first highs and then subsequent lows were recorded. The four quarters of the first year are numbered 1–4 and those of the second 5–8.

What is impressive now is that in all classes but manufactured foodstuffs in 1936–1937 the quantity downturn preceded the unit

Table 1. Percentage Decline in Index Numbers of Imports for Consumption by Classes in Three Separate Recessions, Measured from High to Subsequent Low in Quarterly Averages

	1937–1938			1948–1949			1953–1954		
	Quantity	Unit Value	Value	Quantity	Unit Value	Value	Quantity	Unit Value	Value
Crude Materials	44	23	55	25	12	27	13	6	15
Crude Foodstuffs	44	22	51	18	12	22	50	5	41
Manufactured Foodstuffs	37	20	43	16	7	16	27	4	32
Semimanufactures	44	14	48	15	20	30	28	6	31
Finished Manufactures	36	3	31	17	3	19	13	1	13
Total Imports	40	14	46	13	9	20	17	1	14

1937–1938 and 1948–1949 calculated from U.S. Department of Commerce, *Foreign Trade of the United States, 1936–1939* (Washington: Government Printing Office, 1951), Table 14; 1953–1954 calculated from U.S. Department of Commerce, *Quarterly Summary of Foreign Commerce of the United States*, Cumulative Year-to-Date, January–December 1953, and January–December 1954.

Table 2. Percentage Decline from Highest Quarter to Subsequent Low

	1936–1937	1948–1949	1953–1954
National Income	11*	9	3
Industrial Production	34	13	10

* Income Payments.

Source: Survey of Current Business, Statistical Supplements; Federal Reserve Bulletin.

value. This is demand at work. In 1948–1949, quantity preceded in two cases, and followed in three. The two cases where it preceded were crude materials and semimanufactures, where inventory accumulation and decumulation play significant roles. In 1936–1937 all the import indices preceded the downturn of income payments and of industrial production. In 1948–1949 crude materials and semimanufactures turned down before income and production, but both foodstuffs and manufactures simultaneously with or after. In 1953–1954, on the other hand, price declines — very moderate, as Table 1 shows — preceded the recession in quantity, and these were simultaneous with, rather than preceding, the decline in income and industrial output.

These indicia can be no more than suggestive. They support the view of Gertrud Lovasy,[1] that a significant difference between 1953–1954 on the one hand, and 1948–1949 and 1937–1938 on the other, was that prices did not fall in the later period because they had already fallen or were still in course of gently easing. They also are consonant with the findings of H. K. Zassenhaus,[2] that the area impact of the several recessions were different: 1937–1938 and 1948–1949 were hard on the sterling area (because of adverse speculation in raw materials); 1953–1954 was easy for sterling, more punishing to Canada and Latin America. But, while these data have no relevance to one major finding of the other staff member of the International Monetary Fund to study the 1953–1954 experience, J. J. Polak,[3] which deals with other sources of supply of dollars than imports, it does contravene his view that when United States business activity falls, the volume of imports declines by the same amount and value 1½ times as much. The volume and value of imports will behave very differently depending upon the nature of the cycle, and these differences may have fundamental significance for the impact of United States cycles on other countries.

179

EUROPE AND THE DOLLAR

Table 3. Timing of Declines in Import Relatives in Three Depressions (First number represents high quarter, second, low, where numbers 1 through 8 are successive quarters of the two years specified)

	1936–1937			1948–1949			1953–1954		
	Quantity	Unit Value	Value	Quantity	Unit Value	Value	Quantity	Unit Value	Value
Crude Materials	1–6	2–7	2–6	1–7	3–8	1–7	2–9	1–7	1–8
Crude Foodstuffs	1–4	2–8	1–6	5–7	3–6	4–7	5–7	6–8	5–7
Manufactured Foodstuffs	2–5	1–8	2–5	6–8	2–6	3–8	6–8	3–5	6–8
Semimanufactures	1–6	4–8	2–6	1–6	5–8	5–7	2–5	1–6	2–5
Finished Manufactures	2–6	6–8	3–6	4–7	2–8	4–7	2–5	4–5	2–5
Total Imports	2–6	2–7	2–6	4–7	3–8	4–7	2–7	6–8	2–7
				Other Timing					
National Income	3–8			4–8			2–4		
FRB Industrial Production	2–6			4–7			2–6 or 7		

This is by no means the whole story on the difference between 1953–1954 and earlier experience. In addition to speculation in stocks, there was speculation in foreign exchange, directly in 1937–1938; through the "leads-and-lags" in 1948–1949. Such speculation was encouraged by lack of European reserves and overvaluation in the two earlier periods, discouraged by the removal of these weaknesses in the later incident. The period 1953–1954 found Europe stronger in production, as well as reserves, and in alternative sources of supply. Nor was the only change in Europe. The speed of recovery from 1949 under built-in stabilizers and governmental policy correctly argued that recession would not be deep.

It is one thing to explain events in history, another to forecast their path in the future. At the moment, we have too many models.

Notes

[1] Gertrud Lovasy, "Prices of Raw Materials in the 1953–1954 U.S. Recession," *Staff Papers*, February 1957, pp. 47–73.

[2] Herbert K. Zassenhaus, "Direct Effects of a United States Recession on Imports: Expectations and Events," *Review of Economics and Statistics,* August 1955, pp. 231–255.

[3] J. J. Polak, "The Repercussion of Economic Fluctuations in the United States on Other Parts of the World," *Staff Papers*, August 1956, pp. 279–283.

CHAPTER THIRTEEN

BALANCE-OF-PAYMENTS SYMMETRY AND THE DOLLAR*

I

Current economic discussion has failed to evolve an agreed position on the causes of the continued surplus in the current account of the United States balance of payments. Indeed, there is some dispute as to whether this balance of payments is still appropriately regarded as in surplus. If one eliminates special exports, the view is expressed, credits and debits will be approximately in balance without regard to special aid. But to this it must be replied, first, that there remain a variety of special imports as well, such as offshore procurement and occupation expenditures of dollars, which could also be eliminated and increase the surplus. Second, and more significant, is the intensity of the restrictions in other countries against dollar expenditures. These testify to the fact that authorities abroad believe that the demand for dollars at existing prices exceeds the supply. For the purpose of this discussion, it is assumed that they are correct in this thought.

The present article is not designed to resolve the differences between those who believe a shortage of dollars exists and those who think either that it does not or that it would not if monetary authorities behaved rationally. Its purpose is far more limited. It is confined to an exploration of one aspect of the logical differences between the two main positions. In particular, it is proposed to examine the critical distinctions between what may be called the "conventional" view that the current-account surplus of the United States is due to relative inflation outside that country, or to currency overvaluation, and the heretical notion advanced with increasing

* English original of "L'Asymétrie de la balance des paiements et la problème du dollar," *Revue Economique*, March 1954, pp.166–189.

182

frequency that the rest of the world is committed to dollar deficits —
though of varying size and with occasional smaller surpluses —
whatever the course of its monetary and exchange policies, and
whatever the direction of change in the income of the United
States. The question, that is, is to what extent are events in the
United States and in other countries symmetrical or asymmetrical
in their impact on balances of payments.

If the dollar shortage is due to inflation abroad, it can be corrected by deflation abroad or by inflation in the United States. If
it is due to currency overvaluation, it can be corrected by devaluation, though we may rule out currency appreciation in the United
States at this stage of the discussion as outside the realm of practical consideration. If, on the other hand, the dollar shortage has
its roots in other more deep-seated factors, it may persist, or even
increase, whether the rest of the world inflates or tries to deflate —
still allowing some scope for changes in its size — or whether the
United States deflates or tries to inflate. In particular, the view has
been advanced recently that the deficits of other countries are
likely to persist whether the United States enjoys prosperity or
depression. If this be the case, the balance of payments of other
countries may be said to respond asymmetrically to income changes
in the United States.

In what follows, it must be made clear that we are discussing not
partial, but full, equilibrium responses. This makes for considerable
difficulty, because of the wide number of variables which must be
considered, but it enables us to avoid a host of fallacies which lie
in wait for the unwary. Discussion of the dollar shortage abounds
in partial-equilibrium analysis, which leads to special explanations
and one-sided remedies. So widespread is this error that it may
be useful to furnish examples.

The vulgar or journalistic or politician's explanation of the dollar
shortage is that it is due to high tariffs in the United States. Now,
whatever the course of tariffs in that country in the last twenty
years, it cannot be denied that much in the way of reform remains
to be carried out. Lower rates of duty, simplification of customs
procedure (partially enacted into law), and freedom from fear of
sudden changes in duty such as inhere in the escape clause are
eminently desirable. But they have a minor role to play in the
question of disequilibrium. The slogan "trade not aid" is based on
a fallacy.

That this is so is provable by the most elementary exercise. Other countries have tariffs on goods from the United States, without thereby creating a scarcity of their own currency and an abundance of dollars. But the partial nature of the analysis is worth elaborating.

An increase in United States imports at a given level of income, i.e., an upward shift in the level of imports as a function of national income, will lower national income in the United States through the foreign-trade multiplier. This will produce a reduction in United States imports. The first change (increase) is due to a shift of the import schedule; the second (reduction) is due to a shift along the schedule. It is an error to concentrate on the first change and to ignore the second. Whether the first effect will be larger than the second, or smaller, depends upon a variety of factors, such as the marginal propensities to save, import, invest, and the repercussion on incomes and imports abroad. (Abroad, it may be observed, the initial autonomous increase in exports raises national income and leads to an induced increase in imports. If imports from the United States are income-elastic, the increased imports will come particularly from the United States.)

It has been said above that tariffs in the United States should be reduced, or even, with appropriate timing, eliminated. If this will not "cure" the dollar shortage, it will at least provide the most auspicious circumstances for attempting to effect a cure, paying attention to all relevant factors, and not merely to one. The difficulty, as with so many economic nostrums, is that the public and the politicians will be led to believe that the partial solution is a complete one. Other aspects will be neglected. The resultant failure to effect a cure will rightfully irritate and disillusion with the experts both public and politicians.

A series of other partial explanations and solutions may be equally dismissed. R. F. Harrod has maintained that the European dollar shortage would disappear if the price of gold were raised to the same relationship it bore to other prices in the late 1930's. The *Manchester Guardian* of April 13, 1953, stated that the greatest single cause of dollar shortage is the United States farm support program. A widely accepted view is that the dollar shortage of Europe has been caused by the shift in the terms of trade which has taken place since the war. None of this can be accepted; it is all partial analysis. We must examine not only the immediate impact of any change but also trace out its repercussions through the system. Too much faith in any one explanation or remedy is a consequence of the tendency to substitute partial for general explanations.[1] The analysis must proceed *mutatis mutandis,* not *ceteris paribus.*

The issue between those who believe that the balance of payments responds symmetrically and those who detect asymmetry has not been fully joined. Both groups appeal to the weight of authority and of the facts; frequently the scholarly and stimulating (if the two adjectives do not contradict one another) *Surveys* of the Economic Commission for Europe are cited to lend support to the argument. The "symmetrists" are impressed by the successes of Germany, the Netherlands, and to a lesser extent Italy and Britain in improving their balance-of-payments positions with doses of overbalanced budgets, dear money and a retreat from 100 per cent full employment. The "asymmetrists," on the other hand, point to the recurring crises in the world position in dollars in 1947, 1949, and 1951 and to the hard cores of persistent dollar deficit which remains within the over-all balances of such countries as the United Kingdom and Germany.

In any controversy sustained for an extended period, there is much to be said on both sides. Differences between opposing positions tend to be exaggerated for the sake of clarity, and as each side hesitates to concede too much until it is sure of winning concessions of equal importance from the other. There can be no doubt that the payments difficulties of France, Sweden, and Finland have inflation and overvaluation as proximate causes, even if these in turn are symptoms of deeper forces. Devaluation, coupled with control of inflation (if this were possible), would go far to limit their deficits. Moreover, the European-wide dollar deficits of 1947 and 1948 have been reduced to very much smaller proportions, to such an extent, in fact, that one may feel confident that they can be eliminated with the aid of import and exchange controls. Whether convertibility, liberalization, and balance-of-payments balance can be achieved, however, remains a question. On the other hand, the 1951 experience was discouraging, with its origin in the 1950 Korean raw-material boom which was heralded at the time as liquidating the dollar shortage. Inflation in the United States, com-

185

bined with stockpiling and inventory accumulation, briefly corrected the dollar scarcity and then led to a greater one.

But our interest in what follows is less in the facts or in recommendations as to convertibility than in the logic of the argument. The conventional view which favors deflation and devaluation appears to assume that the impact of other countries on the United States, and of the United States on them, is symmetrical. Inflation abroad leads to United States surplus; inflation in the United States to United States deficit. The believers in persistent dollar shortage, on the other hand, appear to detect a fundamental asymmetry or asymmetries in the operation of the present-day international monetary system.

II

Let us examine first some of the asymmetrical views. Two, both of importance, may be referred to, one put forward by the distinguished Secretary-General of the Organisation for European Economic Cooperation; the other by the anonymous members of the Secretariat of the United Nations, which, on matters concerning economic development, frequently adopts unconventional and provocative views. Both positions may be illustrated by quotation:

M. MARJOLIN:[2] It is (therefore) most improbable that a depression starting in Europe would have serious consequences for the United States. But it is certain that even a minor depression in the United States would have far-reaching consequences for Europe. This happened in 1949, when a minor recession in the United States produced a fall in European exports which, for some countries, reached 40 or 50 per cent of their total exports to the United States. The situation is, in the case of inflation, the same in reverse. Inflation in the United States immediately results in a considerable increase in demand for imported raw materials. With the United States bidding up raw material prices, Western Europe is automatically forced to pay higher prices for the materials that she needs; consequently the internal price structure of the European countries starts moving upwards.

UN:[3] Longer cyclical movements in the terms of trade give broader scope to the play of inflationary effects of rising prices on the economy of primary producing countries while subsequent recessions magnify the deflationary effects of falling prices. In the absence of compensatory or unrelated variables, (footnote) primary producing countries are likely to suffer from both the recessions and the recoveries of industrial countries, without obtaining the full measure of real income gains that attend recovery in industrial economies.

Footnote: For example, a public investment programme of a compensatory character or large-scale private investment related to the development of natural resources.

The position sketched by M. Marjolin is really unclear. What happens to the terms of trade of Western Europe when the United States is depressed, and how much of an offset is this to the direct effect of loss of exports? This question was widely debated during the 1930's as regards the United Kingdom. The general conclusion emerged from that experience,[4] and is still generally regarded as valid by such authorities as *The Economist* that the loss from the decline in income abroad is greater than the gain from improved terms of trade.[5] If this relationship still holds today, what of the obverse? Why should not the gain from increased incomes of Western Europe's customers offset the loss in terms of trade from increased import prices? M. Marjolin has asserted that the system works asymmetrically, but he has not explained how.

The nature of the asymmetrical behavior in primary-producing countries is even more obscure. The writers of the tract, as one may characterize a document so filled with exhortation to action on the part of underdeveloped countries, are urging some kind of compensatory domestic investment policy. The analysis presumably supports the policy. But it is not clear what kind of compensatory investment policy is meant. If investment is expanded when exports are high, this will stabilize the balance of payments, but exacerbate fluctuations in national income. If, on the other hand, investment is undertaken when exports decline, stability is gained for domestic money income but the balance of payments deficit is accentuated.

Apart from this fundamental obscurity in the writers' point of view, the mechanism by which the underdeveloped countries lose both ways — in world prosperity and in world depression — is not described. It must differ from that of M. Marjolin for Western Europe, since the terms of trade behave differently in the business cycle in the two cases. For primary-producing countries, the terms of trade improve in prosperity and become unfavorable in depression; for Western Europe, the converse. The authors from whom we quote fail to make clear why favorable terms of trade are inflationary in the one case (primary producers) and unfavorable terms of trade in the other. The asymmetries inherent in their system are clear in neither case, but differ one from the other.

In addition, moreover, the asymmetries in each case differ from those of the United States. Whether the United States be regarded as a primary producer in international trade, because of its exports of wheat, cotton, and sporadically coal, or as an industrial country, its balance of payments can behave neither in the fashion described by the United Nations Secretariat nor like Western Europe, as interpreted by M. Marjolin. Whatever the behavior of the terms of trade, the underdeveloped countries, and Western Europe, according to these authors, have deficits in prosperity and depression alike. These deficits are not recorded with each other. They must therefore take place vis-à-vis the United States. Why the primary producers and Western Europe behave differently in their balance of payments from the United States — if this asymmetry in fact exists — is not explained.

III

Our dissatisfaction with the explanation of asymmetries in the behavior of the balance of payments thus far furnished us must not lead us to jump uncritically to the position that balances of payments behave symmetrically. This is a possibility. It may be further the most desirable operating hypothesis for national monetary authorities and for such an institution as the International Monetary Fund. But it does not follow that because some descriptions of asymmetrical behavior are unclear, the behavior in question is symmetrical.

While one may criticize the asymmetrists in logic for failing to explain the nature of their asymmetry, no such criticism is possible of the opposing point of view. Logic is all on the side of symmetry. The symmetrical position can be controverted only by the facts.

There are two ways to use the facts in weighing the symmetrical position. One is to try to form an over-all impression of the weight of the evidence as it bears on the major thesis. We have already suggested the futility of this procedure: both sides of the debate appeal to different selected facts, or even use different interpretations of the same facts. Facts, moreover, are not unambiguous; the cold hard facts are generally lukewarm and flaccid.

The alternative used here is to explore the logical implications of the symmetrical view and to see if there is not some point at which balance-of-payments difficulties become systematic, or some statements which even those who are generally "liberal" economists find difficulty in accepting, whether as description of the world, as prescription for policy, or as prediction of the future. To the extent that we can find logical implications of the symmetrical view which cannot be accepted, the symmetrical view may require modification.

If balance of payments in all countries behaves similarly, or if, as may be possible under the symmetrical position, the differences among them are random, it follows that

(*a*) The degree of dependence of one area on the other must be of the same general order of magnitude. In the first place, the ratio of exports to national income must not differ too widely so that changes in foreign imports have roughly the same initial impact on income. In the second, the marginal propensities to import and save on which depend the secondary repercussions on income arising through changes in exports or domestic expenditure, and the foreign repercussion which controls tertiary changes, must again be of comparable dimensions.

(*b*) The development of the national money income must not systematically differ between the United States and the rest of the world. This applies both in the business cycle, and in the secular long run. To limit ourselves to the former, by way of illustration, it follows that the United States is as likely to initiate inflations as primary producing countries or the mature countries of Western Europe, and that inflation is as likely to go as far in the United States as abroad, if not farther. Conversely, there can be no systematic differences in the susceptibility of the two areas to deflation, either in initiation or extent.

(*c*) Whatever the development of income, systematic differences in the demand of the two areas for each other's goods must be reversible. If the demand of primary producers for United States goods is highly income elastic, for example, it must be elastic both in periods of rising and falling income alike. In similar fashion, price elasticities must apply both to rising and falling prices.

(*d*) The incidence of innovations of a sort likely to spread internationally must be randomly distributed. The introduction of new goods or new methods of producing old goods which are likely to be adopted abroad must not be concentrated on balance either in the United States or in the rest of the world.

(*e*) The supply response of the United States and the rest of the world must not differ so as to produce disequilibrium. For example, in periods of rising prices, there must not be supply elasticity in agricultural production and coal in the United States, and supply inelasticity in Europe and the underdeveloped countries.

It is of course possible that systematic differences between the United States and the rest of the world in one of these respects may be offset by opposite differences in one or more of the others, to leave the system still fully symmetrical. While this sort of coincidence is possible, it is not likely. The various aspects of the economy listed — and especially (*a*) and (*b*) — are not unrelated. The forces making for systematic differences in one, if they exist, are likely to operate in the same, not the opposite, direction in another.

To list the logical requirements of a symmetrical system is enough to throw some doubt on the question of whether the real world behaves in this way. There can be little disagreement, for example, with Marjolin's statement that a depression in the United States is more important for Europe than a depression in Europe for the United States, which presupposes that the mutual dependence discussed in (*a*) is not in some sort of rough balance, as required by a symmetrical system. François Perroux especially has developed some fruitful ideas concerning the "dominance" of the United States, arising from the fact that the course of its economy influences other countries, while they have only a limited impact on it.[6]

But the symmetrists may not be daunted by this list. Let us put them then a question or two. Assuming that effective monetary and exchange policies rigorously applied succeed in curing the dollar deficit of the rest of the world to the point where special aid is eliminated and special restrictions on dollar imports are removed, starting from this equilibrium is it just as likely that the dollar will become superabundant as scarce? If it be agreed that United States economists and public servants have no greater wisdom and skill (respectively?) than those of other countries, will the United States have to be as careful to prevent balance-of-payments deficit as will the economists and administrators of other areas? Assuming some redistribution of the world's gold supply, will the directors of the International Monetary Fund be as likely to be called upon to supply the United States with sterling, pesos, francs, and piasters as the rest of the world with dollars?[7]

As we have indicated, the matter can hardly be resolved by appeals to the differing models of the international payments system, nor by "proving" from an infinity of facts that one model fits the facts of the world better than another. There are facts enough for both. But the logical postulates of the symmetrical model, made explicit, help to show how broad must be the framework of the economy it attempts to portray.

IV

If there are asymmetries in the international payments mechanism, as I think, some analysis of what they may be appears to be called for, to escape the melange of income and price relationships furnished us by the United Nations experts and M. Marjolin. I have tried in other connections to set out parts of the apparatus.[8] I trust I may be forgiven if I assemble these parts here briefly and fit them into some illuminating recent contributions by others. The whole will not furnish a complete and general statement of the position, which is too complex to lend itself to easy description. It may help the analysis to progress, however, to furnish a rapid resume of the present analysis.

1. An adult country (the United States in this instance) is subject to "secular stagnation," and underdeveloped and matured countries to "secular exhilaration or inflation," relative to each other. There need be nothing absolute about the deflation or the inflation. The crux is simply that at any one time the United States is deflated, and underdeveloped and Western European countries are inflated, *relative to one another*. The causes are to be found in the facts of savings and investment propensities in both groups of countries. In the United States, savings are high, when employment is relatively full, because income is high and because of institutions like corporate and personal ambition, life insurance, and mortgage amortization. In underdeveloped countries savings

191

are low because of the low level of income, and such savings as do accumulate due to skewed income distribution are unlikely to be made available inside the country as an offset to productive investment. In addition, of course, the cumulative inflationary path destroys the institutions which build savings. In matured countries, savings are relatively low because of redistribution of income in favor of consuming groups, and because of limits to the size to which entrepreneurs wish to see their concerns grow (in France, at least). Capital consumption is believed widespread among upper income groups in Britain who have maintained certain essentials of their standard of living — such as education — despite the sharp reduction in their income after tax.

Investment opportunities outside of the United States are those available in the United States plus the distance by which present capital facilities per capita in the United States exceed those abroad. This statement would need to be qualified by a number of considerations such as relative population growth. But the position is no longer that factor proportions differ sharply from country to country. Every country wants to use the technology of the country with the highest capital intensity, and short-run obstacles such as lack of complementary resources or adequately trained labor are not allowed to defeat it.

With savings smaller and investment opportunities larger than in the United States, the underdeveloped and the matured countries tend to be inflated relative to the United States, or what amounts to the same thing, the United States tends to be deflated relative to them. This is not to say, I repeat, that the United States is at all times deflated, or the other groups continuously in a state of inflation.

2. Given this long-term or secular position, from which of course there are exceptions, the short-run position emerges as follows: The United States is content to permit its balance of payments on current account to be in surplus, so far as the forces shaping its income are concerned. Income is in equilibrium where

Savings = Domestic Investment + Foreign Investment (positive)

The underdeveloped countries and the matured countries, in turn, find it easy to adapt to a balance of payments deficit on current account, for

192

Savings + Foreign Borrowing or Disinvestment = Domestic
Investment

When an underdeveloped country experiences an increase in exports which turns the foreign balance temporarily positive, national income is stimulated. If domestic investment is poised on the brink of an expansion, either in the export or in the domestic sector, the fillip to national income given by the expansion in exports may lift investment and income to the point where the positive balance is wiped out.

Conversely, when exports in the United States decrease, or imports increase, it can happen, though perhaps most economists would regard it as unlikely, that investment, poised on the brink of a downturn, is reduced in the export or import-competing sectors, or in the domestic sector, to leave the balance of payments still in surplus. There may be something, then, of a tendency for the underdeveloped and matured countries to overadjust in income to balance-of-payments surpluses, and underadjust to deficits; and for the United States, conversely, to overadjust to deficits and underadjust to deficits.

3. Connected with this question of saving is a factor which Ragnar Nurkse has recently brought into prominence in international economics, the demonstration effect.[9] The demonstration effect was developed by Duesenberry originally, to assist in explaining why the consumption function rises through time despite secular growth of income, when at any one time consumption falls as income increases. As people become aware of the elements of high standard consumption of others, their satisfaction with a given level of real income is reduced, and their consumption out of income increases. Nurkse attributes fundamental importance to the demonstration effect in international trade under modern conditions of widespread communication. In the nineteenth century, when the theory of international trade was formulated in its classic form, it was assumed that factor proportions, factor prices, and standards of living would differ from country to country — that they were in fact entirely unrelated. This is no longer the case; and an improvement in the standard of living of labor in the United States will reverberate abroad.

One way to handle the demonstration effect is, like Nurkse, to

193

relate it to savings in underdeveloped countries. Another is to suggest that it makes for an asymmetry between the income elasticities of demand in international trade between the underdeveloped and matured countries on the one hand, and the adult countries or country (the United States) on the other. If money incomes in the two groups of countries move in the same path, cyclical disequilibrium will be produced by different income elasticities. In prosperity, the country or countries with the higher income elasticity will have a deficit; in depression, a surplus. It requires a wider movement in income to achieve equilibrium, on the part of the country (class of countries) with higher income elasticities.

The demonstration effect may have further implications of asymmetry. An article with high-income elasticity in both directions, i.e., for income increases and income decreases, is a luxury. For it, income elasticity is symmetrical. But there are goods which start as luxuries and gradually become incorporated in the rising minimum standard of living. They are readily added to the standard of living and reluctantly dropped. They are income-elastic for increases in income, income-inelastic for income decreases. If a country should count a large number of these sorts of goods among its imports, an increase in income would send imports way up; a decrease in income would not produce much decline. This may further be a potential source of asymmetry and disequilibrium in world balances of payments.

It is of course possible that an asymmetry in income elasticity of demand can be offset by an opposite asymmetry of income development. A matured area like Western Europe can compensate for its highly elastic demand with respect to imports from the United States in prosperity by limiting the expansion of income during this phase of the cycle; and for its inelastic demand (with respect to income) in depression, by deflating further than the United States. For this to be accomplished in the face of a tendency for more inflation and less deflation, however, calls for strenuous and effective policies.

4. Thus far we have left price and the terms of trade out of account. This may be justified analytically, either by assuming that all prices are constant, as is usually done with national-income analysis, or by assuming price elasticities equal to unity so that whatever price changes occur in international trade have no effect on the outcome. But these assumptions cannot remain in force. The

194

difficulty arises, as is clear in the case of the Marjolin and United Nations quotations with which we began, in trying to integrate models with incomes and prices both variable.

It is hard to see any reason why prices or the terms of trade should behave asymmetrically. While not all primary products have flexible prices, nor are all prices of manufactured articles slow to change, the normal expectation is that primary products will move in a wider amplitude over the cycle than manufactures. Over a given cycle, and measuring from the average for the cycle, what is lost on the downside from low prices for the seller is gained in prosperity; and the same holds true in reverse for the buyer.

Some asymmetry might be introduced by elasticities of demand which differed for different phases of the business cycle. But this seems an unlikely pattern. For basic foodstuffs, the price elasticity is probably low; for nutritional foods, high. The price elasticity of raw materials is likely to be low, taking them as a whole. For the single small producer or country on a world market, it is of course far higher. Where a number of products compete, moreover, it is higher especially if time is allowed. The elasticities of manufactured products run over a wide gamut, but nothing suggests a likelihood of asymmetries.

An important difference may be made in the response to a price change by the speed with which it takes place. It is well known, of course, that the elasticity of demand and supply changes with the passage of time. As time is allowed for expectations to stabilize, consumers and producers will act in response to a change in relative prices, whereas in the short run they are not as likely to. But this is a somewhat different point. *The Economist*[10] recently noted that the 1953 improvement in the terms of trade of the United Kingdom had been peculiarly favorable because of the fact that it took place slowly. A sharp drop in import prices might be as beneficial to Britain as a low one, provided that the response abroad were the same; but the differences in speeds lead to wide differences in reaction of the countries whose exports are affected. When time is taken to adjust prices, the producers in the sectors affected can shift into other occupations, the standard of consumption of international goods can be modified slowly, and British exports are likely to be better sustained than if the decline in import prices had been precipitous. But it must be emphasized that these differences resulting from different rates of change are subtle and tricky, in their intimate connection with such difficult aspects of economics as anticipations, retaliation, and induced responses, and not much can be said about them with confidence.

It is nonetheless unlikely that the United Nations Secretariat is right in thinking that the difficulty with rising export prices occurs when they continue for long periods of time. It is true that induced responses tend to eat up the benefits of rising export prices, and, if the monetary mechanism of the country decrees, may more than eat it up. But this is a fault of the monetary mechanism and not of the relation between time and export prices. A rise in export prices in the short run will improve the balance-of-payments position and the state of exchange reserves, but only in ways which cannot be sustained beyond the partial equilibrium stage. The longer the terms of trade are favorable, the greater the opportunity, which may not be taken advantage of, to reap benefits in consumption, investment, and balance of payments at the same time.

While then there may be asymmetries in the responses of price movements of similar amplitude compressed into different time spans, it is difficult to find similar asymmetries between responses to rising and falling prices as such. Any asymmetrical monetary or financial response is likely to have its roots in the asymmetrical posture of the financial position. If rising import prices are inflationary, falling import prices should be deflationary, unless the monetary and fiscal system are so poised that any disturbance to an unstable equilibrium must result in inflation.

5. An interesting contribution to the theory of disequilibrium related to prices has recently been put forward by Professor Hicks.[11] Following up a point of J. H. Williams, his thesis is concerned with the effects of differential rates of productivity on the terms of trade and accordingly on equilibrium. In the nineteenth century, he claims, increases in productivity occurred in Britain at a faster rate than elsewhere, but in export lines. This resulted in an increase in the supply of exports and a reduction in their price. Britain's net barter terms of trade were reduced, though not necessarily its double factoral terms of trade, and other countries were enabled to increase their standards of living without increasing their productivity, in the first instance, and without deranging their balances of payments. The present difficulty, Professor Hicks contends, is

that productivity improvements in the United States are import-biased. They thus tend to substitute domestic production for imports, reduce the exports of other countries, and create balance-of-payments havoc.

It is hard to accept this proposition, despite its ingenuity. This is one case where it seems clear that a theory leaves out an important portion of the relevant facts. It is true that there have been important inventions which displaced imports of raw materials. Whether the effect of innovation on imports is random, some, like the tire, leading to increased imports of rubber, or on balance reducing them, as plentiful capital in the United States is substituted for increasingly scarce special categories of land,[12] it is by no means clear that United States innovation has affected imports more than exports, or that export-biased invention may not be disruptive of balance-of-payments equilibrium as import-biased.

There is first of all the demonstration effect, in which it is sufficient to mention the world spread of the automobile, refrigerator, jeep, bulldozer, and Coca-Cola. If the United States introduces new goods into international trade and into the standards of living of the world, this will require a reduction in other United States exports or an increase in imports to restore equilibrium. Disequilibrium may persist if new goods are introduced not at random by one country or another but systematically and consistently, on balance, by the United States. While the mechanism of adjustment may function adequately to any one disturbance, by the time that adjustment is being accomplished, a new disturbance has supervened.

But new goods are by no means the sole disturbing innovation on the side of exports, as H. Tyszynski has pointed out in a penetrating article on world trade in manufactures.[13] One method of improving a country's balance of payments is to gain a comparative advantage in goods newly entering into international trade — the structural effect. The German Enquête Ausschuss of 1926, quoted by E. Staley in his *World Economic Development*,[14] made much of this. But it is equally effective to use an innovation to reduce costs in an industry producing standardized goods long accepted in international trade. The extent to which this will turn the terms of trade unfavorable, and how the increase in productivity will be shared internationally, depend upon a number of factors such as

197

the price elasticity abroad for the cheaper product, the income elasticity for imports in the innovating country, etc. But to the extent that a new comparative advantage is gained or an old one strengthened, import-competing industry abroad must adapt, and balance-of-payments disruption ensues. The fact has been neglected that an important part of the dollar's strength in the postwar period has been due to this sort of cost-reducing innovation in the export industries, which Tyszynski calls the "competitive effect."

During the interwar period, adjustment was proceeding through the elimination of exports in which the United States had the smallest comparative advantage — agricultural supplies. But the agricultural revolution which attended the war, and saw the victory of commercial farming which is capital-intensive over the subsistence farm which is land and labor-intensive, has restored the comparative advantage of the United States in wheat and cotton, and eliminated comparative disadvantages in Turkish-type tobacco and flaxseed. The farm-support program, based on the maintenance of the net barter terms of trade between agriculture and industry (rather than the double factoral terms of trade) complicates the issue; but there can be no doubt that the production of wheat and cotton in the United States is price elastic — which it is not elsewhere — and that the principal inputs are capital.[15] The dual economy with two different sets of factor proportions has practically been eliminated from American agriculture.

Moreover, similar changes in production techniques have occurred in other standard goods. Open-cast mining in coal with 50 cubic yard power shovels, for example, has made this industry capital-intensive. Were it not for the high transport costs, American coal would be knocking at European doors continuously, and not only in periods of shortage. And even textiles. The American textile industry has always had a protected market in Cuba and the West Indies, and this has explained persistent exports in a labor-intensive industry in which the comparative disadvantage of the United States was obvious, though narrowed by high tariff protection. Since World War II, however, it is by no means clear that United States textile exports are a hothouse product. As the industry moved South to obtain cheaper labor, it appears to have attempted to economize that labor, despite its low cost. The result is that exports are appearing in successful competition in open markets. Textiles are well known to be a footloose industry in which transport costs play a minor role. Proximity is not the explanation, therefore, of the fact that United States textiles now outsell British in Canada.

From the point of view of the balance of payments, trouble is created either way, by shrinking imports or by expanding exports, unless the price elasticity of the latter is unity or less. With higher elasticities, the terms of trade of other countries are improved, but their balance of trade is worsened by export-biased as well as by import-biased innovation, if such a distinction in fact be valid.

6. It remains to decide whether to ascribe any importance to the Marjolin and United Nations views that bad terms of trade are inflationary, and so are good. The answer, of course, lies in the rest of the system. Higher export prices are inflationary in their effects in attracting resources into exports, and in the increased expenditure induced by increased incomes of the resources already there engaged. Still a further influence in the direction of inflation may be exerted by monetary expansion based on enhanced international reserves. When import prices rise, however, only one of these particular inflationary influences is at work, the pull of higher prices exerted to attract resources into import-competing industry. In a quasi-monopolistic society, whether these monopolies pervade the market for goods organized by cartels, or those for factors organized by trade unions, an attempt may be made to pass on higher costs of industries using imports in the form of higher internal prices; and this may succeed, to the extent that the banking system uses the higher prices as the basis of expanded credit. But there are deflationary influences as well: especially the import surplus, the loss of international reserves, a signal to the banking system to contract. Only if this response has become weakened and if the domestic market is noncompetitive, is it likely that the adverse terms of trade will be on balance inflationary. This is hardly a price response. It seems more appropriate to regard it as an income response of an economy poised on the brink of inflation.

V

This discussion of the logical requirements of symmetrical and asymmetrical behavior in balances of payments and the possible sources of asymmetry which might make for persistent dollar shortage bridges no gaps in the discussion and provides for no synthesis of views. This was not its purpose, which was rather to eliminate certain logical inconsistencies on the part of the asymmetrists and to point out the logical implications of the opposite view.

The general conclusion is that if there are asymmetrical responses in balances of payments it is best to look for them in the underlying phenomena of income behavior, demand elasticities with respect to income, i.e., consumption behavior, and supply innovations, rather than in some alleged response to prices.

The point may be underlined with a very loose analogy that must not be pressed too far in describing dollar shortage. There are two possible reasons for persistent losses on the part of a gambler playing a game which is theoretically even. Either the coin has two heads, or his adversary has persuaded him to keep score on the basis, "heads I win; tails you lose." In the first case there is asymmetrical behavior of the system; in the second case, there is an asymmetrical response to a perfectly symmetrical phenomenon. In a discipline governed by some degree of logic, it is to the first rather than the second sort of phenomena to which we must look.

NOTES

[1] This applies especially, of course, to the advocacy of devaluation as a remedy for balance of payments deficit as was brilliantly exposed by S. S. Alexander in "Effect of a Devaluation on a Trade Balance," International Monetary Fund *Staff Papers,* April 1952. The point of course has long been obvious in France.

[2] Robert Marjolin, *Europe and the United States in the World Economy,* Durham, N.C., Duke University Press, 1953, p. 94.

[3] Report by the Secretary-General, United Nations, to the Economic and Social Council, "Repercussion of Changes in Terms of Trade on the Economies of Countries in Process of Development" (E/2436 of June 11, 1953), para. 47.

[4] See, for example, R. Hinshaw and L. A. Metzler, "World Prosperity and the British Balance of Payments," *Review of Economics and Statistics,* November 1945.

[5] A difference may be made by the speed of the decline in price. This will be discussed later.

[6] See *Le Plan Marshall,* Paris, 1948, and "The Domination Effect and Modern Economic Theory," *Social Research,* June 1950.

[7] The articles of Agreement of the International Monetary Fund provide for a collection of currencies of all member countries on the assumption that, size for size, one country is as likely to have a deficit as another. It is the failure of this assumption to be realized, in my view, which has been responsible for the inactivity of the Fund, based on its inability to fit the conditions of the real world.

[8] *The Dollar Shortage,* New York and Cambridge, John Wiley & Sons and The M.I.T. Press, 1950; and *International Economics,* Homewood, Ill., Richard D. Irwin, Inc., 1953, esp. Chapter 22.

[9] Ragnar Nurkse, *Problems of Capital Formation in Underdeveloped Countries,* Oxford, Basil Blackwell, 1953.

[10] "Commodities since Korea," July 11, 1953, p. 115.

[11] *Oxford Economic Papers,* Vol. 5, No. 2, June 1953, pp. 117–135.

[12] For a discussion of this point, see *The Dollar Shortage, op. cit.,* Chapter 2.

[13] "World Trade in Manufactured Commodities, 1899–1950," *The Manchester School,* September 1951, pp. 272–304.

[14] Montreal, 1942.

[15] See T. W. Schultz, *The Economic Organization of Agriculture,* New York, McGraw-Hill Book Co., Inc., 1953, pp. 126 ff.

CHAPTER FOURTEEN

THE ROLE OF THE UNITED STATES IN THE EUROPEAN ECONOMY, 1919–1950*

I. Introduction

The economic relations between the United States and Europe in the interwar and postwar periods are so complex that it is impossible to give a coherent account of them in chronological terms. The history of each successive period would have to be written in so many dimensions that continuity between periods would be lost. For this reason, a functional approach has been adopted in what follows.

The time continuum is not wholly discarded, however. Within the account of the evolution and resolution of separate problems, some ordering in time is possible. In addition, several of the problems dominate a particular period, and their discussion can take place in sequence. Immediately after Versailles, gold distribution, exchange stabilization and interest rates were in the forefront of interest. In the middle and late twenties, the focus of attention shifted to war debts and reparations. The depression brought a new change in which unemployment received major emphasis. The present discussion begins then with the monetary problem, continues with capital transfers, and proceeds to employment. Other issues in foreign trade and the interaction of European and American economic institutions which are thereafter treated, lack a chronological focus and occupy relatively the same places of prominence throughout the period.

* Scheduled to appear as "Le Rôle des Etats-Unis dans l'économie euro-péenne," a chapter in *L'Europe du XIXe et du XXe siècles: problèmes et interprétations historiques,* Volume VII, Milan, Marzorati, 1965 (?) (submitted January 1954).

The difficulty with this functional approach is that each aspect is partial. There is no total theory of international economic relations into which money, capital movements, transfer, employment, trade, and institutions can fit. Perhaps such a one is evolving from the theory of economic development on which much work is going forward; but it is far from complete. At the present stage of economic history, all that exists is the series of partial approaches. Their sum, while not an integral whole, may nonetheless serve to convey the outline and dimensions of the relationship.

It is important to emphasize at the outset that to concentrate on one set of international relationships in the world economy is to run great risk of distortion. Perhaps it is inevitable that an American writer will emphasize the impact of the United States on Europe (and that a European writer would tend to minimize it). But to select this topic for study is itself to understate the extent to which the two economies are separate, independent, and inert in their mutual relations. It is not true that every time the Secretary of the Treasury sneezes, the economy of Europe jumps, nor was it true in 1919 nor in 1939. Any impression to this effect in what follows is erroneous, but doubtless inevitable.

II. *The International Monetary Problem*

Prior to the First World War, the unchallenged monetary center of the world was the City of London. Following the second, new foci of the international monetary mechanism, the International Monetary Fund and the International Bank for Reconstruction and Development, were established at Washington, D. C. The contrast epitomizes two changes in the monetary sphere: one across the Atlantic, the other from the financial to the political capital of the monetarily reigning country. The shift of decision-making in the world of money from the Bank of England to the United States Treasury Department, however, was accomplished slowly and through many stages.

The international monetary problem immediately after World War I had two main aspects. There was first the question of the stabilization of European exchanges; second, the relation of all currencies to gold. Each question was related to domestic inflation in Europe and throughout the world. Stabilization was impossible until inflation had been brought under control. The expansion of means of payment through inflation, moreover, changed the relationship between currencies and gold, and altered the adequacy of the existing gold supply. Both aspects of the problem were also linked by another means. It was necessary for each country to have sufficient reserves before the international value of its currency could be reestablished.

The halting of inflation posed a problem of varying severity.[1] In Germany it was intimately tied up with reparations (and their sabotage), the occupation of the Ruhr, and the passive strike of Ruhr industry against the French occupation. The United States contribution to a solution of the problem was sponsorship of the Dawes Plan, involving a repudiation of the mark and of debts dominated in marks, and the establishment of the Reichsmark with a stabilization loan. How much the unintentional saddling of the burden of the war on the middle class, whose savings in bank deposits and government bonds were wiped out, contributed to the rise of Naziism and the Second World War remains an unresolved historical issue. At this time, the United States had no responsibility for German inflation, nor could Charles G. Dawes, or other bankers or economists, have had much insight into the possible political consequences of all-out inflation.[2] The bankruptcy of the *rentier* in the continuous French inflation and successive devaluations further played a key role in weakening the cement of French society. But we are dealing with monetary problems of the narrower, more technical framework within which they were conceived and treated at the time.

United States participation in the stabilizations of the 1920's was largely confined to the provision of certain loans privately, and the Dawes intervention. Sympathy existed. No voice was raised against the stabilization of the pound at par — even that of Keynes in Britain was not unambiguous in its expression[3] — an overvalued rate which later came to be regarded as a calamity of some size. British reasons for parity were rationalized in terms of London as a financial center, the reconstruction of earnings from insurance, banking, commissions, and interest on deposits. But it is now considered likely that the basic reason was one of national pride and prestige. British prestige required a pound sterling at par, just as British prestige after World War II prevented the British from repudiating sterling debts to a host of small countries, many of which had been politically dependent. But British prestige suffered a body blow in the coal strike of 1926, along with the British economy. Here the postwar parallel was a natural phenomenon — the frost of 1947 which emphasized the frailty of the British economy.

Economists who are beguiled by the monetary mechanism, as are most, tend to make much of the action of Benjamin Strong, the governor of the Federal Reserve Bank of New York, in lowering the rediscount rate in 1927, after the disastrous strike of 1926, in an effort to help the British maintain the overvalued pound at its newly won parity. Whether the reduction of the New York discount rate had much or anything to do with the subsequent overexpansion and the boom in the United States may be doubted, but the case is widely cited as an illustration of the incompatibility of domestic stabilization with the international gold standard.

The British overvaluation of the pound was accentuated by the undervaluation of the French franc by the Poincaré government in 1926. The part played in this episode by French disillusion over reparations, the large floating debt and the psychological theory of foreign exchange, need not detain us. The impact was important. Certain aspects, like the stimulus to American tourists, buoyed by the New Prosperity in the United States, were salutary. The ultimate effect on the pound after the Bank of France converted its sterling balances (illegally counted as part of its reserves) into gold in 1930 was disastrous. But here again the United States took no part. As far as the country as a whole was concerned, it could be said to have hardly been aware of technical European economic problems.

United States interest in European exchange rates began in a strangely negative fashion, when President Roosevelt scuttled the London World Economic Conference of July 1933, by refusing to contemplate exchange-rate stabilization which would tie the value of the dollar. This was an act of economic isolationism, paralleling the rejection of the League Covenant a decade before. The President at the time was strongly influenced by a pair of economists, Warren and Pearson, who held the theory that prices in the United States could be manipulated by changes in the price of gold. With the United States in deep depression and the gold value of the dollar having just been altered, the President was wary of commitments until he obtained a clearer view of the impact of the exchange rate on business in the United States. Six months later, having experimented with the Warren-Pearson theory with limited success, he might have been ready for such a conference. Two years and six months later, indeed, the United States was anxious to take part in international monetary stabilization.

The opportunity for United States participation in European currency stabilization was presented by the defeat in September 1936, of the last efforts of the gold bloc to maintain the parities established in the 1920's. Use was made of it to conclude a Tripartite Monetary Agreement among the United States, Britain, and France, with the adherence of the Netherlands, Belgium-Luxemburg, and Switzerland. The substance of the agreement was limited: each country pledged itself to assist in the general stabilization process, and to give certain technical assistance to others, of a type which would not theretofore have been withheld, if sought. Much of the publicity which attended the measure was due to the reversal of the attitude of the United States, led to a considerable degree by the Secretary of the Treasury, Mr. Morgenthau. No longer suspicious of European plots to manipulate the dollar, the United States government took a pleasurable interest in helping to manipulate European currencies in useful directions.

The contrast of this attitude developed just prior to the Second World War with that of the early period is complete. One further step was taken in the Bretton Woods agreements which attempted to stake out international monetary procedure to be followed after World War II. Exchange rates became matters for international determination or, at the very minimum, discussion and clearance with the officials of the International Monetary Fund in Washington. Whether the experience also led to the illogical and impractical conclusion that competitive exchange devaluation is undesirable, and explains the resistance of the Fund to new parities for European currencies, prior to the summer of 1949, is a highly debated subject of current interest.

The question of stabilizing currencies in terms of gold was actually addressed before that of stabilizing them in terms of each other. The Brussels and Genoa conferences of 1920 and 1923 were called for the explicit purpose of examining the question of the adequacy of world gold reserves. From these conferences came the gold-exchange standard, a means by which gold could be economized by holding reserves not in gold but in currencies convertible into gold. The world had been on a gold-exchange standard in the nineteenth century without knowing it, since sterling had been as good as gold. The necessity to think about the adequacy of gold stocks was in part a reaction to the views of economic historians: these had been explaining the prosperity of the sixteenth century in terms of the accretion of gold from the new world, and the depression of 1873 to 1896 as due to the failure of significant new gold discoveries, after 1849 and prior to the South African and Alaskan strikes. It was further, however, a tacit admission of the weakness of sterling. The rationalization of the gold standard and the gold-exchange standard was needed to make the shift from the sterling to the dollar standard.

The change in the status of the United States from a debtor of Europe before the war to a creditor after the liquidation of debts and the granting of war and postwar loans ineluctably led to a change in the international unit of account. The League of Nations Economic Secretariat, for example, reckoned world trade of different countries in dollars, not sterling, beginning with its first studies of world trade and balances of payments in 1925. The devaluation of the dollar in March 1933 led for a time to the use of the hideous statistical device of the "old gold dollar," as the illusion was preserved that it was the value of gold which was significant. But already by the end of the 1930's this notion had been discarded. The international unit of account was the dollar; and if the gold price of the dollar changed, it was the value of gold which was altered, not the value of the dollar.

The successive depreciations from 1931 to 1936 accomplished the change in the value of units of exchange to dollars which the Brussels and Genoa conferences had faced, though this had not been their purpose. Some voices were raised in Europe, particularly Britain,[4] after the Second World War, for a similar increase in the price of gold in terms of all currencies, as a means of stimulating gold production which had suffered from rising costs. The purpose was not one of increasing the value of gold reserves behind national currencies, to avoid deflation, as had been the case in 1920 and 1921. It was rather to raise the value of new gold production, in which Britain had an indirect interest through her capacity to earn gold by selling goods to the Union of South Africa and Rhodesia.

Such a move in 1953, however, required action mainly by the United States. The depreciation of sterling in 1931 had been followed by the depreciation of the dollar in 1933. The devaluation of sterling in 1949, followed by that of a number of European currencies, in varying degrees, had had no significant reaction in the United States leading to the depreciation of the dollar. An increase in the price of gold in dollars in 1953 would have been followed by similar changes in other countries to leave the world network of exchange rates unaltered.

But the United States was not interested in a new increase in the price of gold. One reason for this attitude was the memory of the gold scare of 1936–1937, when a number of European central banks and Treasuries, in addition to private money markets, believed it likely that the United States would lower the price of gold because of the heavy flow of gold to the United States from Europe in exchange for dollars. Purchasers of dollars against European currencies, seeking profits in the New York stock market, or escaping confiscation, threatened or feared at the hands of an increasing Nazi power, were joined by speculators buying dollars with gold in the hope of an appreciation of the dollar or fear of the depreciation of gold. The gold scare increased the movement which gave rise to it. The United States Treasury resisted the temptation offered by public monetary scepticism in the United States to reduce the price of gold, but lost interest in further manipulation.

Such episodes as the Tripartite Agreement on exchanges and the gold scare were minor foci of interest in the economic relations between the United States and Europe. Their counterparts in the action taken under exchange provisions of the International Monetary Fund and the discussion of the world gold price after the Second World War are even more remote from the heart of economic affairs. Monetary matters continue to hold a fascination of the intricate and complex mechanism. In the postwar period, the most glittering of these toys with which Americans and Europeans joined in playing was the European Payments Union. But the central issues lay elsewhere. During the depression, the quantity of money was found to be a poor means of control of the economy; cheap money policies eliminated discount rates as a method of influencing exchange rates; and exchange control was substituted for rate-adjustments and the more subtle manipulation of discount rates.

Interest in international monetary issues in the narrow sense of exchange rates, the supply of money, and the role of gold, which had been high immediately after World War I, sank to a low level.

The "rediscovery of money" within national economies after 1950, and the increased importance given to the rate of interest, discount policy, and the quantity of money in preventing inflation internally, were not matched on the international front. Central bank action to manipulate discount rates was directed almost exclusively to domestic conditions, and without regard to the strength or weakness of foreign exchanges. The connection between inflation and balance-of-payments weakness was well understood, but the international monetary problem became subsumed in other more general formulations of the economic relations between states. International monetary theory as such failed to provide a framework in which to explain the course of events.

III. International Capital Transfers

The relations between the United States and Europe can be interpreted in terms of changes in their respective roles as a producing area with a surplus of goods and a consuming area with a deficit. Prior to the First World War, the United States had been an avid borrower of European savings. Capital had been short, investment opportunity along a wide frontier, high. While the United States had outstripped Great Britain as a manufacturing nation in absolute terms in the 1870's,[5] relatively speaking, it was still very underdeveloped; down until the First World War it continued to need vast numbers of people and large amounts of capital from abroad to combine effectively with its endowment of land.

During and after the war, the United States repaid a large portion of the accumulated debt to and investment capital owned by Europe. In addition to the direct relationship, there was a shift in their respective positions vis-à-vis third countries. Before 1914, London was the world capital market. After 1919, New York shared with London and then took on the main burden as the world's center for long-term loans. New York failures in this respect led to the shift of the source for long-term capital to the Export-Import Bank and the International Bank for Reconstruction and Development in Washington.

But the development was more complex than this sketch suggests.

209

Had no war taken place, the change in the respective roles of Europe and the United States would probably have occurred anyhow, but at a slower rate. The theory has been advanced that war does not change the direction in which a country is likely to go, but only the pace. A declining creditor nation loses its assets faster due to war; a rising creditor nation increases its holdings. This theory must be treated gingerly; it is true that the level of foreign lending of Britain in the period 1900 to 1913 could not have been maintained in the light of the growth of productivity in the United States and in Germany — much less the rate of growth of foreign lending — but the war abruptly put a period to it. World War I, however, did more than speed up the pace of change. It created certain problems — those of reparations and war debts.

The reparation clauses of the Treaty of Versailles had their origin in the 5 billion indemnity of 1871 exacted of the French by Germany. This amount was paid by France. In consequence, the attempt was made by France to collect reparation for the wider devastation of World War I. Voices were raised against the size of the indemnity from the beginning. The United States renounced any share in reparation, aside from ships; Keynes denounced the settlement as unworkable, although as Mantoux has correctly pointed out, the possibility that the payments would be made was reduced by Keynes' protest which justified German ca'canny.[6]

The collapse of the mark in 1924 following the occupation of the Ruhr led to the Dawes Plan, for a stabilization loan and a new attempt at meeting a scaled-down level of payments. The growth of New York lending made possible the meeting of this schedule through 1928; German states and municipalities borrowed in New York the exchange needed by the Weimar government to meet its reparation obligations. With the sudden cessation of long-term lending in 1928, as investor interest shifted to the New York stock market, these payments became more difficult to effect; the German banks borrowed at short term in New York for a while, but with increasing difficulty, and at increasingly higher rates. Ultimately it became impossible to meet the Dawes schedule, and a new scheme, again with American sponsorship, was worked out under the Young Plan. Payments under this arrangement were reduced once again. The first payment was not transferred, but represented the German counterpart of Allied deposits in the institution created for the purpose of transfer, the Bank for International Settlements. The following year the collapse of European currencies led to the Hoover moratorium of June 1931.

While the United States had not accepted reparation from Germany, it refused, until tacitly in the Hoover moratorium, to acknowledge any connection between the debts of its European allies to it and their receipt of reparation from Germany. The European view, on the other hand, was that Germany should furnish the Allies the wherewithal to make their payments to the United States, due on loans contracted during and immediately following the war. (Of these, the postwar loans for assistance were the larger. But both reflected the greater availability of goods in the United States than in Europe, relative to the demands for them, late in and immediately following the war.)

Whether Germany could have paid reparations to France and Britain in the absence of war debts and of United States lending to Germany is dubious. The conditions under which France paid the indemnity to Germany in 1871 were not repeated. In any event, the condition that Germany pay in dollars which could be used to requite war debts to the United States made it impossible to continue reparations after the total cessation of borrowing. Neither Germany nor Europe had the surplus of goods over the demand for them needed to effect a payment abroad, as had the United States during the war and Europe during the period prior to the war.[7] Nor was it likely that the United States could furnish during the 1920's, as it certainly did not during the period after 1929, the demand for more goods than it was producing. On the contrary.

The transfer of capital to the United States in the 1930's proved even more awkward than the reparations question. No simple waiving of an obligation by the United States could halt the flow. Gold was paid out by the European central banks; gold was received in increasing amounts by the Federal Reserve system in the United States. Deflation, however, was not pursued in Europe in the light of the disastrous experience of 1932. After reserves had been exhausted, specie payments were suspended. To prevent exchange depreciation, resort was had to exchange control. In Central Europe control over capital movements and current payments came early in the decade; for the United Kingdom, Scandinavia and the gold bloc, late when war had broken out. After the war, however, only Switzerland was able to dispense with exchange control over capital, at least towards the United States. (In fact, Switzerland was obliged to adopt informal controls to prevent capital inflows from the United States.) Given the difficulty of effecting the capital transfer from Europe to the United States, the transfer problem was obviated by preventing it from taking place legally.

Moratorium to halt contractual movements owed by governments in Europe to the United States, and exchange control to prevent private movements, put a stop to current flows of capital. The next step was to prevent the necessity for such future action by forestalling the accumulation of further debts. The surplus available in the United States could be transferred to Europe during the Second World War. In this direction there was no obstacle. But transfer in the form of loans involved the contraction of debts, giving rise to the need for a subsequent investment in the opposite direction. For this it was foreseen that transfer would be difficult. The answer was Lend-Lease and the subsequent financial settlement of claims and relief assistance. The major charges for material assistance rendered by the United States to the countries of Europe were canceled in consideration of the European contribution to the defense of the United States. The consolidation of obligations into loans was required in certain limited cases: peacetime goods still in the pipeline, or on order, and for surplus ships and war assets; but the capital amounts were kept low and the time period stretched to twenty-eight years.

Later the grants of assistance from the United States to Europe under the provisions of the Economic Cooperation Act, offshore procurement of military equipment under the North Atlantic Treaty Organization, military transfers under the Mutual Assistance Act provided other means of transferring United States surpluses to make up European deficits without incurring obligations. The first of these was of a peacetime character, though it contained an echo of the dislocations arising from World War II. Others, like Lend-Lease, were effected in the light of the defense exigencies of the North Atlantic treaty.

If there was no dearth of devices for transferring United States surpluses to Europe, so long as a defense emergency could be said to exist, the same was not to be the case with respect to third areas. The United States displacement of Europe as the source of capital

212

for the rest of the world was limited geographically, and after the breakdown of the foreign bond market in New York in 1930, ineffective in scope.

The geographical limitation in United States lending after 1945 was largely a function of Britain's maintenance of the sterling area. Within the sterling area, the United Kingdom provided funds. Outside, capital transfers were not allowed. The scale of lending within the area varied. On occasion it was restricted by the Capital Issues Committee for financial reasons. At other times the freedom of private capital movements in sterling, repayment of sterling balances accumulated during the war, and the provision of dollars from its pool to meet the deficits of the member countries of the sterling area meant that capital transfers from London to the sterling area took place on a considerable scale. To the extent that dollars provided by the United States were used in these transfers, the United States made its surpluses available to third countries in the sterling area through grants to Britain.

At Moscow and Potsdam in 1945, the United States tried — unsuccessfully, as it turned out — to avoid establishing a pattern of reparations which would have repeated the experience of the 1920's. In particular, it was anxious to steer clear of arrangements under which United States relief grants or loans to Germany permitted the Soviet Union to receive current reparations from that country, as the private loans to Germany in the 1920's had enabled Germany to pay reparations to the Allies (which in turn, be it remembered, effected payments on their obligations to the United States). A similar attempt was made halfheartedly to prevent aid to the United Kingdom being siphoned off all over the world, to the extent that the Anglo-American Financial Agreement of 1946 provided that the United Kingdom would attempt to scale down the capital amount of sterling balances accumulated by members of the area during the war. But the other means by which the United States surpluses were made available to third countries were not subject to negotiation, and the attempt to settle the sterling-balances question failed.

As for the ineffectuality of the institutions devised by the United States to replace Europe as a provider of capital to third countries, it is too soon to be categorical. From 1825 to 1913, the foreign bond served as the major institution of lending from Europe. In ten years, from 1920 to 1930, the New York market abused the institution to the point where the foreign bond market fell into desuetude. This outcome was contributed to by defaulting nations, but many of these had been encouraged in overborrowing by New York investment bankers. The London market had overlent in its time — in 1870 to 1874 and 1885 to 1889, among others. But in each case, after halting the outflow of funds for a period, the transfer of capital was renewed.

Early in the 1920's, a large flow of capital, coupled with managerial and engineering experience, moved abroad from the United States through direct investment, i.e., ownership or exercise of control in corporations operating abroad. This device was not unknown to Europe. But it was developed by the United States to a far greater extent. Transfers were made to Europe and Canada, as well as to outside areas. Whereas in Europe, the ownership of foreign corporations had been limited for the most part to companies working for export to Europe, or facilitating such exports, as in the case of canals and railroads, in the United States many more such corporations took United States products abroad. Instead of expanding imports, they enlarged exports. In this way, they may be said to have exacerbated rather than relieved balance-of-payments instability.

United States direct investment was sustained fairly well during the depression and immediately following World War II. A change occurred between the two periods, however. In the first, restrictions on United States exports in many countries encouraged attempts to serve existing markets with new domestic facilities. The second emphasized import-increasing investment rather than export-substituting, and was directed away from Europe. Of particular importance were United States investments in the Middle East in oil (which required, however, a complementary investment in refining facilities in Europe).

Direct investment has been criticized for its failure to contribute to the capital needs of third countries outside the United States which Europe is no longer in a strong position to fill. To a considerable extent, these investments are made with a small original equity, supplemented by local borrowing and the subsequent plowing back of profits. British and Dutch investments in tin, rubber, vegetable oils, and petroleum were originally of this sort, to be sure,

214

and earned high dividends on original investments. The importance of direct investment, however, lies not in providing capital to balance the excess supply of goods in the United States relative to the excess demands in Europe and the underdeveloped areas. Its international contribution of capital is limited and confined to the early period of the investment. But direct investment has effects in other directions: stimulating capital formation in the borrowing area through increased savings out of profits, and especially disseminating production and distribution techniques throughout the investment relationship.

The decline of international lending contributed to the severity of the depression of the 1930's, and in turn was caused by it. While default on foreign indebtedness was never unknown, especially in the United States, the depression developed new techniques of partial default through foreign-exchange regulations. Interest on obligations was paid in local currency, deposited in blocked accounts, and profits on direct investments were made transferable in carefully limited measure. German ingenuity at devising restrictions almost kept pace with the market's capacity for evading them. Some forced investment resulted out of profits which could not be transferred into the currency of the investor. This again failed to contribute to the problem of meeting the current international imbalance, and, further, it stored up new debtor-creditor problems for the future.

The decline of the foreign bond and the limited capacity of foreign direct investment led to the development of governmental institutions for matching the United States surplus and the European deficit. The first of these was the Export-Import Bank in the United States, initiated as a stimulus to foreign trade in the United States, and developed after World War II into an institution to provide relief loans to Europe and developmental loans to underdeveloped areas, particularly in Latin America. The second was the Bretton Woods International Monetary Fund and Bank, created from the merged plans of Lord Keynes and H. D. White of the United States Treasury. In the event, these institutions proved to be inadequate to meet the problem of international transfer after the war, despite the work of Lend Lease and Mutual Aid in keeping down the burden of debt due to war. The result was the necessity to extend the lend-lease technique into peacetime or cold war, and to make grants in aid in place of loans. While this technique satisfactorily effects the transfer, it meets objection both in the United States, where peacetime international transfers are questioned, and in Europe, which dislikes the necessity to receive what is regarded as charity. The technique fits the material exigencies of the problem, but is regarded by both parties as less than appropriate to the sociopolitical relation between them. Accordingly, the transfer problem remains a problem: either United States surpluses and European deficits must be eliminated or some other means of financing them must be found which accords with national sensibilities.

The scope of the transfer problem has been sharply reduced since its peak after World War II. At times United States purchases of military equipment and for occupation troops stationed abroad coupled with remaining restrictions on imports from the United States have enabled European countries to earn surpluses in trade with the dollar area. But the nature of the problem remains the same: the world seeks solutions for increasing European earnings of dollars, not United States earnings of European currencies.

A final point: on one view, the problem goes beyond that of simply eliminating the European deficits, actual or repressed. In a wide section of opinion the objective for Europe is to regain its position as an area of surplus, investing annually in underdeveloped areas, along with the United States. There would be growth in European investments in the United States and Canada, as well as United States and Canadian investments in Europe; but the main United States-European position would be balanced, as both supplied capital to the rest of the world. As already noted, a beginning in this direction has been made by European investments in South Africa and elsewhere in the British Commonwealth, and by the discharge of sterling debts; thus far these capital outflows to third areas have been more than balanced by capital inflows from the United States. But the possibility is envisaged that Europe will attain the status not only of a nonborrower of the United States but that of a creditor, like the United States, of third countries.

IV. The Problem of Depression and Unemployment

In the 1920's, the major preoccupation of economists was the transfer problem. In the 1930's, the center of attention shifted to the question of employment. The change was marked by intellectual

216

retooling. In the 1920's, and before that as far back at least as Adam Smith, the main engine of economic analysis was the price system. The revolution in economic thought stimulated by the depression and associated largely with the name of Lord Keynes, was to focus attention on movements in national money incomes.

Immediately after the war, there was a worldwide shortage of goods which resulted in a short-lived commodity boom. Prices and incomes rose precipitously. In 1920, however, inventory accumulation stopped, expectations of further price increases were revised, and the price inflation collapsed. This almost forgotten boomlet and recession are interesting for European-American economic relations only because of their lack of impact upon them. Successor periods of upswing and setback in 1937–1938, in 1948–1949, and 1950–1951 produced convulsions in United States imports which were communicated to Europe both directly and indirectly via the primary-producing areas.

Then began in the United States the vast boom of the 1920's. Belying the monetary historians (inasmuch as it was based upon a world gold supply thought exiguous at the time), it is ascribed by income theorists to the buoyancy of long-term business investment in newly developed goods, as the electrical age, the chemical age, and *par excellence* the automobile age, were ushered in. (These same theorists were at pains to explain, ten years later, why the level of investment in the United States was suffering long-term decline.) In retrospect, signs of exhaustion of upward momentum began to appear as early as 1925. In that year residential building slackened after the collapse of the Florida real-estate bubble, and prices of primary products began to slip. But these cracks in the facade of the golden age were not visible at the time. A stock-market analyst who correctly predicted in 1928 that a depression was inescapable lost most of the confidence of his followers, since the boom in securities really began about this time, with the first million-share days.

The unevenness with which American prosperity was communicated to Europe depended primarily on exchange rates and capital movements. The overvaluation of the pound sterling in 1925 kept Britain exports low, interest rates high, and business depressed. After the French inflation of the early 1920's, the undervalued rate for the franc established *de facto* in July, 1926, by the Poincaré government led to a prolonged boom, fed by the tourist movement. Governmental and business investment in Germany was maintained at a high level by borrowing from the United States — at long term through 1927 and at short term in 1928.

While these deviations occurred, the European economy functioned in a setting of world prosperity. Primary-producing countries were good customers for European products, based on the high incomes derived from their exports and in many cases using loans which the New York market forced on them. The world economy operated effectively under the stimulus of high national income in the United States.

The 1929 crash abruptly changed the position. Grain prices had begun to edge off in 1925. The cessation of foreign lending in 1928 occasioned difficulties abroad as American investment funds were diverted into the New York stock market. But the cumulative decline in short- and long-term investment in the United States from 1929 to 1933 produced havoc, for separate countries and for the world economy as a functioning mechanism.

Much of the blame for the collapse of the world economy is assigned to the Smoot-Hawley Tariff Act of 1930 and the retaliation to which it gave rise. These produced a cumulative constriction of the world economy, it is thought, in which no country could regain prosperity. This view is probably superficial. There is no adequate account of the great depression and of the respective roles of domestic and international forces as they interacted. Measures to contract imports may have served as *causa proxima,* but the *causa causans* was the declining spiral of long-term investment in the United States, aided by banking weakness, and the impact of this decline on the world was more significant than the superficial increase in tariffs.

The decline in United States income decreased United States imports both from Europe and from European customers in third areas. In combination with the decline in capital exports which preceded, it forced other countries to deflate their national incomes, and ultimately to take other steps to correct their international accounts — exchange control, the Ottawa conference and Empire preference, quotas on commodity imports, and finally currency devaluation. The devaluation of sterling, moreover, had repercussions back on national income in the United States, leading to the ultimate devalu-

218

ation of the dollar. The decline in wheat and cotton prices, as a result of devaluation in 1931, in combination with the weakened state of the small separate agricultural banks in the United States, gave a new turn to the deflationary screw in the United States just when it was thought that conditions were picking up again.

The depression in Europe was not as deep as in the United States and the recovery was more extensive in the 1930's. A number of factors contributed to this result. The boom in Germany, cut off from the world market by an autarkic system of exchange control, barter and clearing, and reequipping its army, was one. There was general rearmament after the occupation of the Rhineland by Germany in 1936, with the stimulus this gave to the iron and steel and engineering industries. Foremost, however, was the fact that long-term investment failed to recover in the 1930's in the United States to 1928 levels.

An increase in income in the United States has two effects, one on incomes abroad, and one on world prices. The first of these is always favorable for Europe. The second may or may not be favorable, depending upon whether the prices at which Europe sells rise more than the prices at which it buys, i.e., whether her terms of trade are favorable or unfavorable. If raw materials and food prices remain relatively low, while manufactured prices are high, Europe gains at the expense of the primary-producing areas. For Britain, this means that income which would otherwise have been spent on food and basic materials can be diverted to other uses. In combination with the depressed condition of the 1920's, and a backlog of overdue housing and industrial construction, the improved terms of trade gave Britain a construction boom which spread to Scandinavia via expanded timber imports.

A more extensive recovery in the United States is not as favorable for Europe as a limited one. As the postwar experience has shown, a United States boom which imposes a strain on the primary resources of the world, and raises their prices, turns the terms of trade against Europe at the same time that it increases European exports directly and through third countries. The unfavorable effect is unlikely to offset completely the favorable one, but the net result is less satisfactory than that in which recovery proceeds less far and leaves some slack in primary-products prices. The difference for Europe, it may be observed, is not against the United States —

or against only those sections of the country which sell wheat, cotton, tobacco, oil. The intensity of the recovery in the United States affects the distribution of real income between Europe and primary-producing areas. Both suffer in United States depression; but in limited recovery Europe gains more than underdeveloped areas; in full recovery, the other way around.

An account of the events affecting the levels of national incomes in the United States and in Europe must not obscure the real change which took place between 1914 and 1929. In 1914, the course of money income was determined by expenditure on investment and consumption in Europe. In 1929, the determining center had shifted across the Atlantic. Exchange rates, capital movements, or action to isolate the national economy from the world might permit an apparently independent course to be pursued. Slight and subtle differences of degree might have important effects on the nature of the final result for Europe. But the course of world income after 1929 was determined in the United States.

V. The Structure of Foreign Trade

In the economic relations between Europe and the United States, the first decade of the interwar period may be regarded as dominated by the transfer problem; the second, by unemployment. The temporal prominence of these problems, however, must not be allowed to obscure the effects of changes which took place during the two wars themselves, and over the period, which were fully as important. These changes occurred in the fundamental factors affecting the "Wealth of Nations" — the related aspects of capital accumulation, entrepreneurship, innovation, and productivity. In their international aspects, these factors may be said to determine the structure of foreign trade.

The loose generalization has been made that the United States developed mass production in the First World War and mass precision in the Second. Neither part of the statement is strictly true. The origins of mass production go back to Eli Whitney and the interchangeable parts of the Springfield rifle. At the turn of the century British observers were studying the differences between British and United States plants.[8] In 1900, Germany imported agricultural machinery and tools from the United States — albeit in amounts of only $1 million each. The reduction of $1,000 in the price of Ford automobiles reaching out for a mass market occurred in 1907. And even in 1936, Junker engineers were surprised that pistons on American radial airplane engines were machined to exact tolerances, as were the balls for ball bearings, while similar accuracy of fit in Europe was achieved only by painstaking matching of parts by hand.

War is nonetheless a hothouse of economic change. Given the seedlings of invention, war produces developed plants like the automobile, the telephone, the airplane. Consumption is changed as well as production, as the cigarette and wrist watch testify. Parallel to these changes of World War I, the Second World War developed jet propulsion, atomic energy, electronics, and in the field of production, automatic controls.

These changes were not by any means all initiated in the United States. J. A. Schumpeter has made a distinction between invention and innovation, the one connected with a discovery, the other with its practical applications. European invention and American innovation have been a consistent pattern since World War I, or even since 1900. Radio furnishes a classic example. But examples of invention and innovation on a single side of the Atlantic are abundant: synthetic gasoline and rubber in Europe, to cite an example to parallel jet engines and rockets; the airplane and the automobile in the United States.

The introduction of new products is an important source of changes in the structure of foreign trade. The *Enquête Ausschuss,* an inquiry conducted by a German commission to examine the German economy in 1925, concluded that the strength of the American economy was due to its concentration in exporting on products new in international trade.[9] On this showing, Germany did fairly well, but Britain lagged far in the rear with coal and textiles. A recent investigation[10] has suggested an emendation: to new products should be added new methods of producing old products. The Balfour Committee, established to investigate the health of the British economy, was troubled by the inability of British industry to obtain capital and its failure to maintain its plant in an efficient and modern state.[11] Professor Hicks of Oxford has advanced a theory, not generally accepted, that part of the difficulty occasioned by American industrial leadership is that its innovations tend to take place in import-competing lines, which displace foreign exports, while Britain's innovation was export-biased in the nineteenth century, and cheapened the imports of its customers.[12]

Discussion of differences between Europe and the United States — which were not so wide between the United States and Germany, perhaps, as they were for the rest of the Continent, ran in terms of standardization of product, organization of the factory, and incentives to efficiency. Complex issues are bound up in each of these expressions, which cannot be investigated here. In standardization of a product, for example, it has been claimed that the United States has a wider mass market than Europe because of a leveling upward of incomes, or because of a leveling downward of popular taste (which may be interconnected) or because of manufacturer's efforts to combine for standardization, or for many other reasons. Similarly, the efficiency of the large factory organized for mass production, so satirized by René Clair and Charlie Chaplin, has been ascribed to work simplification, efficiency engineering (Taylorism); while some investigation of higher productivity per worker in the United States has emphasized the drive of the American worker on farm and factory for an increased standard of material well-being, to the efficiency of the foreman class, or to professional training of the engineering supervisors who stand between the owners and the workers.[13]

Whatever the fundamental explanations for the rise of mass production in the United States and its slower development in Europe, the impact on international trade between the areas, on the allocation of resources and the prices at which goods are traded, has been evident and important. New products developed by the United States can be bought by Europe only by borrowing, or, with the trade balance preserved, by enlarging exports or reducing other imports. The method of achieving balance through enlarged exports had to be triangular, in considerable part, because of United States protectionism. This protectionism was in part an intellectual carry-over from the infant-industry days, when United States industry was growing strong; in part it represented a concession to national defense, to maintain certain new industries, especially in chemicals and optical instruments which had been built up behind that most effective protective mechanism, the total disruption of trade in war; and partly, midway in the period, to the Smoot-Hawley tariff act already mentioned. Europe could spend less for American products: here a distinction is necessary between those goods it was prepared to substitute home products for, largely luxury foodstuffs like fruit (but also lard); those which it was prepared to buy abroad, but only at lower prices, like wheat, and those items of machinery and consumers' durable goods which it regarded as fundamental to its standard of living, and which it found hard to dispense with. Protection and imitation helped here; imitation which led to the development of a distinctive production. Thus, for example, United States automobile output, which ultimately resulted in imports of European cars into the United States. But in other producer and consumer lines, American imports were not lightly cut off.

The mutual relationship between Europe and the United States was not symmetrical. Europe depended upon the United States for a wide range of goods not easily foregone; United States imports from Europe were luxury products, like tourist travel, hand-made articles of high value for a limited market, and a few specialties. Czechoslovakia furnished one example of a country attempting to penetrate the United States market with mass-produced inexpensive shoes pottery, and leather goods, in its effort to reduce its trade dependence on Germany. The success of Switzerland in marketing watches there despite the tariff was another.

As a part of its adjustment in this respect, Germany went in for borrowing from the United States. This was not as true of the rest of Europe. But the same relative result was reached by the reduction of European lending to the rest of the world. In 1913, the rate of European overseas investment reached a peak: the British investment alone was on the order of $1 billion a year, which in terms of modern purchasing power would amount to more than $2½ billion. The development of new products in the United States helped to induce Europe to consume and invest at home all of its production (in the case of Germany, more), and even to consume overseas capital.

Behind the rise in American industry and the decline in foreign trade of its agriculture was a marked shift of factor proportions and comparative advantage. One relationship remained unchanged: the halting of immigration in 1921 and 1924 kept labor relatively abundant in Southern and Southeastern Europe and scarce in the United States, during the interwar period as before World War I.

223

But the position of land and capital in the United States was altered, and with it the historic basis of United States trade policy. The shift closely paralleled the movement which led to the repeal of the Corn Laws in Britain in 1846. But there was a difference.

The repeal of the Corn Laws had been due to a transfer of political power from the landed gentry to the rising commercial and industrial classes. The former wanted high prices for grain; the latter were interested in free trade partly as a means for depressing wages, but primarily, in the light of modern explanation, to expand their total trade. British customers spent in Britain all the pounds they could get hold of — whether by borrowing in or exporting to London. Increased imports therefore meant increased exports, and a gain for industry at the expense of agriculture.

In the case of the United States, however, there was no need for the Reform Bill of 1832 to accomplish the political shift. The industrial north effectively maintained power during the whole period. When capital was the scarce factor so that United States comparative disadvantage leading to imports lay in goods embodying capital, protection raised the prices of the import-competing goods produced in the north, and the incomes of New England and Middle Atlantic industrialists. Free trade would have been of benefit to the south and west, but they were politically submerged.

With the rise of capital accumulation during the First World War, however, the position and interests of regions within the United States changed. Capital, not land, became the abundant factor, and labor remained scarce, or moved into that position from the intermediate one. Large-scale industries, interested in exporting farm machinery, automobiles, business machines, tires, petroleum, were not served by protection which, rather, limited their potential markets. Small-scale industry in textiles, gloves, watches, ceramics, and similar labor-intensive areas retained their interest in protection; but they were left behind by the industrial giants.

Cultural lags made these changes slow to result in political action. The movement to freer trade had to be led by the Democratic Party and southern statesmen, even though the interest of agriculture in the movement had been reduced, and the growing parts of the industrial South, in chemistry and textiles, could have been said to need protection. Moreover, the Republican party, especially in the Middle West, largely opposed the Reciprocal Trade Agreements Program, enacted in 1934, despite the importance of the area in machine tools, automobiles, tires, and other export items.

The emphasis on the reciprocal nature of tariff reductions underlines the interest in the United States in exporting. Like the British movement of 1850 to 1860, culminating in the Cobden-Chevalier treaty, the United States embarked on an attempt to reduce barriers to world trade. In addition to the reciprocal trade agreements of the 1930's and after World War II, it collected governmental signatures to the principle of freer trade in connection with its war and postwar financial arrangements — the famous Article VII of Lend Lease, the Atlantic Charter, etc. — and led the abortive movement for the International Trade Organization. But to the extent that dollars made available to foreigners were spent, as was the case with sterling in the seventy-five years to 1913, the emphasis on the reduction of tariffs abroad is unnecessary. The export interests sell abroad as much as the country buys and lends.

The rise in the comparative advantage in mass-produced articles has effects on agriculture, as well as on labor-intensive industry. The old export advantage in these fields was reduced, and American farm products were squeezed out of the foreign market. Agricultural produce fell from 50 per cent of total United States exports in 1913 to 25 per cent in 1938.[14] Farm policy and farm export policy became a serious internal political problem, with important repercussions abroad. Whether the United States held farm prices high at home and dumped abroad, as the McNary-Haugen bill vetoed by President Coolidge called for, or sold at the same price in both markets, and supported these prices, was of considerable importance to European producers and consumers, with divergent interests. The issue, in a new guise, is alive in 1953.

But the persistent squeeze on agriculture did not last. World War II brought a new revolution in certain branches of United States farming. The great increase in productivity in industry brought about by increased capitalization spread to the growing of wheat, cotton, tobacco. Capital was applied in the form of machinery and fertilizer. In 1945, the United States produced 33 per cent more farm produce than in the period of 1935 to 1939, with 15 to 20 per cent less labor.[15] The gain in productivity in agriculture in this period outstripped that in industry.

New production techniques were devised in the United States, even in European staples like coal and textiles. The increase in miners' wages in the United States led to mechanization. In textiles, the movement of the center of gravity of the industry from New England to the South Atlantic states in search of cheaper labor was accompanied by the adoption of new labor-saving techniques. These industries, previously regarded as land- and labor-intensive, respectively, became capital-intensive, and therefore industries in which the United States had a comparative advantage. [. . .]

In all these changes, events in the United States lead; the task of Europe was to adapt. Nor was adaptation made easy by tariff protection, administrative regulation, and government preferences in the United States. With each new comparative advantage there is automatically created a comparative disadvantage. But it is not always obvious in which direction it lies, nor is it clear that the commercial policy of the United States assists in finding it. One important disadvantage lay in minerals in which Europe's interest was an indirect one, effected through its ownership of mines in third areas. Here, however, the United States was in a better position to expand mineral output through capital development, since it had more capital. In lines directly affecting Europe it gradually became apparent after World War II that Europe had a comparative advantage over the United States in the construction of especially designed turbines for electric power installations. These machines, like ships, involve the use of a lot of skilled labor. European concerns could underbid those in the United States on contracts in the United States and in third countries. In these cases, however, the fact that credit was more easily available in the United States than in Europe — and that much of this credit was tied to the sale of American goods, and the Buy-American Act which imposed a 25 per cent price preference for American products — made it difficult for Europe to exploit the difference. In ships, of course, the defense needs of the United States led to subsidies to domestic yards.

The interwar period as a whole saw an irregular increase in productivity in the United States at a faster pace than in Europe. As already suggested, the causes of this development are rooted deep in the social structures of the two societies. The result of the unevenness was to change the structure of foreign trade in ways which have been sketched. Analysis of the more profound influences on war-making capacity, political power, and world leadership lie outside the scope of this chapter.

How the changes in productivity in the United States, plus those proceeding somewhat more slowly in Europe, will affect European terms of trade with the world is a vital subject for Europe. Mention of the terms of trade above has been limited to their cyclical behavior. But the long-term trend is important to Europe. Europe's terms of trade improved from 1870 to 1900, as European technological improvements in land and ocean transport brought the world's supplies cheaply to its doors. A further improvement in the 1920's was due to the delayed result of large-scale investment in primary production in the first decade of the century, and to the resultant overexpansion of agriculture, ultimately realized when European production regained its prewar output. The depression as already indicated, brought still further gain, and was the basis of the British construction boom.

The improvement in Europe's terms of trade from 1870 to 1938 enabled it to increase its consumption and capital expenditure at a faster rate than the improvement in its productivity. This benefit hid the stagnant course of productivity from view. It further left Europe unprepared for the sharp reversal which took place in World War II. This reversal was due to the expansion of manufacturing capacity outside Europe, the improvement in manufacturing productivity, and the strain on the world's raw material capacity, which had been neglected, imposed by reconstruction and high economic activity in the United States.

A sharp debate is taking place on the prospect for the terms of trade. W. Arthur Lewis[16] and Colin Clark[17] foresee a continuation of the worsening of terms of trade between manufactured goods and primary products. They look to increased productivity and capacity in manufacturing, and the sluggish response of supply to price increases in agriculture outside the United States, coal in Europe, and mining in a few other areas. On the other hand, the Food and Agriculture Organization and the Economic and Social Council of the United Nations and its functional and regional commissions take the view that the world needs price supports for foodstuffs and raw materials.[18] They apparently are impressed by the buoyancy of

227

agricultural production in North America, and of mining output in many underdeveloped parts of the world under the influence of the United States, and to a lesser extent European capital. The outcome will only in part be determined by action in the United States and in Europe. But the interwar benefits derived by Europe from the development of the terms of trade are not assured.

V. Economic Institutions and Policies

These four areas — money, capital transfer, prosperity and depression, and the structure of foreign trade — encompass the major effects of the United States on the European economy in the interwar period. Most of these, it may be observed, are effects which were not purposeful or contrived. In the one area, however, the United States has tried to exercise influence and leadership, in suggestions to Europe that it adapt American economic institutions and follow United States economic policies. The results have been limited. American institutions and policies have been adopted in other fields, particularly the military, but to a considerable extent in international political organizations, as well. In consumption, as in production, United States institutions spread to Europe, some slowly like chewing gum and Coca-Cola, some more rapidly like the refrigerator. But for all its evangelism in the field of economic institutions and policies, its espousal of the British liberal tradition, albeit transmitted into a peculiarly American form, the United States has not been able to "sell" its abhorrence of public ownership, its antitrust policies, nor its belatedly avowed — not universally practiced — Manchester liberalism in trade. In particular, immediately after the Second World War, it tried, and failed, to lead and push Europe into an economic union to duplicate, on the Continent, the vast internal market of the United States.

Some institutions of American origin, adopted in Europe, led to disaster. Such, for example, was the 40-hour week, adopted by the Front Populaire in France under Daladier in 1936, with crippling effects on French industry, and a new demonstration of the truth that income cannot be increased ahead of productivity. It is not, therefore, true that institutions selected by Europe from those available will succeed because they are adapted to an indigenous setting. Many more, like the corporation and the labor unions, pursue different lines of development on the two sides of the Atlantic, with

228

the points of difference occasionally being sharpened, occasionally blunted, by trans-Atlantic comparisons. Young economic historians in the United States have lately emphasized the importance for France of the reluctance of the entrepreneur to allow his firm to grow beyond family size, as in the United States, with a consequent limit on its capacity to adopt economies of scale.[19]

European voices have been raised against the path followed in Europe, toward interference with the workings of the free market, and public ownership.[20] These works, in English, probably have their best sale in the large market of the United States. It seems evident, however, that the swing to more conservative governments in Europe after 1950 had its origin not in any pressure from the United States or intellectual acceptance of the superiority of the arguments for freer enterprise, so much as in dissatisfaction with the rate of progress made by Socialist governments in European reconstruction. Even the German liberalism did not accurately reflect the views of the United States: there the impatience with controls in such matters as foreign trade and exchange convertibility went well beyond the limits which the United States was inclined to urge in practice, whatever its views, while German industry chafed under the anticartel laws promulgated by the German government under the direction of the United States, and prepared to remove them or at any rate ignore them in practice.

The peak of the United States intervention in the formation and creation of European economic institutions was reached in the field of economic integration after the war. In this period, the United States with difficulty restrained itself from requiring abandonment of un-American views on the nationalization of industry, in which experiments were going forward in France and Britain. It insisted, however, upon more "integration" into a single market, urging customs union on Europe, both European-wide and later partial bilateral agreements, and supporting the subsequent French initiative to convert the movement into one for functional integration, industry by industry. Earlier, United States initiative and insistence in the face of British indifference or opposition had led to the creation of a number of separate functional bodies, the European Coal Organization, the European Emergency Economic Committee, and the European Inland Transport Organization, later merged, again in response to an American suggestion, into the Economic Commission for Europe, a regional commission under the United Nations Economic and Social Council.

It must not be thought that the inspiration and suggestion for economic institutions all came from the United States. The Bretton Woods institutions were devised, as already mentioned, from parallel suggestions in the United States and in Britain. And in the middle thirties, the United States borrowed the British notion of a stabilization fund, although equipping it with gold rather than with credit so that it was completely unable to perform the function for which it was intended. The Keynesian views on oversaving which originated in Europe have application primarily to the United States, and cannot serve as a guide to policy in Europe. The major fact, however, is that the conscious impact of the United States on European economic institutions and practices, from small beginnings in the interwar period, rose to great prominence and power. This influence was associated, of course, with the provision of economic assistance to meet the European deficit of production below consumption and investment. When that assistance ceases, however, it is hardly likely that the concern of the United States for the European economy, its functioning and its institutions, will immediately or completely evaporate.

VI. The Dominant Economy

The interwar period was one in which the world center of economic impulses moved from Europe to the United States both in the mutual relations between the two areas, and in their economic impact on third areas. In the field of monetary policy, income determination, and economic institutions, the United States is not obliged to respond to changes in Europe; Europe on the contrary is required to react, positively or negatively, to changes in the United States. In foreign trade, change emanates from the United States; adaptation must be made by Europe.

A French writer has characterized the United States as a "dominant economy."[21] This dominance is not to be found in mere size or in wealth, or in military or political power. It resides in the fact that whether it wills it or not, the United States by all its actions affects what goes on in Europe, without being affected in turn by European events.[22]

The theory of the dominant economy, however, overstates the

position in one respect. The balance-of-payments position of the United States is the mirror image of that of Europe (and the rest of the world). It is true that Europe cannot consume and invest more than it produces unless the rest of the world — United States, colonies, and third countries — produce more than they consume and invest. It is equally true that the United States cannot produce more than it consumes and invests at home, as it has continuously since 1915, unless Europe borrows, accepts aid, or joins the United States in making their combined surpluses available to the under-developed parts of the world. The dollar shortage of the rest of the world is one of the major problems faced by the United States, and in this respect, Europe has a sensible economic impact on that country.

VII. *Stages of Development*

The theory of the dominant economy, presupposing that one country must always dominate, falls short of full explanation on another showing. Switzerland in Europe has an economic position resembling that of the United States in many respects: it is a creditor with surpluses to invest abroad; it is an innovator in foreign trade, or when it adapts it does so with an inspired and creative response which is very different from passive acceptance in a stereotyped pattern.[23] The other neutral and unoccupied country in Europe, Sweden, resembles Switzerland in these respects.

While the vast size of the United States, compared to Sweden and Switzerland, may make it dominant, and the two neutrals are unlikely to impose their consumption or production patterns on the rest of the world, the three countries may all be at the same stage of economic development. Much attention has been devoted to the early stages of development; thus far little has been devoted to the later stages. Economists have been concerned with the transition of a "young debtor" country to a "young creditor," the former borrowing and the latter repaying and lending. The opposite side of the shield is the overinvestment of the debtor and the undercon-sumption or underinvestment of the creditor. The stage of transition from mature creditor, which balances production and domestic spending, and thus does not need to consume foreign capital or seek foreign aid, to overmature creditor, needs exploration. It would appear, however, that all the European belligerents, but not the

European neutrals, have made this transition over the course of the period.

Thus far, moreover, little account has been taken of the evolution and change in the capacity for innovation in the several stages of development.[24]

Anthropomorphic analogy is dangerous in social science, as in history, and yet, used with care, it may be suggestive. If the stages of development are divided into youth, maturity, and old age, it may be recognized that youth consumes and invests more than it produces. It also is acquiring existing skills, but devises few that are new. Maturity is the period of greatest production in which consumption falls short of total output. Some of the surplus is made available to the young; some set aside for old age. Maturity is a period, moreover, when new techniques are developed, new products developed to satisfy old and newly created wants. As the aging process goes forward, however, capacity for production shrinks faster than the desire for consumption. The ability to innovate declines. The result is the necessity to consume past savings, or to seek the aid of vigorous maturity.

How far the theory of development can be applied to the relations between the United States and Europe in the interwar period remains to be tested carefully. At the present stage, it can only be remarked that the extension of the theory of development into stages of decline looks promising. It also suggests that the relationship between the United States and Europe is destined to change as the vigor of the United States declines.

In his well-known posthumous essay on the economic position of the United States,[25] Lord Keynes predicted that the balance-of-payments position of Europe would shortly be ameliorated by the development of higher standards of consumption in the United States, standards that would rise faster than productivity. There can be little doubt that this outcome is inevitable, as the United States ultimately crosses the line dividing maturity from age. The history of the period up to and immediately past World War II, however, leaves the prediction of Lord Keynes in error as to timing.

NOTES

[1] See League of Nations, *The Course and Control of Inflation after World War I,* Princeton, 1945. This masterly account of the interrelations among inflation, exchange stabilization and international lending, largely the work of Ragnar Nurkse, is generally unknown to economists, much less to people professing other disciplines.

[2] Brilliant contrast is afforded with the period after World War II. Here the United States had both a share in responsibility for inflation in Germany, beginning with Occupation on June 2, 1945, and divided counsels. The chaos school, which reached a zenith of influence at the time of the revelation of concentration-camp atrocities, argued strongly that German inflation should be allowed to proceed unchecked, to let the German people suffer in their turn as other countries occupied during the war had been systematically looted through inflationary devices. In the end, however, the United States took a lead in promoting monetary reform, including a capital levy for the purpose of equalizing war losses, and preventing further dispossession of the middle class.

[3] See J. M. Keynes, *The Economic Consequences of Mr. Churchill,* London, 1925.

[4] See, for example, R. F. Harrod, "Imbalance of International Payments," International Monetary Fund *Staff Papers,* Vol. III, No. 1, April 1953.

[5] League of Nations, *Industrialization and Foreign Trade,* 1945, p. 13.

[6] See J. M. Keynes, *The Economic Consequences of the Peace,* New York, Harcourt, Brace and World, Inc., 1920; and Etienne Mantoux, *The Carthaginian Peace or The Economic Consequences of Mr. Keynes,* Oxford, Oxford University Press, 1946.

[7] This is not strictly accurate. The German economy developed a large export surplus after the cessation of foreign borrowing. This was achieved in European currencies, however, not in dollars, and only by means of a rigorous deflation which led to 5 ½ million unemployed, or 30 per cent of registered workers, and to Hitler.

[8] See A. Shadwell, *Industrial Efficiency,* London, 1906; and Reports of the Mosely Industrial Commission, Cooperative Printing Society, Ltd., Manchester, 1903 (cited by G. Hutton in *We Too Can Prosper,* London, Allen & Unwin, 1953).

[9] Ausschuss zur Untersuchung der Erzeugungs und Absatzbedingungen der deutschen Wirtschaft, *Handel,* Berlin, 1927.

[10] H. Tyszynski, "World Trade in Manufactures, 1899–1950," *The Manchester School,* September 1951.

[11] Committee on Industry and Trade, *Final Report* (Cmd 3282) H.M.S.O., 1929, pp. 50, 179 ff., and *Factors in Industrial and Commercial Efficiency,* H.M.S.O., 1927, *passim.*

[12] J. R. Hicks, "An Inaugural Lecture," *Oxford Economic Papers,* Vol. 5, No. 2, June 1953.

[13] For a popular, and rather badly organized, discussion of productivity, see Graham Hutton, *We Too Can Prosper, op. cit.*

[14] The United States droughts of 1936 and 1938 may have brought the latter figure unduly low, but not by more than one or two percentage points. See H. B. Lary, *The United States in the World Economy,* United States Department of Commerce, Bureau of Foreign and Domestic Commerce, Washington, 1943.

[15] See T. W. Schultz, *Agriculture in an Unstable Economy*, New York, McGraw-Hill Book Co., Inc., 1945, p. 6.

[16] W. Arthur Lewis, "World Production, Prices and Trade, 1870-1960," *The Manchester School of Economics and Social Studies*, May 1952.

[17] Colin Clark, *The Economics of 1960*, New York, Macmillan Co., 1942.

[18] See, for example, Food and Agriculture Organization, *The World Situation in Food and Agriculture*, Rome, December 1953; United Nations, Experts report on *Measures for International Economic Stability*, 1951; Economic Commission for Latin America, United Nations, *The Economic Development of Latin America and Its Principal Problems*, 1949.

[19] See J. E. Sawyer, "Social Structure and Economic Progress: General Propositions and Some French Examples," *American Economic Review*, Vol. XLI, No. 2, May 1951.

[20] See, for example, F. A. Hayek, *The Road to Serfdom*, Chicago, University of Chicago Press, 1944, and J. Jewkes, *Ordeal by Planning*, London, Macmillan Co., 1948.

[21] See F. Perroux, "Equisse d'une théorie de l'économie dominante," *Economie Appliquée*, 1948, pp. 242–300.

[22] For a similar official European (and French) view, see R. Marjolin, *Europe and the United States in the World Economy*, Durham, N.C., Duke University Press, 1953, esp. Chapter V and pp. 92ff.

[23] One of the most inspired adaptations in Europe was that by Denmark in the 1870's and 1880's to the decline in the price of wheat. This took the form of a shift into butter and bacon raising, but required the invention of the milk-separator, the creation and spread of the cooperative, to combine large-scale marketing with small-scale production, and depended upon the extension of the Folk-High School movement. For a discussion of economic adaptation by a Danish author, making little use of this example, see C. M. Wright, *Economic Adaptation to a Changing World Market*, Copenhagen, Einar Munksgaard, 1939.

[24] See, however, W. W. Rostow, *The Process of Economic Growth*, New York, W. W. Norton & Co., Inc., 1952.

[25] "The Balance of Payments of the United States," *Economic Journal*, June 1946.

CHAPTER FIFTEEN

THE MECHANISM FOR ADJUSTMENT IN INTERNATIONAL PAYMENTS— THE LESSONS OF POSTWAR EXPERIENCE*

I

The grand design for the machinery for adjusting international payments in the postwar period, embodied in the Bretton Woods agreement, was derived from the lessons of the thirties. The task of establishing a new international economic and financial framework was regarded as one of reconciling the requirements of domestic and international equilibrium. Domestic equilibrium meant chiefly full employment. International equilibrium meant chiefly the avoidance of large and persistent national surpluses and deficits in external accounts. The two guiding principles were that no country should be prevented by balance-of-payments difficulties from pursuing domestic policies of full employment, and that no country should be permitted to adopt "beggar-thy-neighbor" measures for exporting unemployment. These principles were adopted to assuage the widespread fear that after the war the United States economy might sink back into depression and that the United States government might not take adequate compensatory measures to correct deficiencies in aggregate demand. One central objective was to develop a postwar framework which would prevent American depression from again becoming world depression. Another was to free trade from the trammels of quantitative and price interferences and to establish a framework conducive to the development of world trade and investment.

* Emile Despres, coauthor. From *Papers and Proceedings, American Economic Review,* Volume XLII, No. 2, May 1952.

The methods for reconciling these parallel objectives were (1) the creation of an international pool of liquid reserves to help meet cyclical balance-of-payments difficulties; (2) exchange control to prevent "hot-money" movements, thus eliminating speculative amplification of balance-of-payments disturbances; (3) discriminatory restriction on dollar imports if cyclical disturbances in the balance of payments were of sufficient size and duration to exhaust available reserves; (4) exchange-rate adjustments to correct persistent or "fundamental" disequilibrium; and (5) with the two foregoing exceptions, the rule of fixed exchanges rates with current payments free of quantitative restriction and discrimination.

Some of these rules, acceptable in principle, proved difficult to effect in practice. Thus, for example, speculative capital movements were proscribed in many countries but took place nonetheless as the ingenuity of the speculators exceeded or led in time that of the exchange controllers. Some took on the character of a rule of thumb, clung to even at the sacrifice of its objective. The emphasis on par values of exchange established to promote trade, for example, led to the conclusion in some quarters that it was desirable to protect par values at whatever cost, even if it meant severe restrictions on trade — a point which was put in this way by Guy Orcutt.

For the most part, however, discussion in Britain and the United States revolved around the question whether the new facilities and new rules would be adequate to prevent a repetition of the experience of the thirties. Some considered that the rules conceded too much to the predilections of American exporters for multilateralism and left insufficient room for the use of discriminatory direct controls; others felt that too much had been conceded to the planners and neo-Schachtians. Initially, however, there was general agreement that the problem was to maintain balance-of-payments equilibrium on the one hand and the domestic level of effective demand on the other.

It would be easy to conclude that the Keynesians, in their international as in their domestic planning, were concerned with imaginary rather than real dangers and that the fault was not with their economics but with their judgment. The postwar difficulty on this showing was not lack of effective demand but a plethora. Consumption rose to a new relationship with income, because of backlogs of demand, liquidity maintained by wartime accumulations of money and government debts which could not be repudiated, and, in some countries, a shift of income in favor of spending and against saving groups in the society. Investment responded to the shortage of capital, which had been seriously underestimated, and, at least through 1948, to postwar reconstruction needs. Government expenditure and business investment were then held at high levels by the unforeseeable military expenditures which followed the invasion of South Korea.

But the fault with the Keynesian tradition has not been solely one of forecasting. Two other demerits can be charged against it. In the first place, in the thirties it produced near unanimity that deflation was a wrong method of correcting balance of payments under all circumstances. Cultural lag carried this view into the late forties. Secondly, the economic problem in a world of excess demand is not simply the obverse of the problem in a world of depression. Exports come to be thought of less as added employment than as a cost; and imports lose their character as producers of unemployment and are regarded as real income. More than this, however, the world of full employment is a classical world where the problems of allocation of resources and the distribution of the gains of trade, neglected in depression, come into their own. The roots of present balance-of-payments difficulties do not lie solely in excess demand, as some anti-Keynesians and even pro-Keynesians think, but in this fundamental area. The real questions today are structural.

II

Before we turn to these structural problems which involve the price system, however, a further comment may be in order concerning income adjustments and the effects of depression.

The Keynesian view of the world of depression was limited to industrial countries where the impact of depression is different from its impact on producers of primary materials. Under the system which evolved in the nineteenth century, a large part of the burden of maintaining interregional and international equilibrium was borne, not by the financial centers, but by debtor, primary-producing regions at the periphery. A reduction in the flow of capital to the periphery usually preceded or accompanied a decline in external demand for primary products; thus subjecting their balances of payments to double pressure. The effect, however, was not chiefly upon the level of employment, owing to short-term inelasticity of output, but upon terms of trade, volume of imports, and, consequently, real income.

Primary-producing countries frequently adjusted their external accounts through exchange depreciation rather than deflation, but this did not obviate the loss of real income. The only choice open to them was to accept the loss through lower export prices or higher import prices. Meanwhile in the industrial regions the cheapening of imports subject to inelastic demand bolstered expenditure for domestic goods and helped to counterbalance the loss of employment resulting from the falling off of exports.

Insofar as industrial countries are concerned, however, it is ironical that Britain and Western Europe should be so fearful of another American depression. Capacity to control effective demand — at least to the extent of preventing it from declining — could be used to offset secondary income effects resulting from loss of exports. If economic assistance were not forthcoming or were available in insufficient amounts to finance deficits, the dollar deficit could be reduced or removed by devaluation or discrimination. The overall position of Western Europe, however, would be improved by the movement of the terms of trade in favor of manufactures and against agricultural products and raw materials. It is the primary producers rather than Western European industrial countries which should fear American depression.

Popular confusion on this point has been caused by the behavior of the sterling area, which lumps the United Kingdom industrial balance of payments with those of Commonwealth primary producers and hides the separate movements in each. Rising raw material prices build up the sterling balances of the primary producers; declining prices bring them down. Britain, as banker for the area, gains gold and dollars from rising prices as in 1950; loses from falling as in 1949. But high raw material prices, after primary-producing countries have adjusted real consumption to them, no longer benefit the banker qua banker; if the adjustment is excessive, so that balances are drawn down, as has been the case in 1951, the banker may suffer. And Britain and Western Europe suffer from high prices of primary products and gain from low in their other capacities as producers and consumers. Only a partial offset to these fundamental effects is afforded by the change in income from overseas investment, now much reduced from prewar and from the nineteenth century.

III

The exclusion of deflation from the armory of weapons for adjusting balance-of-payments disequilibrium has not been rigorously maintained. Room was found in the postwar period for what is not an unrelated process — disinflation; and deflation which produced unemployment, while perhaps less effective in limiting imports from the dollar area, has been found useful in reducing balance-of-payments deficits within the European trading area. For the most part, however, economists have searched elsewhere and for a relatively painless device to bring about balance-of-payments adjustment. In advocating restriction of investment, Harrod assumed that much of the investment taking place was of low productivity. Proponents of exchange rate adjustment have expressed faith in the elasticity of demand for industrial goods. Advocates of discrimination have assumed that reciprocal discrimination could easily be negotiated. There is, however, nothing in economic theory to support the faith that balance-of-payments maladjustments of a structural nature can easily or cheaply be corrected, even if the appropriate mechanism be chosen.

An impressive technical literature (e.g., Lerner, Mrs. Robinson, Metzler, Hirschman, and Meade) has developed during and since the war, stipulating the conditions under which devaluation improves the balance of payments of a country. To this has been added an expanding series of articles — especially by Frisch and Alexander — comparing the efficacies of devaluation and discrimination and suggesting the optimum method of discrimination. Broadly speaking, devaluation will improve the balance of payments of a country only when, including real-income effects, the sum of the elasticities of its demand for imports and the world's demand for its exports is greater than one; and import restriction improves the balance of payments of a country more economically than devaluation, i.e., with less loss in real income, so long as the gain in welfare from an additional dollar spent on imports is less than the welfare cost of earning an additional dollar through exports. If, on the other hand, the domestic value of the added imports is greater than that of the goods which must be foregone as exports in order to obtain them, then it pays to devalue rather than to restrict imports further.

These developments in theory were accompanied by a spate of work in the field of measurement (e.g., Tinbergen, Adler, and Chang) culminating in the conclusion, rather widely accepted, especially by Orcutt, Machlup, Haberler, and Viner, that the pioneering efforts in this area left much to be desired. Few economists are willing nonetheless to hazard the judgment that the elasticities are high over-all, except perhaps in the long run.

It is important to observe, however, that this is partial-equilibrium analysis and therefore of limited relevance. Modern proponents of devaluation are prepared to concede that the elasticities of demand may be low in the short run, but they count on their being higher over time. This involves a reversal of the older view of the matter. It used to be thought that depreciation would be effective in correcting balance-of-payments disequilibrium only in the short run. Over time, when full equilibrium had been reached, it was thought that this transitional gain would have been lost because of the long-run inflation of costs and prices. The job is not only to "halt the inflation and adjust the exchange rate," if this can be done, but also to keep down domestic prices and costs as resources are transferred into export and import-competing industries and in the face of the rise in import prices. Partial-equilibrium analysis is not sufficient. With its use, depreciation assumes too readily that the price system will be effective in persuading countries to accept the loss in available goods and services entailed to getting rid of balance-of-payments deficits.

The advocates of discrimination fall into two none-too-clearly divided groups. One would ignore the price system altogether as a guide to the allocation of resources and maximization of real income. Bulk buying, discriminatory promotion of high-cost production to save foreign exchange, and quantitative restrictions in general are viewed as the prerequisite to effective internal planning. The difficulty with this view is that price comparisons lose their meaning as a guide to resource allocation. The criterion of "economizing foreign exchange" in directing new investment and allocating resources may waste productive energy, lower real income, and even worsen the balance of payments. Since the balance-of-payments problem is one of achieving the least costly adaptation to changed external conditions, i.e., of minimizing the loss of real income, discard of the price system may leave the planners without effective guides to the allocation of resources and distribution of output.

The other group chooses to use the price system rather than discard it, to take advantage of inelasticities to improve real income. An extreme example of the attitude employed is found in the advocacy of exchange appreciation, not discrimination, by Harrod and by the Economic Commission for Europe to secure more favorable terms of trade for Britain and Western Europe. If there are low elasticities of demand for exports and of supply for imports, then monopoly and monopsony gains are possible from restricting exports and imports respectively. The monopsony gain from restricting imports may be at the cost of increasing unemployment due to loss of complementary resources rather than leading to a gain in employment, as in a depressed world. But the beggar-thy-neighbor tactic of subsidizing exports, which flourishes in a depressed world, is replaced by that of holding them back.

There are a couple of things wrong with this prescription for world trade. In the first place, it leads to retaliation. The neo-Schachtians and the liberal critics of German bilateralism failed alike to recognize that the system persisted because it had real attractions for Germany's trading partners. In a depressed world, additional exports produced additional employment, additional imports, and additional real income, at whatever terms of trade. Second, the all-around adoption of restrictions on exports and imports leads to an impasse in trade negotiations — witness the difficulties of the Andes Agreement between Britain and Argentina — and involves the loss of real income all around. Some monopoly gains are possible for raw material producers, particularly vis-à-vis the United States and by means of the multiple-exchange rate device. But there are limits to these gains, as Argentina knows in linseed and Canada in newsprint. And the possibility of Western Europe effecting monopoly or monopsony gains at the expense of either the United States or primary-producing areas may be excluded in a world of full employment.

This concludes what little we have to say about the adjustment mechanism in a narrow sense confined to the balance of payments.

The rest of our paper focuses attention not so much on the balance of payments as on the underlying phenomena within the country experiencing balance-of-payments disequilibrium.

IV

In a classical economic world of full employment, two questions present themselves. One, from the point of view of the world as a whole, is whether the resources of the world and of each country are allocated to the production of the right goods. A second, which is related to the first, is how total income is distributed among factors within a country and among countries. A world concerned with real income, as ours now is, must have regard to both these questions.

As an aid to the analysis, we may perhaps distinguish between structural disequilibrium at the goods level and structural disequilibrium at the factor level. Disequilibrium at the goods level means that relative goods prices do not reflect the allocation of factors among various industries appropriate to existing factor prices. Disequilibrium at the factor level may arise either because a single factor receives different returns in different uses or because the price relationships among factors are out of line with factor availabilities.

Some of the difficulties at the goods level are due to monopolistic competition, already discussed in connection with discrimination. Included among these by a number of writers is the increasing-returns case. This is a favorite of the underdeveloped countries. In addition to monopolistic competition, however, the price system may suffer because of excessive factor response, typically found in the cobweb theorem, or in factor rigidities which permit no response. Part way between, perhaps, is the difficulty which occurs in products of long gestation, like coffee, where short-run inelasticity is combined with long-run excessive response, occurring years after the cause of the stimulus is forgotten. These defects in the price system have recently been examined by Professor Haberler.[1] While the price system admittedly falls short of its smoothly efficient ideal, he concludes that in the absence of any superior alternative its defects do not constitute an argument for its abandonment. It must be conceded, further, that the demerits of the price system by no means constitute a positive argument for planning. If private

242

enterprise is too little responsive to increasing-returns situations, public authorities find many which ultimately prove illusory. Planners face the same rigidities in factor responses that price will encounter, and in the absence of large windfall profits will provide little stimulus to correct allocation. And planners, perhaps more than entrepreneurs but certainly as much, are as likely to infect each other in particular situations with their own enthusiasm and overrespond to price stimuli and their underlying significance.

The price system never operated without making mistakes. Economic Darwinism regarded the losses under competition as the price paid for progress. With large units directing resources, however, whether under oligopolistic competition or under planning, the penalties of error are increased manyfold and a lower tolerance for mistakes has been developed.

The workability of the price system, however, depended on submission to its verdicts. The invisible hand carried out the judgments of an impersonal fate from which it was impossible to appeal and against which it was useless to struggle. The growth of monopolistic competition and government interference, which exposed the hand and showed the fate to be personal, has changed this. The price system has been undermined in a fundamental respect. Its decisions are known not to be *ex cathedra* and infallible.

Structural disequilibrium at the factor level involves questions both of resource allocation and use on the one hand and of income distribution on the other. We shall discuss first the case of disequilibrium between factor prices and factor endowments, and then the case of unequal remuneration to one factor in different uses despite mobility between uses. Both cases, it need hardly be pointed out, are different from the classical case of noncompeting groups, where immobility exists among occupational groups.

The disequilibrium of Italy and Germany arises from lack of complementary resources. Given the technology in use, these countries lack capital and have an overabundance of labor. In one view, the solution to their problem is capital imports and emigration, to establish the factor proportions appropriate to prevailing factor prices. An alternative is a change in relative factor prices. This would result in changing the least-cost combinations of factors in all uses and the relative prices of goods, thus altering the volume and composition of exports and imports. In the absence of change in either factor endowments or factor prices, balance-of-payments adjustment means unemployment of the redundant factor, and full employment leads to balance-of-payments deficit.

Factor disequilibrium in which factor proportions are out of line with factor prices poses a problem which is out of reach of measures of discrimination and for which devaluation is likely to provide an inadequate solution. Except in the case of slight disequilibria, moreover, capital imports and emigration are not likely to occur to the extent necessary to justify existing factor prices and technology. Strenuous deflation with high interest rates, which will raise the return to capital and lower that to labor, is hardly attractive as a social and political policy. In addition, it faces the disability that elasticities of substitution of labor for capital are almost certainly low. Capital, for example, can be shifted among industries only slowly, as depreciation takes place. The alternative aspects of the disequilibrium, however — the deficit and the unemployment — require solution urgently.

Germany and Italy are, in a sense, special cases. But it must be remembered that most Western European countries have been hovering close to the same type of structural unemployment. The combination of a full employment level of domestic demand for manufactures, limited exports, and American aid to finance a part of the needed primary products is providing a sheltered market for Europe's output. But when and if Western Europe must shift from domestic capital formation, military production, and American aid to exports and self-support, it is questionable whether Europe's full employment requirements for food and raw materials can be paid for by exports of manufactures. At best the process will produce a marked worsening of terms of trade. If external grants and loans are not available, other European countries may face structural unemployment or underemployment of the work-relief type.

A similar disequilibrium, partial in nature, may be detected in underdeveloped countries. In these, the export sector of the economy, which may have access to foreign capital, will frequently employ factor combinations which yield relative marginal productivities different from those in the subsistence sector. In consequence, labor and land will receive a higher return in exports in combination with foreign capital than in the rest of the economy where it works with scarce domestic capital. In Venezuela, for example, labor will earn more in oil than in domestic enterprise. In Cuba, foreign capital participates in the sugar export economy but not in tobacco; so that different factor proportions and factor returns exist side by side in exports.

The existence of different returns in different sectors of the economy need raise no particular problems for the balance of payments. It may, however, raise serious problems of other kinds, both economic and social, as pointed out by F. Ortiz in *Cuban Counterpoint: Tobacco and Sugar* (New York, 1947), pages 1–93. The difficulty, however, is that these countries are tempted to use the technology and factor proportions appropriate to the export sector in development projects for which foreign capital is not available. In these cases, the result is structural disequilibrium which is reflected either in balance-of-payments deficit or in a large degree of unemployment or underemployment in the subsistence sector of the economy.

The dual-economy case is representative of the first type of disequilibrium in which factor prices are out of line with factor proportions if we focus attention on the subsistence sector of the economy. If, however, we look at both sectors and if labor moves between the subsistence and export sectors as production for export fluctuates, we approach the second type of disequilibrium: unequal prices for one factor in alternative uses. Wage rates are higher in the export sector than in the subsistence economy. The general case of failure of factor prices to reach equality in different uses, however, is that presented by Manoilesco (*Theory of Protection,* London, 1931), which has recently received renewed discussion in connection with underdeveloped countries.[2] In this model, the level of wages in the manufacturing or import-competing sector of the economy is assumed to be higher than in the primary area engaged in exports and subsistence, owing simply to wage rigidity in manufacturing. There are no barriers to entry and the supply of labor for manufacturing is highly elastic at the established wage rates. On this assumption, the marginal transformation ratios between primary products and manufactured goods deviate from the corresponding price ratios.

Manoilesco regarded this situation as one calling for protection of manufactures, to induce a shift of underemployed agricultural labor into industry. It should be pointed out, however, that if expansion of industrial output requires additional capital as well as labor, it is necessary to weigh the gain in real income from such investment against the gain which would result from an equal amount of output-increasing investment in agriculture. But it is also important to examine the position in demand. If the elasticity of demand for primary-products exports is low and the marginal terms of trade lower than the average, the higher apparent return to capital in agriculture at the average terms of trade is illusory. In this case a further reason exists, from a national point of view, for shifting resources from an overcrowded, underemployed agriculture.

The following analysis, overdrawn for emphasis, may be suggestive of how the Manoilesco case may apply to the real world and its structural disequilibrium at the factor level. Western Europe has been a densely populated area with limited natural resources. Its relatively high real income per capita in the past has come in large part from its gains from trade. Western Europe has concentrated in the production and export of industrial goods in exchange for primary products; the exchange ratios have overvalued industrial goods and undervalued primary products in comparison with their transformation ratios. Rostas' comparison of prewar productivity in the United States and the United Kingdom, for example, shows that real income in the United Kingdom was much higher relative to the United States than industry-by-industry comparisons of productivity would suggest. A major element in the explanation for this phenomenon was the relatively greater concentration of British resources in "high value-added" items; i.e., a more favorable product mix.[3] Colin Clark indicated the same phenomenon in another light when he showed the far lower average return available in the United States in agriculture as compared with industry (see *Conditions of Economic Progress,* London, 1951, second edition, Chapters IX and X, especially pages 395 and 440 and following). This lower return reflects disguised unemployment, not throughout agriculture as a whole, but in some major sectors of American agriculture.

In the last ten years, there has been a considerable narrowing of the gap between the returns in occupations in which wages and prices are relatively high and rigid and those in which they are low and flexible. This narrowing has been almost world wide, in developed and underdeveloped countries alike. Its importance for income

246

distribution, present and prospective, should not be underestimated. With some notable exceptions, both industrial and primary-producing countries have attempted to increase their real income by directing labor and capital into those lines which are characterized by high and rigid wages. A large part of the problem of international equilibrium turns on the question whether, if these trends continue, manufactures can be exchanged at their customary terms for primary products.

The question has been postponed for a time by the prolongation of American aid to permit the expansion of military production. The military program provides an outlet for highly fabricated goods at the same time that it intensifies the demand for raw materials. When and if there is a return to a more nearly peacetime economy and if the output of manufactures is sustained through domestic full employment policies, it may well be that the share of world income going to primary producers will be much larger and that of fabricators much smaller than in the past.

The demand for full employment in the industrial countries is irresistible. In practice, full employment means a level of demand sufficient to keep high-wage industries operating at close to capacity, and a concentration of investment to expand these industries. As a result of full employment, along with expansion of manufacturing plants, restricted immigration, mass education, and growing labor mobility within countries, industrial countries are drawing a larger and larger share of their resources into the traditionally high-wage lines of activity. In this the underdeveloped countries insist on joining, through emphasis on industrialization. At the same time, they are unwilling and will not need to accept the former terms of trade. The scarcity premium which manufactured goods have enjoyed over most of the last 150 years is in process of being lost.

V

A smoothly functioning system of international payments requires that all countries follow the same set of rules. This will be done if the interest of each of the separate countries, as each views it, is identical or parallel with the interests of all others; or if each country is prepared to carry out measures against its interest, either because of ignorance or because of faith in the ultimate identity of the national and the cosmopolitan interests.

The present full employment world is one in which neither of these conditions holds. On this account alone, no return to gold, nor to flexible exchange rates, to regional free trade, to bilateral monopoly, or to anything else, by itself, will provide the basis for a successful system of international adjustment.

Even if there were a consensus, a major difficulty would remain. The two major schools of thought — the price economists and the planners — have accepted too simple a view of the nature of the problem. We have examined structural disequilibrium at this length because of our view that neither therapy, universally accepted and skillfully applied, would fully meet the maladjustment nor the balance-of-payments problem. International capital movements and migration of labor are unlikely on an adequate scale, as both schools would agree. While the record in governmental loans and grants has been remarkable, no accepted criteria have been evolved in surplus countries, and they remain a limited and unreliable substitute for the international capital movements of the nineteenth century.

Fundamentally, the mechanism of adjustment includes all the processes by which new patterns of resource use and the distribution of gains from trade emerge in response to continual changes in technology, resource endowments, and demand. Price economists tend to focus exclusively on the problem of resource allocation; planners on that of international income distribution. But these problems are inseparable. A workable system of international payments must both allocate resources and distribute income in some fashion which countries and factors within countries are willing to accept.

More time is needed after the breakdown of the nineteenth century system to see how a new workable mechanism will evolve. If one kind of consensus should emerge, the world may settle on new terms of trade, preferably after increases in productivity have converted an absolute to a relative decline in the standard of living for Western Europe. Another possibility is a shift of resources in both industrial and primary-producing countries into raw materials and foodstuffs, and an increase in relative efficiency in these lines, to restore the terms of trade to which the industrial sections of the world have become accustomed. Still a third alternative is the evolution of some regular system for redistributing income internationally, as this is now done interregionally within a country, to

248

offset the most inequitable results of malallocation of resources where it exists and to ease any hardships of adjustment to appropriate resource allocation and terms of trade.

NOTES

[1] See especially "Some Problems in the Pure Theory of International Trade," *Economic Journal,* June 1950, pp. 223–240, and "Real Cost, Money Cost and Comparative Advantage," *International Social Science Bulletin,* Spring, 1951, pp. 54–58.

[2] See Gottfried Haberler, "Real Cost, Money Cost and Comparative Advantage," *op. cit.,* and Jacob Viner, "Lectures on the Theory of International Trade" (mimeographed, 1950), pp. 60 *et seq.*

[3] L. Rostas, "International Comparisons of Productivity," *International Labor Review,* September 1948, pp. 283–305, especially pp. 295–296.

CHAPTER SIXTEEN

INTERNATIONAL
MONETARY STABILIZATION*

So far as can now be judged, four principal factors of disequilibrium will exist at the conclusion of the period of relief and reconstruction after the war, to plague the establishment and maintenance of a free system of international trade and exchange:

1. The distribution of international monetary reserves will be more distorted than in the prewar period.

2. International liquidity will be more difficult to accord to national capital assets, not only because of shortages in foreign reserves, but also as a result of the increase in internal liquidity in all countries.

3. The long-run shift in the relative prices of finished goods and primary products, which has resulted in a steady worsening of the terms of trade of countries dependent upon exports of agricultural and raw commodities, appears likely to persist.

4. The "chronic world shortage of dollars," due partly to the height of American tariff protection and partly to the economic stagnation in the United States during the 1930's, but resting fundamentally upon the fact that the rest of the world feels the need of American products in greater value amounts than the United States requires foreign commodities, is likely to be accentuated as a result of the changes during the war.

Considerable progress toward the reconstruction of free, stable, and multilateral international economic relations will have been achieved if problems of war debts, including the costs of financing relief and reconstruction, are overcome by treating national war expenditures in behalf of allies as direct costs of war which do not

* From *Postwar Economic Problems*, Seymour E. Harris, ed., New York, McGraw-Hill Book Company, Inc., 1943, pp. 375–395.

give rise to international obligations.[1] An attempt to collect reparations from the defeated enemy, which would further complicate the problem of international economic adjustment, is also unlikely to be made on the basis of past experience. Yet it should be remembered that the disintegration of the international economic system during the interbellum years continued to take place at a rapid pace during the decade of the 1930's, after war debts and reparations had passed from the international scene as live issues.

Crucial Problems for International Stability

The inability of the world to cope, prior to Sept. 1, 1939, with the four factors of disequilibrium just listed was fully evidenced by the growth of bilateralism, trade discrimination, foreign exchange control, and clearing agreements. The war in its progress to the end of 1942 has accentuated the potential disruptive powers of these factors in the postwar period.

1. The facts relating to the concentration of monetary gold in the United States, the loss of British gold, foreign balances, and foreign securities, the accumulation of blocked sterling by Empire and other countries, etc., are too well known to require repetition. It may be noted, however, that the Lend-lease Act in the United States and the Canadian provision for a billion-dollar gift to Britain, both initiated because of the inability of the United Kingdom to finance its North American purchases out of income or capital, have halted British losses of foreign assets in these countries.

2. The problem of international liquidity, familiarly known before the war as the "hot money" problem, has been effectively disposed of for the period of the war by foreign exchange control. If exchange controls are to be removed after the war, however, the problem must be dealt with. Even apart from the question of confidence in currencies, hot money will be troublesome because the proportion of liquid to total assets[2] has grown enormously in all countries. Currency in circulation, central bank deposits, commercial and savings bank deposits have increased markedly, while physical capital assets have been consumed for war purposes. At the same time, the distinction between government debt and cash has narrowed as governments have given explicit and tacit undertakings of stability of interest rates during and after the war. Savings bonds in the United States can be redeemed 60 days after issue at

any time without notice, and similar special securities have been sold to the public in many countries. Ordinary government bonds are so widely held by the public, corporations, and banks that any reversal of the cheap-money policies pursued during the war would be likely to meet with extensive political opposition and endanger the safety of important national institutions. Cheap money has been adopted as an immutable policy of finance during the war when capital is scarce; it would appear virtually impossible to dispense with after the war when the need for capital is reduced, the danger of deflation threatening, and a heavy load of war-contracted debt must be carried by governments.

If money remains cheap after the war, government debt in the hands of the public in all countries will be convertible into cash with a low risk of loss on principal. The increased liquidity of national assets will accentuate the problem of providing international liquidity. Capital flight will be a greater peril to a country's international monetary stability. If free exchange markets are maintained, the ease of converting national assets into cash will lead to increased attempts to distribute the risk of capital loss internationally.

3. The trend in the terms of trade against primary products in favor of industrial goods may be expected to continue after the war, unless further steps are taken to correct it, because of the wartime expansion in agricultural and raw-material capacity and the accelerated development of manufactured substitutes for natural commodities.[3] That this trend has been disturbing to the maintenance of international trade equilibrium under an open system cannot be doubted. The shrinkage of markets in general gives monopolistic advantages to markets which remain available. By making full use of the power of their bargaining position, large-scale importing countries can require the countries from which they buy to buy from them. Once involved in bilateral clearing, moreover, primary producing countries are vulnerable to attempts further to reduce agricultural and raw-material prices or to raise quotations on industrial goods. The long-run shift in the terms of trade has opened opportunities for government intervention on a discriminatory basis in the pricing and distribution of goods in international trade.

The reasons underlying this movement in the terms of trade can be illustrated by reference to agricultural products. The inclusion of raw materials complicates the analysis but does not greatly modify its conclusions.

The terms of trade have moved against agricultural products and in favor of industrial commodities because of differences in the institutional organization of production in the two fields, on the one hand, and in the character of the demand for them, on the other. The differences in the organization of production need not be elaborated. In various quarters it is urged that they be narrowed by national and international acreage controls and international agreements to stock-pile surpluses on the "ever-normal-granary" principle, as far as agriculture is concerned,[4] or by the destruction of monopolistic practices in industry. The fact that the demand for agricultural products as a whole is relatively inelastic and the demand for industrial products relatively elastic, however, presents a far less tractable problem. As productive efficiency improves in agriculture, factors of production must be shifted out of agriculture into manufacturing or service industries, because the demand for agricultural products is limited; as productive efficiency increases in industry, on the other hand, an over-all expansion in industrial output as a whole is possible.[5]

The possibility of technological unemployment in agriculture calls into question a fundamental assumption on which the case for international specialization rests. Greater efficiency in agricultural production can raise the real income of a country dependent upon exports of the agricultural product only if labor freed from the land is able to migrate abroad, or, where migration is impossible for political reasons or for inability to accumulate the capital initially called for, when industry is developed within the country. This industry need not be so efficient as industry abroad. The real income of the country will be increased if, at some level of costs, labor displaced from agriculture can produce industrial products previously imported to enable part of the proceeds of an unchanged volume of exports to be spent upon other types of imports.

If neither migration nor industrialization occurs, the terms of trade of the country experiencing an increase in productive efficiency in agricultural products will move against it, and the country will have made no gain from the increased output. The terms of trade may even move so far that the country experiences a net loss in real income as a result of an increase in efficiency in the exporting industries.

4. The concept of a chronic world shortage of dollars is perhaps too complex for full analysis in a paper of this length. That a

shortage exists is supported by the fact that the balance of payments of the United States has recorded surpluses on current account in all but 2 years since 1919 and the fact that the merchandise trade balance of the country has been favorable each year since the large-scale capital imports of the 1870's. The small balance of payments deficits in 1936 and 1937 occurred during a period of heavy inventory accumulation and drought.

The difficulties encountered by foreigners in obtaining adequate supplies of dollars are "blamed" on United States tariff policy or on the fact that during the 1930's United States recovery lagged behind that of other countries as compared with 1929. These explanations fail to make clear why a new equilibrium is not established when United States tariff barriers are raised, after simply a transitional shortage of dollars; and they fail to push the analysis of higher United States income and ensuing higher imports to the impact of these in turn on the purchases of foreign countries in the United States.

At basis the explanation for the chronic world shortage of dollars is to be found in the technical superiority of the United States in the production of many goods necessary to a high modern standard of living and to the natural desire in other countries to raise real incomes faster than the basic conditions of their economic productivity justify. The United States has large and fairly balanced natural resources, relatively modern and efficient capital equipment, a comparatively small population in relation to natural resources and capital equipment, but a large domestic market for the output of its own mass-production industries. The United States can produce a variety of producers' and consumers' goods with a price and quality advantage so great as to be almost absolute. The advantages of other countries over the United States in the production of other industrial goods are relatively narrow. Under these conditions, the law of comparative advantage can establish equilibrium in international trade only with great difficulty, especially since technological advance is being made in the United States and abroad at a rapid pace.

The fact that other countries want to increase their standard of living faster than the facts of their economic productivity justify can be expressed in the statement that the demand of the rest of the world for American manufactured products[6] is highly elastic with

254

respect to income and price, whereas the United States demand for foreign products is relatively inelastic.[7] It can be demonstrated that disequilibrium in trade relationships will be brought about if national money incomes increase by a similar percentage in two countries, one of which has an inelastic demand for the goods of the other, while the demand of the latter for the goods of the former is elastic. If the ratios of exports to national income in the two countries also differ, further disturbances result.

Assume country A with a low marginal propensity to import (low elasticity of demand for imports with respect to income), and country B with a high marginal propensity, trading exclusively with one another. From a position of equilibrium in trade, an autonomous rise in national money income of an equal percentage in relation to the preexisting level occurs in each country. A's imports from B will rise somewhat, but B's imports from A will rise considerably. National income in A will receive a further stimulus from the favorable balance of trade; national income in B will tend to decline from the new level. If a new trade equilibrium is to be established (assuming no change in the exchange rate, demand schedules, or other conditions of trade), national income must rise still higher in A, decline in B, or both. If the original increase in national money income were sought in both countries, say, in order to eliminate a certain amount of unemployment, and a strenuous attempt made to maintain it, the equilibrium of the trade position cannot be restored.

When A has a low marginal propensity to import and is only slightly dependent upon export trade, and B a high marginal propensity to import and is heavily dependent on exports, adjustment becomes much more difficult. An autonomous rise in the national incomes in A produces a small increase in imports from B. The rise in B's exports, however, results in an increase in incomes in B, most of which in turn is spent for imports from A. This rise in imports may be larger than the increase in exports which prompted it, with the result that the original stimulus to the favorable balance of trade in B eventually produces an unfavorable balance. The maintenance of trade equilibrium in a world where these conditions obtain is a difficult task.

It may be suggested that the United States has a comparatively low propensity to import and a low ratio of exports to national income, whereas the rest of the world has a relatively high elasticity of demand for United States exports of manufactured goods and a relatively high ratio of exports to income. If this be true, and if the foregoing analysis be applicable to the postwar situation, additional dollars made available to foreigners by increased United States imports may lead to a greater increase in foreign expenditures for American products, leaving the world still short of dollars. This is not to gainsay the desirability of lower American tariffs, since the shortage would still occur at higher levels of real income. It simply underlines the conclusion that a reduction of the American tariff is not of itself an adequate solution for the world shortage of dollars and that the earnest admonitions of the rest of the world to the United States that it "live like a creditor nation" fail to come to grips with the fundamentals of the problem.

Three Unorthodox Solutions

The types of solutions appropriate to the problem of establishing and maintaining a free system of international trade and exchange after the war may be illustrated by the analysis of three recently advanced proposals: (1) the Feis plan, (2) the Twentieth Century Economic System, and (3) pool clearing.[8] These are all variations of an essentially similar idea, to use international clearing as a substitute for or a complement to an open exchange market.

Feis's plan, which he describes as a suggestion for a "Trade Stabilization Fund or Budget," calls for the United States to make $3 or $4 billion available to foreign nations as a minimum annual budget for payments to the United States for goods, services, or debts. This sum would be allocated among various foreign nations by negotiation. Foreign countries drawing against the minimum credit assigned to them would credit the United States with an equivalent amount of their own currencies, computed at agreed rates of exchange, or of other foreign currencies as agreed upon. These credits in turn would be drawn upon as the United States spent dollars — which would be paid in to the authority handling the plan — for foreign goods and services. If a balance of dollars credited to foreigners, or of foreign currencies credited to the United States, were left unspent at the end of a specified period of time — Feis suggests 2 years — the unspent sums would be canceled. As the use of the plan developed, it would be expected that all countries would credit all other countries with minimum budgets of local currency at the beginning of each trade year, at agreed rates of exchange alterable by negotiation. Feis also anticipates that private markets for foreign exchange, free of government control, would grow up outside the confines of the minimum budgets, to provide media of international payment for capital movements, trade in excess of minimum requirements, gold flows, etc.

The plan outlined in *A Twentieth Century Economic System,* endorsed by the London Chamber of Commerce,[9] involves less elaborate machinery. It starts with an international convention, in which the participating countries agree on a series of exchange rates. Exporters draw foreign currency bills against foreign purchasers, discounting these bills for local funds with their respective national exchange-control authorities, which debit the importing country. Importers make payment for purchases from abroad in local currency to their respective exchange authorities, which credit the exporting country. The exchange control of a country with a surplus of exports over imports vis-à-vis another country builds up a claim on that country which can be reduced only by importing further amounts of its goods. Otherwise the latter is entitled to cancel the credit after 7 years.

The author states that multilateral trade could be provided by the creation of an international exchange, where blocked credits in one country could be canceled against debits in another at the conventional rates. He is opposed, however, to holding all credits and debits with the international exchange. He considers it important that countries owning uncanceled credits recognize in which countries these have arisen, in order that they can "take steps to clear those credits either by taking more imports or restricting exports to them."

The third proposal, that for pool clearing, is similar to the Twentieth Century Economic System plan but is shorn of its strongly bilateral tendencies and without specific provision for the cancellation of unused surpluses. Each country establishes a national clearing fund, and together all countries establish an international clearing office. Exporters obtain payment by drawing bills on importers abroad and discounting these bills at the national clearing fund. The latter pays the exporter by borrowing local funds from the central bank and registers a claim with the international office. Importers pay their national funds for foreign merchandise. In this case the national fund repays loans to the central bank, and its credit at the international clearing office is canceled. The international office regards net claims from all net exporting countries as offset by balances accumulated in net importing countries as a whole, without identifying particular claims with balances in particular countries. The persistent accumulation of deficits by a country will require: (*a*) the funding of deficits into loans or exchange depreciation, in the case of countries the trade of which is only technically out of balance; (*b*) enforced depreciation or exclusion from the system on the part of countries continuing to import but unwilling to export; or (*c*) no action at all, *i.e.*, the continuous accumulation of balances in the case of countries ready and able to sell abroad, but from which the world is unwilling to buy. Surplus countries run some risk of loss through depreciation of the claims they have amassed against deficit countries. It is felt that they can be relied upon to increase their imports from the world as a whole (not the deficit countries alone), in order to keep down cumulative and unmanageable surpluses which represent barren investments and run the risk of loss.

These brief summaries fail to do justice to the specific plans put forward but may indicate their broad outlines. In general, the proposals are designed to relieve countries with chronic deficits in their balances of payments on current account from the sole necessity to undertake adjustments and to shift the bulk of the burden to surplus countries. The Twentieth Century System is frankly bilateral; the Feis plan tries to rid itself of evident bilateral features by leaving room for the negotiation of balance transfers; pool clearing makes a valiant attempt to avoid bilateralism,[10] but it is not at all certain that the plan would operate successfully in this connection.[11] All three systems depend upon foreign exchange control to ensure that trade transactions are in fact handled through the mechanism set up for the purpose; the Feis plan ostensibly leaves room for freedom of exchange transactions outside the trade stabilization fund, but these transactions have to be examined to ensure that they do not include deals which belong inside, say, imports on the part of a country which has credits abroad to be used up. The Twentieth Century System is not opposed to trade adjustments in the form of export restrictions by surplus countries:

the Feis proposal, put forward to assure countries of import minima, and pool clearing are evidently averse to this method of adjustment.

To get back to the four factors of disequilibrium:

1. All three proposals evidently fill the immediate need of countries which will be left after the war without adequate monetary reserves. If any of them were adopted, no nation need retain its controls over trade transactions for fear of being unable to pay for imports or in order to reconstitute a monetary reserve of appropriate size.

2. The Twentieth Century System and pool clearing meet the problem of international liquidity by providing for exchange control which presumably forbids any but official capital movements that are undertaken to fund surpluses and deficits in balance of payments. Provision under the system could, of course, be made for more latitude in capital movements. The Feis plan purports to allow for freedom of exchange transactions outside the "trade stabilization budget device." It is evident, however, that exchange surveillance is required outside this area, and it is not clear how the plan expects to make movements of short-term capital manageable outside the system. In all three cases, the meeting of the problem of lacks of monetary reserves will serve to increase confidence in currencies, at least for a period. If deficits pile up continuously against a country, however, a movement of the exchange rates may be anticipated, at least under pool clearing, which would provide a stimulus for exchange speculation. Under these conditions, the exchange control necessary to operate the system at all would probably be used to prevent short-term capital movements on private account.

3 and 4. Where these proposals fall short of providing an adequate basis for the reconstruction of international stability in world trade and exchange is in their lack of correctives for the deep-seated factors of disequilibrium discussed above under the headings of the trend of the terms of trade against primary producing countries and the chronic world shortage of dollars. The proposals rely on various means of adjustment: (a) consciously promoted increases in imports by surplus countries; (b) consciously promoted decreases in exports by surplus countries; (c) exchange depreciation on the part of deficit countries, or exchange appreciation on the part of surplus countries; (d) the conversion of unsettled

balances into gifts from surplus to deficit countries.[12] The effectiveness of these measures of adjustment may be tested against the two disequilibrium factors.

(a) To rely on increased imports by industrial countries to correct the shift in the terms of trade against primary-producing countries is futile in the long run, since at higher standards of living a country wants a greater proportion of industrial goods relative to primary commodities. In the short run, the position is complex. An industrial country with substantial resources, engaged domestically in primary production, may benefit by shifting resources from, say, agriculture to industry, importing more agricultural products from abroad. In this instance, the migration of labor from agriculture to industry occurs within the surplus country rather than from the deficit to the surplus country. In highly industrialized countries like the United States, however, a shift of labor from agriculture to industry is already taking place to adjust for the increased efficiency of domestic agriculture. It has not proceeded in peacetime fast enough to absorb all the domestic labor freed from agriculture; it is difficult to see how it could be speeded up, in view of the economic barrier to such migration on private account — lack of capital — and because of political and institutional frictions. The inducement to a more thoroughgoing shift provided by the piling up of current account surpluses under, say, the pool-clearing scheme, would have little effect in view of the domestic resistances.

If a country like the United Kingdom were to accumulate surpluses under the pool-clearing scheme, there would be almost no incentive to increase agricultural imports. The operation of Engel's law in the long run makes it impossible for these schemes to solve the problem of adequate terms of trade for primary products.

Will surpluses accumulated by the United States under the pool-clearing scheme lead to increased imports by the United States which will be sufficient to correct the chronic world shortage of dollars? The analysis of the dollar shortage above suggests that it will not. The United States could import more finished goods at any level of production, can import more raw materials at higher levels of production, and might import more agricultural products to the extent it succeeds in moving factors of production already engaged in agriculture into industry. But these increased imports will raise money incomes abroad and will produce increased demands for American products in excess of the original increases in American imports.[13] The chronic shortage of dollars would remain, albeit at higher levels of real income throughout the world, and the United States would continue to pile up surpluses.

The gold accumulated by the United States during the 20 years prior to the war has not succeeded in inducing an expansion of United States imports which was not followed by an equal or greater rise in exports. This gold represents an investment as cumulative and as barren as claims on foreign countries and is increasingly recognized as such by the man in the street and in vaudeville jokes. Perhaps claims on an international clearing office would provide a greater inducement than gold to stimulate imports. In any event, it may be doubted that increased imports would correct for long the world shortage of dollars.

(*b*) The adjustment of trade through reductions in exports by surplus countries has already been shown to fall short of the desires of the authors of two of the proposals under consideration. To limit exports of industrial products to primary producing countries will, of course, widen the terms of trade between primary and industrial commodities. The same measure fails to solve the problem posed by the world chronic shortage of dollars, since the demand for dollars is in effect an insistent expression of the deemed need for American goods. To reduce the amount of goods available would meet the problem, but in a highly unsatisfactory fashion.

(*c*) The author of the plan for pool clearing gives great weight to exchange depreciation as a solution for deficits which arise as a result of trade disequilibria. "Experience shows that the elasticity of *total* demand for import and of the *total* foreign demand for a country's exports is always such that, at one point or another, depreciation can effect a balancing of trade." Issue may be taken with this statement on two counts. Some experience, that of Germany in 1922 and of the United States in 1932, suggests that exchange fluctuations need not result in a balancing of a trade position; in addition, the type of trade adjustment brought about by depreciation may not be the most desirable one.

Rather than recount the complicated experience of Germany, a possible case to be encountered in the postwar period may be examined. Assume that country X has lost foreign assets, on the earnings of which it depended for a considerable proportion of its income from abroad; X is resolved to maintain its standard of living, and in fact to improve it through a nationwide program of reconstruction and rehousing; it has an unfavorable position in export markets, the demand for its products being relatively inelastic with respect to price, and many of its exports are manufactured of imported raw materials; X's demand for other imports is inelastic since these consist of foodstuffs and raw materials for domestic consumption. Under these circumstances, depreciation will be slow in raising the value of exports and may increase the over-all value of imports in terms of X's currency. If, in addition, wage rates are tied to changes in the cost of living, the expansion in the total value of exports may not occur at all. Under these and other imaginable circumstances, exchange depreciation is a very clumsy device and may prove ineffective because of progressive inflation at home.[14]

Exchange appreciation, on the other hand, may be matched *pari passu* by deflation so that the appreciation of the currency does not stimulate an increase in imports nor restrict exports. This is strongly suggested by the experience of the United States when the pound sterling fell from $4.86 in 1931 to $3.12 in 1932, even though the deflation in the United States did not originate solely or mainly in sterling depreciation. Deflation kept up with the appreciation of the dollar, so that the current account balance continued favorable at the highest values of the dollar.

Exchange fluctuations will doubtless correct balance-of-payments difficulties in the usual case, but they do so, like reductions in exports by the surplus countries, by frustrating the economic forces which make for disequilibrium. In the case of countries with trade deficits resulting from a worsening in the terms of trade, exchange depreciation is likely to balance the position by ensuring that the country obtains less imports for a given or slightly larger volume of exports. Such depreciation will redistribute income within the country and may be desirable in diverting real income from the mass of the consumers to export producers. It is hard to see, however, that it can alter, and it may perpetuate, the distribution of the factors of production between primary and industrial occupations which give rise to the growing disadvantage to the exporting groups.

(*d*) The cancellation of unsettled balances may or may not correct the deep-seated disturbances which give rise to trade disequilibria. If the trade deficits forgiven represent imports of capital

262

goods, which will increase the productivity of the deficit countries in appropriate lines, their financing by cancellation will tend to promote long-run equilibrium. If, on the other hand, the deficits arise from consumption and the underlying situations as to economic productivity remains unaffected, cancellation, or making a gift of the surplus, is a palliative which must be maintained so long as the system is kept in operation.

Where there is a long-run tendency for the terms of trade to move against primary products in favor of industry, factors of production must be shifted from agricultural and raw-material production into industry. To the extent that the necessity to make gifts brings this about in the surplus country, which is presumably already largely industrial, the necessity to cancel surpluses will improve the basic situation. But the prospects in this connection are unlikely to provide an adequate solution in the long run, as pointed out under *a* above. Where the deficit (loans) in the agricultural country is utilized to finance domestic industrialization, the cancellation of the deficit produces a real improvement in the situation. If deficits on the part of the primary-producing countries arise from expenditures on consumption goods abroad, the cancellation of such deficits will continue to be necessary in the future.

Similar reasoning applies to the problem created by the world shortage of dollars. If dollars are made available to the rest of the world to finance a higher level of consumption than would otherwise obtain, the system may be counted upon to be a perpetual one. Where, however, the dollars are given to foreign countries to enable them to narrow the gap between their efficiency in production and that of the United States, *i.e.,* to finance capital formation abroad, the cancellation of United States trade surpluses will tend to correct the fundamental disequilibrium in the international trade position.

It is politically difficult to justify gifts from surplus to deficit countries on either of these grounds. An increase in public debt in the United States to finance more effective resistance to the Axis and a somewhat higher standard of living for United Nations is deemed appropriate in time of war on the principle of equality of sacrifice in the attainment of a mutually sought end. In peacetime, with wide variations in the standard of living within the United States, it is doubtful whether use of public funds to increase consumption abroad would be politically supportable, except in cases of desperate need. It would also be politically difficult to justify gifts of capital equipment abroad. Capital equipment is productive and can pay for itself with a portion of the increased output it makes possible. If the United States is not ready to receive added imports when repayment is offered, the funds repaid can be reinvested abroad.

Britain in the nineteenth century had a technical superiority in the production of industrial products and lent abroad on a large scale to finance the spread of industry abroad. If Britain had stopped lending for any reason, while it retained its margin of superiority, there would have been a world shortage of sterling and a plea for renewed loans rather than for Britain to restrict its exports or to "act as a creditor nation." Britain continued to pile up surpluses for reinvestment until the First World War, and has acted as a creditor nation as far as the whole balance of payments on current account is concerned, only since 1914. For Britain to have given away the advantages of its superior productivity during the nineteenth century would have been unthinkable at that time.

To sum up: the three proposals put forward cannot be expected to solve the deep-seated disturbances in international trade and exchange through voluntary increases in imports by the creditor countries, by reduced exports of such countries, or by exchange-rate adjustments. To the extent that these proposals at basis resolve themselves into gifts from surplus to deficit countries, they may or may not help to correct the disturbances. The proposals may therefore be taken as inadequate to meet the basic needs of the postwar period.

Orthodox Proposals

Can international monetary stabilization then be achieved through the more orthodox techniques of gold purchases by surplus countries, or by the formation, by surplus and deficit countries alike, of an international stabilization fund? The system of gold purchases, which the United States practiced from the passage of the Gold Reserve Act of 1934 to the Lend-lease Act, evidently fails to clear the first hurdle — the fact that most of the countries of the world no longer possess adequate gold reserves. On the second score, hot money, the proponents of gold insist that confidence in currencies can be maintained only through basing national currencies on gold reserves.[15] This position is debatable. As far as the tendency for the terms of trade to move against raw-material-producing countries is concerned, gold purchases are on the whole neutral, except possibly in some areas where the alternative to employment in gold mines is more intensive use of labor in agricultural pursuits. The real contribution which the gold purchase system makes, however, is in its easing of the world shortage of dollars. So long as the United States is prepared to monetize gold more readily than other claims upon foreign goods, $1,200 million are made available to the world annually against foreign new gold production.

Despite these advantages to the system of gold purchases, it is abundantly clear after the experience of the last decade that there is nothing inherent in the limping type of gold standard practiced before the war which tends to correct disequilibria in international economic relationships. The open system of international trade based on gold broke down completely in spite of the attainment of new high records by gold production.

An international stabilization fund with large resources would, like the unorthodox proposals, obviate the necessity for a redistribution of international assets and might contribute effectively to confidence in national currencies. The collection of international assets in the fund could be made available to countries with temporary balance-of-payments difficulties for a sufficient period of time to enable disequilibria of an ephemeral character to be corrected. Surplus countries would be paid for their excess of sales over purchases, so long as their original contributions to the fund sufficed for this purpose. Loans by the fund to deficit countries would have to stop, however, when the assets of the fund were fully engaged in unpaid previous loans, unless further contributions from the surplus countries were forthcoming.

It should be observed that neither gold purchases nor an international stabilization fund are far different from the three unorthodox proposals outlined above. Under the system of gold purchases, surplus countries receive payment for their excess of sales over purchases in a conventional commodity which they can monetize. Under the Feis plan, the Twentieth Century Economic System, or pool clearing, however, surplus countries could monetize this excess in a sense by financing it at the central bank. The surplus could, on the other hand, be financed by the national treasury, but this is entirely similar to the policy of gold sterilization followed by the United States Treasury in 1936–1937.

An international stabilization fund requires financing by the contributing countries which can be undertaken out of central bank credit or budgetary receipts. So long as the country maintains a balanced position in trade, the line of credit or collection of assets allocated to the stabilization fund has no effect on the economy. When a surplus occurs, however, new central bank funds are made available on the market, or a budget deficit must be financed (or a budgetary surplus reduced). The result of the surplus is inflationary in its effects on national income, whether under the gold standard, pool clearing, an international stabilization fund, or any other type of conceivable formula.

The strong kinship of gold purchases and an international stabilization fund with the three proposals for righting world trade discussed above does not mean that these devices must inevitably be discarded because the unorthodox proposals were found to fall short of their objectives. Within a limited sphere, an international stabilization fund can make an effective contribution to monetary stabilization, by providing a collection of international assets for short-term use. Its proponents, who claim for it a broader objective, or the perpetuation of monetary stability through a formula — *e.g.,* a country can borrow up to 2 per cent of its national income from the stabilization fund to finance trade deficits, but thereafter in order to qualify for further loans, it must depreciate its currency by 3 per cent — these advocates are simply more timid than the authors of the unorthodox schemes discussed above.

The Need for Long-Term Capital Movements

While some new international monetary machinery, such as a stabilization fund, may make an effective contribution to international monetary stability in the short run, the effective basis for such stability must be found in a revival of long-term capital movements. The authors of the three unorthodox schemes already discussed and most of the advocates of gold standards, international stabilization funds, etc., aim at achieving a balance in the current-account position of most countries and hope to keep these accounts perpetually in balance. In so doing, they are waging war against the fundamental economic tendency for the rewards of like factors of production to move toward equality.

Within an area or region where factors of production have mobility, the tendency for incomes of like factors to achieve equality can be observed in practice as it is recognized in theory. Where mobility does not obtain, it once was possible for unequal incomes to be received by similar factors of production over long periods of time without stress or strain on political or economic institutions.

It may be doubted, however, whether wide inequalities in incomes received by like factors of production can endure for long today without some conscious effort to narrow them. While the physical mobility of the overwhelming majority of the world remains limited, there is great mobility of ideas, including the idea of what constitutes an adequate standard of living. Ease of communication of thought is a twentieth-century commonplace; but the consequence that like factors of production are beginning to insist upon a greater approach to equality of real incomes in spite of lack of mobility is barely beginning to be realized.

The desire for greater equality in standards of living and its continued frustration lie close to the basis of the international disequilibrium of the twentieth century. Primary producing countries insist that if they are capable of producing more goods they should be privileged to consume more of the types of goods they want. Dollars are chronically short because the world wants American products in order to enjoy a high standard of living directly, or in order to have the use of the most efficient tools for producing desired goods.

International monetary stabilization, therefore, must be sought in a wider area than that circumscribed by pool clearing, stabilization funds, gold stocks, hot money, interest rates, or even budget balancing. The need of all countries for adequate monetary reserves may be readily handled if steps are taken to assure that these reserves will not be quickly dissipated by capital flight or through uneconomic imports. Faith in currencies can be restored in the short run, but confidence adequate for an open system of international exchange must wait on a trend which promotes rather than frustrates income equalization.

It must be accepted by the economist that large-scale migration cannot be relied upon heavily to achieve the desired equalization of incomes. Some migration will be possible, from the most densely overpopulated areas in terms of natural resources, capital equipment, and the standard of living to which the population has been accustomed, to underpopulated and developing countries. Principal reliance, however, must be placed upon the spread of capital equipment and modern techniques of production. The movement of the terms of trade against primary products can be halted by improving still further productive efficiency in agriculture and raw materials, at the same time that domestic industrial opportunities are realized as fully as possible. The world shortage of dollars can be met by the spread of American, British, German, Swedish, and other modern production techniques throughout the world, together with sufficient capital to put them into operation.

Monetary stabilization, therefore, rests fundamentally upon the resumption of long-term capital lending on a significant scale. Proposals which ignore the basic problems of stability and aim merely to provide temporizing means to fill the gap in balance of payments on current account are doomed to fail.

NOTES

[1] See *Fifth Report to Congress on Lend-lease Operations* (Washington, 1942), pp. 21–23.

[2] See A. A. Berle, Jr., and V. Pederson, *Liquid Claims to National Wealth* (New York, 1934).

[3] Reviews of Colin Clark, *The Economics of 1960* (London, 1942), which is not yet available at the time of writing, indicate his view that a new shift in the terms of trade in favor of primary products will occur in the near future. This position does not necessarily conflict with that expressed above, since Clark apparently expects the steps necessary to reverse the trend — the expansion of purchasing power and productive capacity in the economically backward areas, and the further industrialization of primary producing countries — will in fact be taken.

[4] See L. A. Wheeler, "Agricultural Surpluses in the Post-War World," *Foreign Affairs*, Vol. 20, No. 1 (October 1941), pp. 87–101.

[5] This discussion omits consideration of population trends, synthetic industry, and other new sources of demand for agricultural products, the role of better nutrition, and many other relevant aspects of the problem. It should be pointed out, however, that malnutrition, for which more production of protective foods is needed, raises the ceiling on total agricultural output but does not vitiate Engel's law. It is further significant for the world problem that Engel's law does not apply where the standard of living hovers at or below the subsistence level. In this area, Malthus's law applies instead.

[6] The foreign demand for American primary products is, of course, subject to the influences of the long-term shift in the terms of trade, as well as to the economic forces in the United States, which have lately assumed politi-

cal forms, tending to bring about equalization of incomes. Compare the shrinkage of American foreign markets for lard, wheat, cotton, tobacco, fruit (other than citrus), etc.

[7] That the American market can be sold by modern methods is illustrated by the success of Czechoslovakia in developing outlets in this country for sales of pottery, glass, shoes, gloves, and other leather goods, during the interbellum years. The "Corporacion para Promocion del Intercambio," organized by American exporting interests in Buenos Aires to promote the sale of Argentine products in the United States, was apparently achieving considerable success in 1941, until shipping difficulties curtailed its operations.

The American demand for raw materials is, of course, derived. The influence of this fact on the course of imports is so strong that the volume of total imports fluctuates closely with the physical volume of industrial output in the United States, as measured by the Federal Reserve index. This relationship is so marked, moreover, that no distortion in the correspondence appears to have resulted from the imposition of the Smoot-Hawley Tariff Act of 1930 or the tariff reductions under the Trade Agreements Act of 1934.

[8] See Herbert Feis, "Restoring Trade after the War," *Foreign Affairs,* Vol. 20, No. 2, January, 1942, pp. 282–292, and Anonymous, *A Twentieth Century Economic System,* pamphlet, London, 1941. The third proposal has been put forward in an unpublished, privately circulated memorandum, and provides for a system called *pool clearing*. It is perhaps unfair to analyze pool clearing, when the reader is unable to test the validity of the analysis against the text of the proposal. The reason for so doing, however, is that the proposal in question is the most able presentation of the basic idea common to the three schemes.

An earlier variant of essentially the same idea is advanced by Edgard Milhaud, *A Gold Truce,* London, 1933. Chapter VII is particularly worth examination as an attempt to answer all possible objections to the plan.

[9] See *Report on General Principles of a Post War Economy,* pamphlet (London, 1942), p. 11.

[10] The objections to an international system of settling trade bilaterally are obvious and compelling. In prosperous times, the United States buys $200 million of tin and rubber from British Malaya and sells that country some $25 million of American goods. To force a bilateral balance would involve a reduction in American tin and rubber imports or an increase in Malayan imports from the United States, the latter in the face of cheaper goods available in the Netherlands Indies, Japan, and perhaps the United Kingdom.

Under the Feis proposal, the interested governments would negotiate the distribution of the British Malayan export surplus against the United States, which would require government distortion of trade unless it were possible to elaborate a system which, prior to the fact, would distribute the surplus in the same way that dynamic forces of a free market would have dictated. The Twentieth Century System also makes allowance for negotiated transfers of balances, but, under the case cited, appears to insist that, if the United States has an over-all deficit, or British Malaya an over-all surplus, some special merit attaches to corrections in the mutual trade between these countries as a means of arriving at the needed adjustments. Subjecting transfers of surpluses and deficits to government negotiation in any case seems to retain the likelihood of trade rivalry and discrimination on a political basis.

[11] If one or two countries accumulate large surpluses and one or two countries large deficits at the international clearing office, it is hard to see how the adjustments on the part of the surpluses countries could avoid being put on a bilateral basis.

[12] It may be noted that, while the various authors do not explicitly rely on expansion or contraction of money incomes as a method of adjustment — such as are called for under the "gold standard," which has been politically repudiated on this account — the three proposals do involve such changes. To take the simplest example, under pool clearing, a surplus country borrows from the central bank, which directly enlarges national income and expands the credit base; the deficit country builds up idle balances at the central bank, which contracts money incomes directly and the credit base. To be sure, further central bank or treasury operations could offset these inflationary and deflationary effects.

[13] The Argentine experience of 1936–1938 reveals the effects of a high dependence on foreign trade and a high propensity to import on the balance of payments adjustments. The North American drought of the summer of 1936 raised world prices of wheat and corn. Argentina with large crops of those cereals enjoyed an enormous export surplus during the 1936–1937 season, using some of the proceeds to pay off debt. After a normal lag, money incomes in Argentina rose sharply. Imports followed the rise in income, and orders were placed for substantial quantities of American automobiles, etc. Even if the gain in exports had been sustained in the following year, Argentina would have found itself with a large import surplus which had to be corrected by foreign-exchange-control measures, directed primarily against imports from the United States.

[14] See Geoffrey Crowther's discussion of the British postwar shortage of dollars in "Anglo-American Pitfalls," *Foreign Affairs,* Vol. 20, No. 1 (October 1941), p. 11: "In the classical theory of the free exchanges a situation of this sort would be corrected by a depreciation of the pound, which would cheapen British goods in America and make American goods dearer in the sterling area. But in this particular case it is questionable whether the remedy would work. British goods do not, in general, sell on price in America. . . . On the other hand, many of America's exports to the sterling area, particularly the automobiles and machinery, are virtual necessities for the maintenance of industry and trade. It would be rash to go so far as to say that there is no rate of exchange between the pound and the dollar which would balance the accounts in a free market. But it would have to be a very severe depreciation, which would hardly be welcome in either country."

[15] See any journal catering to a financial audience interested in gold-mining securities, especially *The Northern Miner* (Toronto), *The Financial Post* of the same city, and *The Financial News* (London).

270

CHAPTER SEVENTEEN

SPECULATION AND
FORWARD EXCHANGE*

I

The attention recently focused upon forward exchange in economic writings, particularly in England, may be said to have been due more to the intricacy of the subject than to its importance. Unlike the forward contract in commodities, which has not as yet been held to have other than technical importance to commodity markets, the forward-exchange contract requires a fair amount of skill at mental gymnastics for its lively discussion — largely because a short position in one currency must sometimes be viewed the other way as a long position in another currency — and has, for this reason, acquired a special literature. It is the purpose of this paper to evaluate that literature in the light of some American banking statistics bearing on it which have not as yet received adequate discussion. Besides calling attention to the statistical material, the paper will attempt in conclusion to examine the contention insistently advanced by certain students, that the forward-exchange market can be used by monetary authorities as a costless device for the accomplishment of certain specific ends.

The American statistical material referred to is found in the *Statistics of Capital Movements between the United States and Foreign Countries and Purchases and Sales of Foreign Exchange in the United States*, published by the United States Treasury Department and covering the period since the beginning of 1935.[1] In these publications the short-term foreign assets and liabilities to foreigners of reporting banks and bankers in the United States are set forth, along with security transactions between residents of

* Published in *Journal of Political Economy,* Vol. XLVII, No. 2, April 1939, pp. 163–181.

the United States and foreigners, and these foreign assets and liabilities are divided by countries and geographical areas and by types of assets or liabilities, whether deposits, short-term loans, acceptances, bills, etc. According to the usual analysis, it should be remembered, a reduction in the foreign assets or an increase in the short-term liabilites to foreigners of the American banks represents an inflow of short-term capital to the United States, while an increase in foreign assets or a reduction in liabilities to foreigners represents an outflow of short-term banking-funds to abroad.

In addition to these classifications, however, the short-term assets and liabilities are separated by the currencies in which they are denominated, i.e., dollars or foreign currencies. Over and above these short-term or "spot" foreign currency assets and liabilities, the forward-exchange contracts of the banks are also reported, showing how much foreign exchange the banks have contracted to buy and sell in the future.[2] These commitments, together with foreign currency spot assets and liabilities, go to make up the banks' position in foreign exchange, which is, moreover, shown separately.[3] These positions of the banks in foreign exchange are evidently a factor to be followed in the analysis of international movements of short-term capital.

Since the commitments of the banks in forward exchange are divided not only by countries and into contracts to buy and sell exchange, respectively, but into contracts for purchase and sale from and to foreigners and from and to domestic customers, it is possible to make a separation between the forward position of domestic customers of banks in this market and that of all foreigners. The difference between the banks' forward contracts to purchase exchange from domestic customers and their forward contracts to sell exchange to domestic customers represents the forward position of domestic nonbanking customers, since interbank contracts, reported by both the purchasing bank and the selling bank, will cancel out. If the banks have sold more exchange forward to their customers than they have bought, these customers will have bought more than they have sold and will be long of foreign exchange in the amount bought forward. The converse, of course, is true if the banks have bought more forward exchange from their customers than they have sold to them. Net outstanding contracts for purchase or sale of forward exchange from foreigners similarly represent the net position of foreigners, including foreign banks, in the forward market of their own currencies and the converse of this position in forward dollars.

As far as foreigners are concerned, however, the forward position of the banking community and others abroad in dollars has little significance by itself compared to their total position in dollars, spot and forward, because it is impossible in the American data to distinguish foreign banks from their customers. The spot liabilities in dollars of American banks are the spot dollar assets largely of the foreign banks, and these may in great part be held as cover for forward sales of dollars to nonbanking institutions and individuals abroad. Thus, if all foreigners are short of dollars in the forward market, this may conceal the fact that customers of banks abroad are long of forward dollars and the banks themselves are short in the forward market by more than this amount, because they hold spot assets over and above the amount of forward dollars they have sold to their customers. For this reason it is uninstructive to measure merely the forward position of foreigners as a group.[4] It is, however, useful to measure the forward position of nonbanking domestic customers of reporting American banks.

The forward positions of the domestic customers of American banks do not give a complete or even a satisfactory partial picture of the speculative exchange positions of this group. There are no published figures of the spot foreign currency claims and debts of domestic industrial and commercial concerns and individuals, and these may be expected to vary with the development of conditions of trade, money markets, political conditions, etc. In many cases changes in domestic customers' forward positions will be directly associated with such changes in spot assets and liabilities, while in other cases an American concern can adopt a speculative forward position without buying forward exchange from American banks, by dealing in significant amounts of forward exchange directly with a foreign bank, by borrowing from foreign banks and selling the spot foreign funds received, or even by buying or selling commodities forward in foreign markets.[5] Nevertheless, since the present investigation is more concerned with the forward-exchange than the speculative aspects of the inquiry, it may be defensible to study the forward positions in exchange of their domestic customers, as reported by banks and bankers in the United States.

273

II

Charts I and II contain several series relating to the exchange markets for the pound sterling, the French franc, and the Dutch guilder together with the forward position of the domestic customers of reporting banks in the United States. The reasons underlying the selection of these currencies are that they present certain related and complementary aspects of the topics under discussion, and that, aside from the Canadian dollar, theirs are the only broad forward-exchange markets in New York. In the three years covered by the charts — i.e., from the beginning of the week ended January 2, 1935, to December 29, 1937 — total sales of pounds sterling by reporting banks in the United States amounted to $17,186,000,000, total sales of French francs to $2,582,000,000, and total sales of guilders to $941,000,000. Of these totals, moreover, 36, 29, and 40 per cent, respectively, represented the proportion of sales of forward exchange to sales of all exchange, spot and forward.[6]

Chart I contains merely two series on the three currencies: the weekly forward position of their domestic customers as indicated by outstanding forward-exchange contracts of reporting banks and bankers in the United States and weekly averages of daily spot rates of exchange. Chart II presents three series: the first consists of weekly averages of daily three months' forward quotations for the same exchanges; the second, of significant rates of interest in London, Paris, and Amsterdam; the third, of the adjusted movement of short-term banking funds between the United States and England, France and the Netherlands, respectively.[7] All the series are integrated chronologically so that the weekly averages of daily spot and forward rates are for weeks ending Wednesday and the interest rates are as of Wednesdays, which are the reporting dates used by the Treasury Department. The three months' forward-exchange rates are quoted in percentage premiums above or discounts below the spot rate of exchange for a full year, to enable their comparison with rates of interest in appropriate money markets.

The most striking feature of Chart I is how markedly the character of the forward market in sterling differs from those of the markets in the French franc and in the guilder. In the forward-sterling market the position of their domestic customers as re-

SPOT RATES AND FORWARD POSITIONS

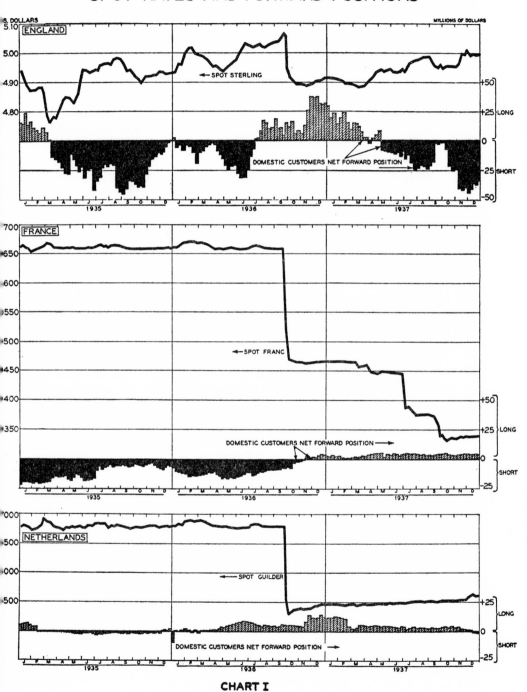

CHART I

ported by banks and bankers in the United States varies within a relatively wide range of $83,000,000, from $45,700,000 short in September, 1935, to $37,300,000 long in December, 1936. Moreover, changes in this position occur rapidly and appear at first glance to be associated in many instances with variations of the spot rate of exchange quoted for the pound. In the forward market for the French franc, on the other hand, the position of domestic customers has varied within a range of only $27,300,000, from $22,100,000 short on January 2, 1935, to $5,200,000 long on May 12, and again on July 14, 1937. This position started considerably short and gradually became long over the period. In the forward guilder the forward position of domestic customers varied within a still narrower range of $18,000,000[8] from $3,-600,000 short on July 3, 1935, to $14,400,000 long on December 23, 1936. In addition, this forward position varied somewhat, going from long to short in 1935, then to long again in 1936, and to short again at the end of 1937. The changes in the forward positions of the American market in the French franc and in the guilder do not appear in either case to have been associated with the movements of the spot rate of exchange, except that the timing of the transition in the position in the French franc forward market occurred shortly after the devaluation of the currency in September, 1936.

The explanation for these striking differences among the various New York forward markets may be found on Chart II in the relation between the rates of interest and the three months' forward rates. There it will be seen that while the forward discount on sterling was not far from the bankers' bill rate in London, the discount on three months' francs, after March, 1935, greatly exceeded the private discount rate in Paris, and the discount on guilders, between March, 1935 and December, 1936, was considerably wider than the private discount rate in Amsterdam. These differences merely mean that interest arbitrage took place freely and was effective in the pound, but that this was not the case with the franc or with the guilder over the twenty-month period already noted.[9]

The bankers' bill rate in London does not give a complete idea of the factors involved in interest arbitrage between New York and London, even if the New York interest return be taken as

INTEREST RATES, FORWARD RATES AND MOVEMENTS
OF SHORT TERM BANKING FUNDS

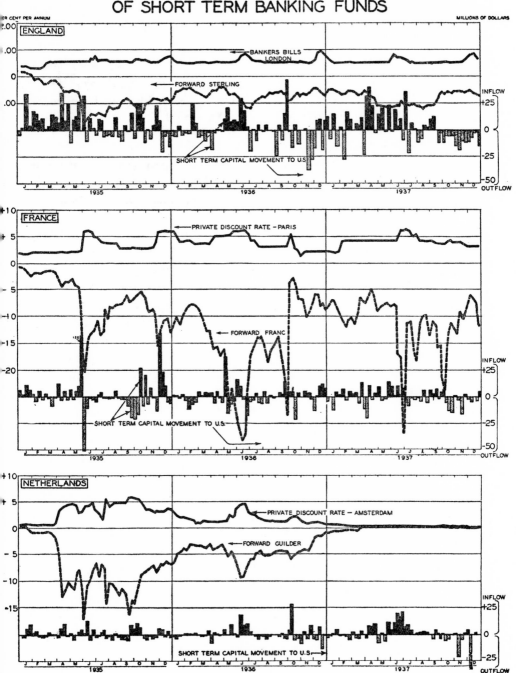

CHART II

zero,[10] for several reasons. In the first place, New York funds placed in London earn a higher return than that indicated by this rate, because London banks, in their anxiety to acquire deposits, pay a higher rate of return on three-month time deposits than they can earn by investing the funds in bankers' or Treasury bills.[11] This means that two London rates would be needed: one to indicate what rate of return New York banks could obtain on their funds and the other to illustrate what interest return the London banks must sacrifice before placing their funds in New York. Second, the money markets in London and New York are not so sensitive that they respond to all spreads between interest and forward rates, but only to those of some size. Einzig gives a figure of ½ per cent, which appears to be approximately correct.[12] In the case of sterling, then, loose limits were set to the fluctuations of the forward discount by the fact that interest arbitrage was prepared to operate to move funds either from New York to London or vice versa, under circumstances in which London banks paid 1 to 1⅛ per cent for foreign deposits, and the London bankers' bill rate held fairly close to ½ per cent, except at the middle and the end of the year when window-dressing by the banks made money temporarily scarce. In the French franc and in the guilder forward markets, restrictions against interest arbitrage by domestic banks[13] and the inability of foreign banks to obtain francs and guilders for the same purpose led to wide discrepancies between rates of interest and forward discounts. The forward market had to clear itself, i.e., a seller of forward francs had to offer a discount wide enough to attract someone willing to buy forward francs — and assuming that imports balance exports, a speculative seller of francs would have to give such a concession that someone would be induced to go long — rather than find itself continually cleared by interest arbitrage or "swap" operations undertaken by banks. Of course, some connection between the spot and forward markets was maintained during these periods. Foreign importers of goods from France and Holland may have shifted from the spot market to the forward, because of the inducement offered by the wide discount, and foreign exporters of goods to France and Holland who had previously sold their foreign currency receivables forward would be induced to borrow in Paris or Amsterdam if possible and thus shift from the forward to the spot market. Similarly, foreign names with international reputations were encouraged to finance their trade in the centers whose currencies were at wide discounts in the forward market, to take advantage of the spread, and by so doing to narrow it.[14] In these ways the demand for forward francs and guilders achieved some degree of elasticity, but this elasticity would have been more considerable in the absence of a prohibition on interest arbitrage.

One more general point may be made on Chart II before returning to a particularized discussion of specific periods in the record of specific currencies. The inflow of short-term capital to the United States for the account of England, France, and the Netherlands appears to be heaviest in periods of widening discounts on the pound, the franc, and the guilder, respectively, or the discount on the foreign currency in the forward market widens (the premium on forward dollars mounts) as the rate of inflow of short-term banking-funds to the United States increases. This relationship is an ordinary one and fails to indicate anything about the part played by speculative forward contracts in the total movement of capital, because, as was stressed above, it is impossible to separate foreign speculative transactions in forward dollars from swap transactions (interest arbitrage) in the American statistics. It should be noted, however, that changes in the forward position of domestic customers of reporting American banks in sterling are sufficiently large to affect the weekly flow of short-term capital between London and New York, while similar changes in positions in forward francs and in forward guilders are small in relation to the corresponding movement of liquid funds between New York and abroad.

III

The interrelation between speculation and the forward exchange may be more effectively set forth by specific examples. The difference between stabilizing and unstabilizing speculation may be illustrated by an example from the experience of the pound sterling in early 1935. How speculation in the forward market can be halted can be shown by the data for the franc in the spring of 1935; and how interest arbitrage reappears in a forward market can be illustrated by the guilder market in December, 1936.

In the early weeks of 1935, Americans (and foreigners) were

still closing out the large short position in dollars which had been built up in 1932 and 1933 and maintained during the greater part of 1934. At the end of 1934 it appeared that the Supreme Court of the United States might invalidate the dollar devaluation by its gold-clause ruling, and this led to very heavy covering of short dollar positions, a sharp decline in sterling, a fall in the premium on forward sterling, its replacement by a discount, and a very large movement of English short-term banking funds to the United States. When sterling reached $4.76 in the week ended March 13, 1935, from $4.94 in the week ended January 2, the position of the domestic customers of reporting banks in the forward market had become short. Thereafter sterling rose but the market went farther short. Prior to March 13 the market had been indulging in unstabilizing speculation (or rather in the correction of previous unstabilizing speculation which had bid sterling up so high); after March 13 the short speculation against the pound, which grew as the pound rose further from $4.76 to a level above $4.90 in May, furnishes an example of stabilizing speculation. Sterling was strong because of the heavy flight of liquid capital to London from the gold bloc; adverse speculation against sterling served to induce another movement of capital to New York so that the net inflow of funds to England was reduced.[15] Gradually, however, the forward market began to reduce its short position in sterling, since the pound continued to be supported by the capital flight from western Europe, until the American forward market, other than banks, actually went long in July, 1936, when average spot quotations for the pound had risen over $5.02. Thus stabilizing speculation itself was followed by unstabilizing speculation.[16]

Few wide shifts occurred in the American market's forward position in francs, and among the largest of these was the reduction in the short forward position from $15,700,000 on June 26, 1935, to $9,100,000 on the following Wednesday. This change may in part have been a reflection of a new attitude toward the likelihood of franc depreciation, on the part of Americans with long-term assets to hedge, with expected franc receivables or with a purely speculative interest in that currency, or it may have resulted from an underlying alteration of the trade or investment situation. Neither of these hypotheses appears to furnish a complete explanation for the relatively large change recorded in this particular week. This change

280

appears to have been due in large part to the fact that many contracts matured at the end of the quarter and were not renewed because the discount on forward francs for three months had increased from an average of about 3½ per cent per annum in April to an average of 12¾ per cent in the week ended June 26 and 10 11/16 per cent in the week ended July 3. At this level the cost of hedging and bear speculation was deemed too high by some individuals and concerns and some contracts taken out in April to sell forward francs before the end of June were closed out.

This high cost of hedging, which of course was responsible for the upward trend of the forward position adopted and maintained by the American market, can be illustrated in another way. If an asset of a fixed amount of francs had been hedged by a forward three months' sale on January 2, 1935, and renewed on six successive occasions on the first business day of succeeding quarters, the loss resulting from the September, 1936, devaluation would have been reduced only by less than half. The spot franc depreciated in New York from $0.0663¼ at the close of trading January 2, 1935, to $0.0476½ on October 1, 1936, or by 187 points. The continued renewal of the forward contract, however, had cost 99⅝ points, or an average of 7¼ per cent per annum over the period. This high cost of hedging and maintaining a hedged position, therefore, induced many to leave their long positions in francs unprotected.

As a final case study, the example of the forward guilder in December, 1936, may be taken to illustrate the effect of the withdrawal of restrictions. After the devaluation of the guilder, the Netherlands experienced a heavy repatriation of funds, a return to easy money conditions at home and a firm market tendency in the guilder. As money rates eased, the discount on forward-guilder contracts narrowed. In November, however, restrictions against foreign and domestic loans for the purpose of buying foreign exchange and against swap operations by the banks themselves appear to have been lifted. This had the effect of increasing the forward long position of the American market from $4,400,000 on November 11, 1936, to $14,000,000 two weeks later. Three months later — i.e., between February 17 and March 3, 1937 — this forward position decreased from $10,700,000 long to $2,500,-000.

When the restrictions on loans to foreigners in the Netherlands were lifted, the American market financed a small part of its trade by discounting acceptances in Amsterdam and covering the exchange risk by buying forward guilders. The discount on forward guilders made Amsterdam the cheapest place in which to finance this trade, and it is likely, although it is impossible to tell at what rate the American firms or individuals were able to borrow, that they obtained credit at less than the forward-guilder discount, which was 3 11/16 per cent per annum on November 12 and 2 ½ per cent on November 24, and thus derived a net profit from their borrowing operations. In the period between February 18 and March 3, 1937, the discount on forward guilders for three months amounted on the average to 0.27 per cent per annum, so that there was no incentive to renew the loans on the forward contracts.

IV

Certain practical as well as theoretical conclusions emerge from this study of the New York market in forward exchange. With respect to individual currencies, it appears first that the managers of sterling have working with or against them a considerable volume of speculative funds willing and even anxious to take exchange positions in the forward market at given or varying levels of exchange. If sterling has been steady within a comparatively narrow range, this speculation is likely to be of the stabilizing variety, and to make the task of maintaining an exchange rate easier, but the task of varying it harder. If the market takes the view that sterling is going to move from one range of fluctuation to another, however, the task of maintaining sterling is rendered more difficult because of this body of funds. In addition, the fact of the willingness to speculate in sterling exchange (and the British willingness to take positions in dollars) enables the managers of sterling to affect the volume and the direction of the movement of short-term funds, when the rate has been steady for a period, by the manipulation of the spot rate. This possibility of stabilizing speculation provides a favorable argument against the gold standard or for wide gold points on the gold standard.

The experience of the franc illustrates principally the evident fact that if the monetary authorities of a country do not make their currency available to outside markets, these markets cannot go short of it beyond the amounts they originally possessed. There can still be an outflow of domestic capital. Einzig has recently insisted again that monetary authorities should not defend a currency by making it difficult to speculate against it, but should even buy their own currency forward as outside markets sell it, if they intend to maintain their currency through the bear attack. He is particularly critical of the Belgian exchange authorities,[17] who, when the belga was under attack in May, 1938, after the downward revaluation of the French franc by the Daladier government, refused credit to banks which themselves speculated against the belga, which undertook swap operations, buying sterling spot and selling it forward, or which loaned spot belgas to their foreign or local customers for the purpose of speculating against the currency. Einzig rests his case on his belief that while a wide discount in the forward market for a currency decreases the amount of forward sales, it increases the pressure on the spot exchange through its psychological effects on liquid capital. Einzig admits that this is debatable, but fails to see that the burden of proof rests on him to prove that the psychological effects of a high discount on a currency in the forward market are more conducive to capital flight than gold losses, increased discount and interest rates, weak spot-exchange rates, or any other of the usual accompaniments of a capital outflow.

If a high discount on forward contracts reduces the amount of forward selling, then it reduces the purely speculative pressure on the spot exchanges, in the first instance, without affecting the valid export of capital. If speculation is permitted in the forward market but is prevented from reaching the spot market by central bank sales of foreign currencies forward, the central bank acquires a contingent liability against its gold or foreign exchange reserves, and the issue is postponed in the forward market possibly as long as three months. At the maturity of the contracts, if the central bank has been able to maintain its currency, the results of its policy will depend upon whether the speculators want to reverse their forward sale, renew it, or whether they have meanwhile obtained spot funds, against which the forward sale had been a hedge, and want foreign currencies delivered to them. In the last case only will the central bank lose gold at the end of the period. If the central bank has been unable to maintain its currency for the duration of its forward-exchange commitments, it will be obliged to sell its currency cheap and buy it dear. Whether or not forward support for the currency should be rendered depends upon the nature and extent of the speculation and the solubility of the fundamental problem which gave rise to the speculation. In the case of the belga, the policy of forbidding credit to banks which aided short speculation was highly successful and the belga crisis was over at the end of May. In the case of the French franc, the charted American forward position from 1935 to 1937 suggests that the wide discount made sales of forward francs by the American market, either for speculation or for hedging, extremely difficult.

No special conclusions follow from the episode of the guilder, although its study indicated how the spot and forward markets can be joined other than through bank arbitrage.

On the theoretical side, perhaps our most significant conclusion is that when it is stripped of its technical refinements and ramifications, the forward contract in foreign exchange introduces no real change into foreign exchange theory. Spot funds are moved between countries when a speculative position is taken in either spot or forward exchange, with the sole exception of the case of an equal and an opposite position being taken by someone else.[18] Covered balances, which Einzig distinguishes sharply from uncovered balances,[19] can be held only because there is a balance of forward purchases of the currency which can be satisfied only by the intermediation of an agency which buys the spot currency and sells it forward.[20] No short-term capital movement can occur without either a change in underlying conditions of trade, its amounts, its directions, or its credit terms, or in a speculative position.[21]

The fact that speculative positions are not freely taken in various currencies is responsible for premiums and discounts on forward contracts and is also what permits interest rates in different markets to remain at different levels. In the absence of all speculation, the forward rate would correspond exactly and automatically to the differences between rates of return in various money markets since at least the interest parity would have to be offered to induce the interest arbitrage necessary to cover exchange risks which cannot be balanced out, and since competition would render it unnecessary to offer more than this.[22] With speculation present, the forward discount can differ from the interest parity and will adjust itself only slowly to changes in it, because a change in interest rates by changing the willingness of banks to undertake arbitrage at going levels will also change the readiness of speculators to undertake exchange risks or to cover existing risks; in an exchange market where the spot rate of exchange is so rigidly fixed that banks, individuals, and commercial concerns do not care in which currency they hold their liquid funds, rates of interest in the two countries become identical as the two money markets merge into one and forward exchange would sell flat, i.e., no one would have any incentive to offer a premium for a contract to buy the other currency and everyone would be willing to sell such a contract at any premium.

Speculation, therefore, is necessary to a forward market, unless that market is to be completely automatic; but a forward market is not indispensable to speculation.[23] Long speculation evidently does not require a forward market, since if one's credit is good (as it has to be in either case) one can borrow at home and buy foreign currencies; while in the case of short speculation one can borrow abroad and sell the foreign currency.

Finally, the conclusion that the technique of the forward market does not result in any essential differences in the analysis of exchange-rate fluctuations, or of international movements of short-term funds, should not be allowed to obscure either the very real contribution the market does make in providing inexpensive opportunities for hedging and speculation or the real character of a forward contract. Forward contracts have an exchange feature and a credit feature, the latter of which has failed to receive sufficient emphasis. If an importer buys forward exchange, he is in effect borrowing at home the money to lend abroad at interest until he requires it; and if the banking system is unable to marry his contract to buy exchange with a forward contract to sell, it must buy spot exchange with its resources and lend abroad until by contract it must make the exchange available to the importer.

This line of reasoning may also be applied in the case of official operations in forward exchange. If the exchange of a country is under attack and the authorities sell foreign currencies forward, they are in effect borrowing exchange abroad and lending it at home. By reducing the discount on their own currency or increasing the premium, they keep those who sell the exchange forward from affecting the spot market, and encourage spot purchases of their own currency from abroad against forward sales. The establishment of forward markets in weak currencies by strong central

285

banks is similar in character. The market would only run one way, i.e., the strong central bank would be called upon only to buy the currency of the weak country, and such purchases would enable the strong country to build up covered balances in the weak country or the weak country to decrease the volume of covered balances it previously felt itself obliged to maintain in the strong country. In either case there is a short-term capital movement from the strong to the weak country and the forward-market device in effect enables the weak country to borrow from the strong. Whether this will be considered desirable depends, of course, on the strong country's policy with regard to short-term lending and on whether the discount on the forward contract in the weak currency adequately compensates the central bank for the exchange risk involved.

NOTES

[1] These data, hereinafter referred to as *Statistics,* were originally published quarterly in Washington, D.C., with a three-month lag. Beginning in January, 1939, they were incorporated in the monthly *Bulletin of the Treasury Department* and are currently presented on a monthly basis, but still with a three-month lag.

[2] See *ibid.,* Tables 47–52.

[3] *Ibid.,* Table 53. The stated position of the banks may differ from the positions computed from spot assets, spot liabilities, and the net of forward commitments if the banks report foreign currency assets or liabilities on their books, which they regard as belonging to their customers rather than to their own position. One such item among assets payable in foreign currencies is "Deposits Abroad for Account of Domestic Clients" (*ibid.,* Table 15).

[4] Since our interest is centered on forward exchange, no statistics are presented of variations in foreigners' total position in dollars. It may be of interest, however, to note this position at the beginning and the end of the period charted below. On January 2, 1935, foreigners owned $536,900,000 in short-term dollar assets (*ibid.,* Report 1, Table 2), but owed American banks $765,300,000 (*ibid.,* Table 17), or were short $228,400,000 of spot exchange. In addition to this, they had sold $397,900,000 in forward dollars (*ibid.,* Table 51), and bought only $112,900,000 forward, leaving them $285,000,000 short forward. Their net position was thus $513,400,000 short. On December 29, 1937, spot claims on American banks amounted to $1,646,600,000 (see corresponding tables in Report 6), spot liabilities to $502,600,000, and their net forward position amounted to $120,100,000 short, giving foreigners a total long position of $1,023,900,000. It should be noted that among the "spot" dollar assets of American banks, or liabilities of foreigners, are included blocked credits in Germany (see Tables 17–20 incl.) amounting to $230,800,000 on January 2, 1935, and to $125,600,000 on December 29, 1937. These and blocked assets in other countries — e.g., in Latin America — should perhaps be deducted from foreign short-term liabilities to United States payable in dollars.

[5] These last two methods might be used oppositely to take advantage of a wide forward discount on a currency. Thus an American cotton-house, for example, could have shipped cotton to France, borrowed against it and repatriated the proceeds of the loan, and sold the cotton forward. The forward market for cotton would reflect the wide discount on the exchange and sell at a premium over spot, and the proceeds of the forward sale of cotton could be used to pay off the loan. The borrowing and immediate repatriation of the spot francs leaves the American concern short of francs, but his forward sale of cotton, in effect a forward purchase of francs, evens this out.

[6] See *ibid.*, Report 6, Table F, p. 11.

[7] Computed from *Federal Reserve Bulletin*, May, 1937 (Table 3, pp. 406–7), and April, 1938 (Table 3, p. 269). The French and Dutch series are adjusted to eliminate the effects of the financing of gold shipments according to the procedure described by the writer in *International Short-Term Capital Movements* (New York, 1937), pp. 250–53.

[8] The $8,700,000 short position appearing for January 8, 1936, appears to be erroneous. It resulted from an increase of $8,900,000 in contracts to purchase from domestic customers, reversed in the succeeding week by a drop of $8,800,000, and had no counterpart, either in contracts to purchase exchange forward from foreigners, in contracts to sell exchange, in foreign currency assets of the reporting banks, or in the banks' global position.

[9] Interest arbitrage is definable as the practice of placing funds on deposit or investing funds in a money market abroad with the exchange risk covered by a forward sale of the currency. Thus if the forward dollar is at a premium equivalent to 1 per cent per annum, a London bank can earn ½ per cent more by depositing funds in New York without interest and selling forward dollars against them than by investing the same funds in bankers' bills in London at ½ per cent. See also P. Einzig, *The Theory of Forward Exchange* (London, 1938), chap. xviii.

[10] Such appears to have been the case, at least until the end of March 1937, despite dealers' quotations of the yield in ninety-one-day Treasury bills at 0.17 per cent per annum. Bills held for foreign account (see *Statistics,* Table 5) presumably represented mostly collection items rather than bills bought for foreign account in the New York market, and this presumption is strengthened by their concentration, prior to April 1937, in Latin America and the Far East. When dealers' quotations on ninety-one-day United States Treasury bills reached 0.60 per cent per annum in April 1937 (see *Federal Reserve Bulletin,* February, 1938, p. 146), foreigners found it worth while to employ their New York funds at interest and Treasury bills held for foreign account rose from $172,000 on March 17, 1937, to $282,523,000 on September 15, 1937 (see *Statistics,* Table 6). Thereafter, interest rates in New York eased off, as $300,000,000 was desterilized from the United States Treasury's inactive gold account, and foreign holdings of Treasury bills fell to $89,315,000 at the end of the year. Since the interest-bearing assets of foreigners in New York formed only a small portion of their total dollar funds, and as no interest is paid on deposits of foreign funds in New York, it seems wise to continue to regard the rate of interest on foreign funds in New York through 1937 as zero.

[11] See P. Einzig, "Deposit Hunting," *Banker,* XLIV (November 1937), 92–97. Unfortunately there are no published interest rates on time deposits which might have been used for the purposes of this chart.

[12] See *The Theory of Forward Exchange,* p. 274. The deposits of London banks in this market were built up when the discount on forward sterling approached or reached 1 per cent per annum. Conversely, when the discount fell as low as ½ per cent, as in the spring of 1938, the sterling balances of New York banks rose (see *Statistics,* Reports 7 and 8, Table 14, which indicate that these balances increased from $37,812,000 on February 23, 1938, to $79,971,000 on June 22).

[13] Newspaper records give June 11, 1935, as the date of the first unofficial steps to curb speculation in France, when the Bank of France decided to discontinue loans on gold, and the Bank of England requested London banks to refrain from forward dealings in gold currencies if they believed the accounts were for speculative purposes (see *New York Journal of Commerce,* June 12, 1935). In July 1935, the governor of the Bank of France drew the attention of the Paris banks to inconveniences resulting from facilitating certain speculative operations for the account of their clients (*New York Herald Tribune,* May 18, 1936). It is likely, however, that Paris banks were asked to exercise discrimination in using their own resources for interest arbitrage or for making funds available to clients for the same purpose throughout the successive crises of the period. Similar restrictions appear to have been in effect in the Netherlands, although probably administered at various times with varying degrees of severity, and their lifting is referred to in the *Wall Street Journal* for December 22, 1936.

[14] This practice was restricted shortly after straight loans to foreigners to allow them to go short were prohibited. During the period of relatively strict foreign-exchange restrictions on the dollar between March 1933, and November 1934, however, American banks were permitted to make dollars available to foreigners not only on goods in transit to or stored in the United States but also on goods in transit between foreign countries or stored abroad. Such loans were considered "legitimate," although they evidently permitted foreigners to go short of the dollar or to earn the spread between the cost of the loan and the wide discount on forward dollars at that time, if they covered their positions by buying forward dollars.

[15] The high price of sterling also served, of course, to induce some of the flight of capital to be directed to New York rather than London in the first instance.

[16] Undoubtedly some of the market's purchases of forward sterling represented cover for loans in London to finance American trade, these loans being induced by the wide discount. To this extent the increase in forward purchases did not represent a change in the New York market's speculative views.

Another example of stabilizing speculation can be found in the last quarter of 1937 when a heavy outflow of capital from the United States took place in response to the rumors that the American administration would devalue the dollar as a recovery measure. The market which was practically even in forward sterling in September, with the spot pound at $4.95, went short at $4.99 in October and November because it did not attach much credence to the rumors.

[17] "Some Theoretical-Technical Aspects of Official Forward Exchange Operations," *Economic Journal,* XLVIII (June 1938), 249–55, and also *The Theory of Forward Exchange,* pp. 386 ff.

[18] The only circumstances under which this exception is important are

those when one position is taken by the public and another by the authorities charged with the management of the currency.

[19] *Foreign Balances* (London, 1938), pp. 109–13.

[20] An exception arises in the case in which banks arrange forward contracts abroad. A New York bank might buy spot sterling and sell the forward cover in London. The London bank asked to sell forward dollars (buy the forward sterling) may be unable to buy forward dollars in the market and hence may buy spot dollars. In this way covered balances in two currencies can be built up simultaneously, without, of course, any short-term capital movement taking place on balance.

[21] H. Barger's remark that "the bull position in a given currency can increase only *pari passu* with the bear position ("Speculation and the Risk-Preference," *Journal of Political Economy,* XLVI [June 1938], 404), is only true on the paper standard in the short run, unless Mr. Barger believes a country goes short of its own currency when it buys gold to finance an inflow of short-term banking funds.

[22] This statement abstracts from imperfections of the market.

[23] The same is true, of course, of commodity forward markets.

INDEX